Erotic Politics

Taking eroticism on the English Renaissance stage as a paradigm for issues of sexuality and identity, these essays examine the nature of sexual definition and desire in early modern culture. Recent studies of Renaissance sexuality have focused on the subversive potential of gender reversal: *Erotic Politics* widens the arena of debate to study the structure and cultural definition of erotic desire. The authors view the stage as a primary site for the display of eroticism and use it to decipher what may be radically different cultural codes and expectations: the Renaissance stage is seen as a decoder for erotic experience, used both to reinforce and subvert expected sexual behaviour.

Any examination of Renaissance sexual eroticism must acknowledge the profound shift in sexual sensibility which took place after the seventeenth century, a shift which produced concepts of sexual dimorphism and 'homosexuality' as a category. Thus, for example, several essays in *Erotic Politics* view the theatrical convention of cross-dressing or transvestism, as a contribution to a distinctively *erotic* dynamics. Contributors argue that such a dynamics served to deconstruct gender itself, leaving conventional categories of sexuality blurred, confused – or absent.

This volume also addresses a crucial theoretical problem in postmodern cultural criticism: how can subjective phenomena, such as Renaissance erotic experience, be placed in their historical, public context? And can this experience be examined without recourse to psychoanalytic theory? In seeking to reposition the conventions and subversions of gender and desire in terms of one another, these essays open up a new and distinctive perspective in the cultural debate.

The editor: Susan Zimmerman is Associate Professor of English at Queens College, City University of New York.

Erotic Politics

Desire on the Renaissance stage

Edited by
Susan Zimmerman

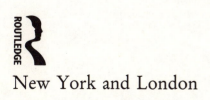

New York and London

First published 1992
by Routledge
11 New Fetter Lane, London EC4P 4EE

Simultaneously published in the USA and Canada
by Routledge
29 West 35th Street, New York, NY 10001

Phototypeset in 10/12pt Garamond by Intype, London
Printed in Great Britain by T.J. Press (Padstow) Ltd, Cornwall

British Library Cataloguing in Publication Data
Erotic Politics: Desire on the Renaissance Stage
  I. Zimmerman, Susan
  792.09

Library of Congress Cataloging in Publication Data
Erotic politics : desire on the Renaissance
stage / edited by Susan Zimmerman
p.   cm.
Includes bibliographical references and index
1. English drama—Early modern and Elizabethan, 1500–1600—History
and criticism.   2. Sex role in literature.   3. English drama—17th
century—History and criticism.   4. Erotic literature, English—
History and criticism.   5. Political plays, English—History and
criticism.   6. Psychoanalysis and literature.   7. Gender identity in
literature.   8. Desire in literature.   9. Renaissance—England.
I. Zimmerman, Susan
PR658.S42E76   1992   92.9710
822'.3093538—dc20

ISBN 0–415–06646–8   ISBN 0–415–06647–6 (pbk)

Contents

Notes on contributors

Catherine Belsey chairs the Centre for Critical and Cultural Theory in Cardiff. She is author of *The Subject of Tragedy* (1985) and *John Milton: Language, Gender, Power* (1988).

Jean E. Howard teaches Renaissance literature and critical theory at Columbia University. She is author of *Shakespeare's Art of Orchestration* (1984), co-editor of *Shakespeare Reproduced: The Text in History and Ideology* (1987), and has written numerous essays on Renaissance drama. Her new book, *Discourses of Theatre: the Stage and Social Struggle*, is forthcoming from Routledge.

Lisa Jardine is Professor of English and Head of Department at Queen Mary and Westfield College, University of London. She is completing a book entitled *Reading Shakespeare Historically*.

Kathleen McLuskie is Senior Lecturer in English at the University of Kent and teaches drama and women's studies. Her work includes an essay on 'The patriarchal bard' and her most recent book is on feminist readings of *Renaissance Dramatists*. She is currently working on a Leverhulme-funded project on the commercialization of drama in early modern England.

Stephen Orgel is the Jackson Eli Reynolds Professor of Humanities at Stanford University. His books include *The Jonsonian Masque* (1965), *The Illusion of Power* (1975) and, in collaboration with Sir Roy Strong, *Inigo Jones: The Theatre of the Stuart Court* (1973). He has edited Ben Jonson's masques, Christopher Marlowe's poems and translations, and *The Tempest* for the Oxford Shakespeare. His edition of *The Winter's Tale* is forthcoming in the same series.

Bruce R. Smith is Professor of English at Georgetown University, Washington D.C., and is the author of *Ancient Scripts and Modern Experience on the English Stage 1500–1700* (1988) and of *Homosexual Desire in Shakespeare's England: A Cultural Poetics* (1991).

Peter Stallybrass is Professor of English and Chair of the Cultural Studies

Committee at the University of Pennsylvania. He co-authored with Allon White *The Politics and Poetics of Transgression* (1986) and co-edited with David Scott Kastan *Staging the Renaissance: Reinterpretations of Elizabethan and Jacobean Drama* (1991).

Valerie Traub is Assistant Professor of Renaissance Drama and Gender Studies at Vanderbilt University. She has published *Desire and Anxiety: Circulations of Sexuality in Shakespearean Drama* (Routledge: 1992), and is at work on another project, *Staging Desire: Discourses of Female Erotic Pleasure in Early Modern England.*

Susan Zimmerman is Associate Professor of English at Queens College, CUNY. She is editor with Ronald F. E. Weissman of *Urban Life in the Renaissance* (1989). Her textual studies of the plays of Shakespeare and Middleton have appeared in *The Library* and *Papers of the Bibliographical Society of America.*

Acknowledgements

I would like to thank Jonathan Dollimore for helping me to conceptualize the Plenary Session of the 1989 meeting of the Shakespeare Association of America that gave rise to this volume; Lisa Jardine for her kindness in introducing me to my publisher; and Janice Price, Publisher in Humanities, Routledge, whose patience throughout this project has been engagingly conjoined with good humour. I am deeply indebted to Leeds Barroll, Catherine Belsey, Jean E. Howard, and Valerie Traub for their generous commentaries on my own scholarship, and to Barbara A. Mowat, whose intellectual support during the project's early stages was critical.

Chapter 1

Introduction

Erotic politics: the dynamics of desire on the English Renaissance stage

Susan Zimmerman

The title of this collection might be viewed as a conundrum: what does it mean to speak of erotic politics, and what is the relationship between politics and desire? There are theoretical assumptions in these juxtapositions: that the inter-subjective realm of desire connects to the public, political domain; that the English Renaissance stage foregrounds the multiple possibilities of this conjunction, shapes each in terms of a 'dynamics' that is available to critical scrutiny. These premises, in turn, suggest a larger problem concerning the production of eroticism, one with particular relevance to the cultural criticism represented in this volume. The crux of this problem may be stated in terms of two related issues: whether it is possible to historicize Renaissance eroticism – or Renaissance sexuality, the larger category of analysis to which eroticism is obliquely but interdependently related[1] – in a wholly synchronic manner; and whether eroticism itself may be anatomized without recourse to psychoanalytic theory.

One influential theoretical formulation of recent date, that of cultural materialism, suggests the dimensions of the problem. Deployed with great effectiveness in the dismantling of liberal humanism and in legitimating a focus on the political context of cultural production, cultural materialism has sought to undermine universal, essentialist notions of human nature; to establish material forces and material relations as the basis for social productions and practices (with particular focus on those of literature and theatre); and to displace the concept of history as a linear, diachronic continuum with the concept of culture-specific, synchronic histor*ies*. Thus, although it borrows from Marxist economic theory, cultural materialism eschews all totalizing narratives, including the narrative of classical Marxism, emphasizing rather the discontinuities and heterogeneity of Foucault's historical 'epistemes'. In this context, any teleology, whether that of the Marxist dialectic or the Christian metaphysics, is seen to reify those transhistorical or transcendental notions that serve the interests of hegemonic structures in their exercise of power.[2]

Not surprisingly, therefore, the status of psychoanalytic theory among adherents of cultural materialism has been exceedingly suspect. Yet, ironically, any materialist theory which insists on a radical historical contingency inevitably establishes a set of binary oppositions (transhistorical/contingent, essential/existential) which not only psychoanalytic theory but also postmodern linguistic theory is distinctively enabled to deconstruct. Moreover, a rigidly synchronic approach to cultural analysis precludes the development of a theory of human sexuality because any theory of sexuality must recognize the interdependence of the material and the representational, and account for the relationship between collective social formations and intersubjective phenomena.

It is then in the arena of sexuality and erotic desire that the problem I have identified is most clearly manifest, as recent cultural criticism focusing on these subjects demonstrates. It would seem that the very terms in which such criticism represents culturally specific constructions of sexuality depend on psychoanalytic terminology and paradigms. Consequently, some scholars of Renaissance sexuality, including cultural materialists, are now attempting to mediate the tension between psychoanalytic and materialist theory. For example, in his ground-breaking study of *Sexual Dissidence* (1991), Jonathan Dollimore, acknowledging that neither materialism nor psychoanalysis, in isolation from each other, can generate an adequate 'account of social struggle and change', positions his own analysis at 'the point where [they] converge with, but also contest each other' (1991: 34).[3]

Dollimore freely acknowledges what appear to be inconsistencies in such a positioning because he recognizes the theoretical (as well as the sociopolitical) dead-end of a narrowly defined materialism. Without some form of mediation between seemingly incompatible discourses, any materialist attempt to historicize sexuality is inevitably vitiated by a reductionist view of materiality itself. If, as postmodern linguistic theory would have it, language (words, sounds, notations) is a material process of signification, then a theory inscribed in the operation of language, such as that of psychoanalysis, is also a theory of the material. More fundamentally, if phenomenology is a delusion and consciousness does not constitute meaning; if signs are determined by their differences from other signs so that meaning derives from absence (what the sign is not); and if a linguistic system of signs (one that does not reflect but produces meaning) is a social formation that pre-exists the human subject, then the disjunction between matter and consciousness is not complete, and the relationship between them is a necessary problematic for any materialist philosophy.

By appropriating postmodern linguistic theory in an elucidation of Freud, and thus recasting psychoanalysis in a materialist framework, Jacques Lacan has served as the catalyst for the reformulation of other materialist theories as well. His influence has been especially marked in such neo-Marxists as Louis Althusser and Fredric Jameson, who have worked to position the Freudian-Lacanian theory of the unconscious within Marxist historical materialism. The legitimation of the unconscious in a material theory of history is of course highly relevant to cultural materialism as well, although here it is not used in the service of a teleological paradigm of historical 'progress'. Indeed, in the end the materiality of the Lacanian unconscious and its centrality in the operation of desire must be accommodated by *all* postmodern cultural criticism, particularly as such criticism focuses on the study of sexuality and erotic desire.

For Lacan, language, sexuality and subjectivity are inextricably connected in a single developmental process, one marked by absence, difference, division and desire. Language is difference and absence: the meaning of the sign depends on what it is not; a sign can only signify by alluding to what is absent (Freud's *fort/da* game). The human subject enters into consciousness from the undifferentiated pre-linguistic state through the agency of language, and in so doing experiences a fundamental split or division: subject and object (I/you) are defined by difference, absence and a sense of loss.

The division is also sexual: the induction of the subject into language coincides with an induction into culturally coded sexuality through the intervention of a third term – the 'paternal metaphor', the Phallus, or the Law. All the mental impulses prohibited by language and the Law, or what Lacan terms the symbolic order, must be repressed: thus consciousness and the unconscious come into being simultaneously in the human subject. Further, in the fissure or gap of the subject's radical split, desire is born. According to the Lacanian paradigm, desire aspires to possess that which is always absent, repressed, or unattainable – the imagined wholeness of the pre-linguistic condition, the misrecognized lost plenitude; it is 'the unuttered residue which exceeds any act that would display it' (Belsey 1992: 93). Originating in the constitution of the human being as a social subject, desire is an endless process of deferment.

By anatomizing desire as the effect of a psychic split in the subject produced by the symbolic order, and by reifying the symbolic order as a material, causal agent in the development of the unconscious, Lacan provided historical materialism with the means to develop what Fredric Jameson calls the concept of a *'political* unconscious' (my emphasis). For Jameson, Lacan provides – as LaCapra puts it – 'a means of linking the apparently individual and private processes studied by Freud to the social and collective phenomena treated by Marx' (1987: 245–6). Further, Jameson reinforces Althusser in identifying ideology as 'the means by which the subject attempts to close [this] gap' (ibid.).

Althusser's influential essay on ideology remains the touchstone for the postmodern revaluation of this classical Marxist concept. In 'Ideology and ideological state apparatuses' (1971a) and what might be considered a companion piece, 'Freud and Lacan' (1971b), Althusser attempts to do for Marx what Althusser claims Lacan did for Freud.[4] That is, Lacan undergirded Freudian technique and practice by providing a theory of the unconscious;

similarly, Althusser sets out to supply a theory for the Marxist concept of ideology. Further, Althusser's reconfiguration of Marx's 'superstructure' comes by *way* of Lacan. In appropriating Lacan's theory of the unconscious to his theory of ideology, Althusser has two objectives: to rescue historical materialism from a discredited positivism and simultaneously to demonstrate that psychoanalytic theory *inheres* in historical materialism. The rescue operation is in effect a takeover.

Althusser links ideology and 'the discourse of the unconscious' (1971b: 212) through the operation of language and the Lacanian symbolic order: 'you and I are always already subjects, and as such constantly practice the rituals of ideological recognition' (1971a: 172). This 'recognition' is, of course, illusory, a misrecognition, providing a false but practically effective sense of personal coherence: 'ideology represents the imaginary relationship of individuals to their real conditions of existence' (ibid: 162). The imaginary relationship, the fantasy, is instantiated in the *lived* relations that subjects have with collective formations, and Althusser contends that these relations are themselves one of the most striking manifestations of the materiality of ideology. Indeed, Althusser's 'interpellated subject' cannot exist outside these formations; thus 'no theory of psychoanalysis can be produced without basing it in historical materialism' (1971b: 190).

For both Althusser and Jameson, the construction of the subject is thus accomplished by unconscious processes which are constituted by social phenomena. Jameson borrows from Althusser in his own conceptualization of 'the ideological representation . . . as that indispensable mapping fantasy or narrative by which the individual subject invents a "lived" relationship with collective systems which otherwise by definition exclude him insofar as he or she is born into a pre-existent social form and its pre-existent language' (1985: 394). In such a formulation the Lacanian process of desire is made to inhere in the operation of ideology.

The Marxist ideological paradigm has been justly criticized as reductive of Lacan's theory of desire.[5] But Althusser and his adherents none the less succeed in laying the foundation for a postmodern *rapprochement* between psychoanalytic and materialist theory, one with an undeniable challenge for cultural criticism. If, in Terry Eagleton's succinct summation of Althusser, 'the fundamental mechanisms of the psychical life are the structural devices of ideology as well' (1991: 185); and if psychoanalytic theory is part of *any* materialist analysis, does not this linkage revalorize the transhistorical, the universal, the essential? To be sure, such terms would apply to pre-existing structures and not to their contents: the 'unconscious' as a structure need not imply an organization of particular meanings. But if structures may be constants, then how are they compatible with the notion of *synchronic* change?

There is, then, a negotiation to be transacted between the subject's pre-existing structures – of language, of the unconscious, of ideology – and the phenomenon of historical change; as well as between individual and collective agency. In a fundamental sense, the transformational process of social change – what LaCapra calls 'creation from contestation' – is a central concern of most postmodern cultural criticism, which assumes that change occurs as a result of social struggle, but that the process of social change cannot be abstracted into a theory of historical linearity. At the same time, the process is not wholly random, as a radically deconstructive theory of history would maintain. If, then, such a transformational process is *not* random, it should be possible to construct a theory for it, one that encompasses these delicately balanced propositions and that also accommodates the 'pre-existing structures' or 'transhistorical categories' of postmodern linguistic and psychoanalytic theory. The construction of this theory is the challenge that confronts cultural criticism today, a challenge to which studies in sexuality and eroticism, such as those in this volume, have lent a new urgency.

To be sure, the problem of historical change is basic to postmodernism itself, and the conceptual cross-fertilization that distinguishes the larger philosophical field is symptomatic of the need for continual reformulation of individual theories in terms of one another. For example, Julia Kristeva and Hayden White address the historical dynamic differently, but in related ways. Kristeva links Marx and Freud in terms of the semiotic concept of production (products and dreams), which 'replaces the concept of linear historicity with the necessity of establishing a typology of signifying practices from . . . the particular models of the production of meaning' (1986: 85). White, also focusing on semiotic systems, describes a related concept – and without hesitating to use the term 'universal': what is universal is not the meaning content of a cultural system, but 'the process of meaning production' (1982: 307). Thus it might be said that 'pre-existing structures', 'transhistorical categories', 'typologies of signifying practices', and universal 'process(es) of meaning production' all represent strategies for repositioning the synchronic and the diachronic in terms of each other, and that to some degree these strategies are related. In seeking to establish a theoretical framework in which sexuality and eroticism – as inter-subjective *and* social phenomena – may be studied historically, this volume provides a compelling rearticulation of the postmodern problematic.

The essays in this volume are concerned specifically with the dynamic of desire on the English Renaissance stage, and with the social and political implications of this dynamic. As Raymond Williams has pointed out, the 'sociology of drama' provides a complex study in material process through its institutions (theatres, their predecessors and successors), its formations (groups of dramatists, dramatic and theatrical movements), its formed relations (audiences within the theatre, and their wider social formations), and its forms (modes of speaking, moving, representing). The function and effects of the theatre – its social significance – lie in the complex interrelationships among these phenomena (1977: 139).

Representations of eroticism on the English Renaissance stage serve well as the nexus for the study of such interrelationships. The drama of the period was heavily occupied – one might say preoccupied – with sexual desire, and the production of eroticism involved every aspect of theatrical production, including the casting and composition of the companies (the transvestite acting convention providing an inescapable and distinctive erotic element); staging, costuming and the use of props and other theatrical apparatus; language, gesture and interpretation. The responses of spectators to the performers and to the plays were also constituent parts of the erotic dynamic, and the composition of the audience an important factor in this interaction, especially with respect to women.

The relationship of theatrical representations of eroticism to 'official' hegemonic discourses on the subject – for example, those of law, medicine, politics and religion – is part of a larger social dynamics that is extremely difficult to analyse. This is chiefly because these formal discourses do not collectively represent a homogeneous cultural coding, nor are the social practices of the period consistent with the proscriptions of the discourses. For example, there is considerable scholarly debate today over what activities constituted 'sodomy' in the Renaissance. Legal definitions vary and court records indicate comparatively few instances of prosecution for this crime, yet religious discourses inveigh heavily against it. Such contradictions are hardly surprising. Since 'the hegemony' in any society – particularly one as economically and socially conflicted as that of the English Renaissance – is a plurality, ideological domination by ruling groups is not likely to be uniform, but rather an organization of disparate meanings which may themselves be internally contestatory.

It is then in contradistinction to a variety of social formations that Renaissance theatre presents what in a Bakhtinian context are carnivalesque representations of eroticism. Unlike the theatrical traditions in England prior and subsequent to the Renaissance, the Renaissance stage, at the juncture between 'emblematic and realist modes' (Belsey 1985: 26) was transgressively carnivalesque in the sense of calling attention to its own artifice. That is, it disrupted the metaphysical fixities of unity, identity and causality by licensing a plurality of contestatory perspectives through the agencies of role reversal, dialogic interactions and experimental sexual fantasy. Such subversion of the symbolic order is pleasurable and revitalizing, an energizing phenomenon difficult to channel and control by official means.

This is not to say that all Renaissance drama challenged some aspect of hegemonic social discourse, nor that transgressive drama was not internally constructed so as to 'contain' its own fantasies. But the theatre itself, inscribed in the mode of the carnivalesque and situated, at least in terms of its public amphitheatres, outside the city's regulatory sanctions, was powerfully enabled to explore the limits of sexual categories and proscriptions. It seems probable that among the many contestatory discourses in the Renaissance concerned with sexuality and eroticism, only theatrical representations provide Bakhtin's 'doubles' or 'parodies' of hegemonic attitudes, and thus theatrical representations should serve as the primary decoders of these attitudes. In the interests, then, of reconstructing the cultural complexity of Renaissance eroticism, the criticism of this volume focuses on the privileged site of the Renaissance stage.

Studies of the English Renaissance theatre, including many postmodern ones, have traditionally foregrounded the dramatic canon of Shakespeare. Notwithstanding the importance of Shakespeare to his time and ours, such a skew, particularly in cultural criticism, is badly in need of correction. Neither the social function of the theatre nor the production of eroticism within it can be anatomized in terms of the *oeuvre* and practices of a single playwright. By repositioning Shakespeare in a more representative Renaissance milieu alongside many of his contemporaries, this volume deliberately expands the theatrical landscape for the study of eroticism.

The primary difficulty in surveying this landscape results from the strong indications that early modern eroticism was fundamentally different from that of today. Consequently, the challenge of deciphering what may be radically different cultural codes for the Renaissance is formidable. In addition to the physical and temporal displacements inherent in any historical study, and the fundamental ambiguity of language itself, the hermeneutics of Renaissance eroticism must accommodate a profound shift in sexual sensibility that took place after the seventeenth century.

Perhaps the most far-reaching symptom of this change was the introduction of a system of sexual dimorphism – the biological separation of the sexes – which renders the categories of 'male' and 'female' essential and 'natural'. Ironically, this cultural construction has been heavily reinforced by the modern deployment of Freudian theory, which has codified and rendered normative certain of Freud's developmental sequences (for example, that of sexual maturation), while marginalizing revolutionary discoveries such as polymorphous perversity and the structure of the unconscious. 'Homosexuality', which according to Foucault did not come into existence as a category until the nineteenth century (and again was misappropriated by neo-Freudians), and homoerotic desire are equally problematic issues for scholars of Renaissance theatrical eroticism. The hermeneutic difficulty in these cases lies less in resisting the temptation to interpret the past anachronistically than in learning to recognize what *is* anachronistic. Paradoxically, any interpretive strategy for reading the Renaissance depends first on the reader's familiarization – however imperfect or partial – with what seems *alien* in that culture. Thus, exploring the significance of the Renaissance theatre is a transformational process in which the clash of cultures becomes a productively reciprocal exchange.

Cross-dressing, or transvestism, is a convention alien to the mainstream of modern theatrical practice, at least in the West, but central to the erotic dynamic of Renaissance drama. Although there is already a sizable literature on Renaissance cross-dressing, it deals chiefly with cross-dressed female figures in Shakespeare and as such with transgressive defiance of patriarchal social proscriptions. The essays in this collection approach transvestism differently, in terms of an erotic dynamics that deconstructs gender itself, leaving conventional categories of sexuality blurred, confused – or absent.

For example, Stephen Orgel examines the figure of Moll Frith – on and off the stage – as a construction of male erotic fantasies which themselves constitute the cultural interpretation of the figure and help to confuse the meanings of 'male' and 'female' in this interpretation. Lisa Jardine argues for the effacement of gender in erotic relationships of dominant-to-dependent; such relationships originate in the early modern household and are represented textually as transvestism. My own chapter explores the power of transvestism to disrupt dramatic fictions by calling attention to its own artifice, thus creating an erotic dynamic based on a distinctively Renaissance fascination with indeterminacy – a fascination also manifest in medical discourse. And Peter Stallybrass anatomizes indeterminacy itself, arguing that at moments of greatest dramatic tension, the Renaissance theatre stages its own transvestism by forcing a confrontation between 'the absences which mark the actor's body' and the 'fetishistic signs of presence' (breasts, wigs, and other prosthetic projections): 'it is not so much a moment of indeterminacy as of contradictory fixations'.

If for Stallybrass the English Renaissance theatre stages its own transvestism, for Catherine Belsey it 'remorselessly dramatizes desire itself'. Belsey's Lacanian analysis demonstrates the frequency with which this theatre problematizes the notion of the self by staging desire's excess – and its destructive potential – in a variety of extravagant modes. Although most of the essays in the volume appropriate psychoanalytic theory to some degree, Belsey uses Lacan to shape a critical methodology that is distinctively suited to the excesses of the Renaissance stage.

A common concern of the collection is the relationship between theatrical eroticism and other cultural productions, and each essay interprets the theatrical dynamic in terms of one or more hegemonic discourses. However, Kathleen McLuskie takes on the *entanglement* of Renaissance discourses as a primary topic, tracing a complex network of connections between discourses of pleasure and desire (*ars erotica*) and those of social regulation and behaviour (*scientia sexualis*). Arguing for the need to combine competing discourses in our effort to problematize Renaissance eroticism, McLuskie points to the commercialization of erotic fantasy in the theatre and in wider arenas of Renaissance culture, a point taken up from a related perspective by Jean E. Howard, who explores the position of women in erotic commerce.

Another pervasive issue in this study of the English Renaissance transvestite theatre is of course homoeroticism. Although the papers by Bruce R. Smith and Valerie Traub on this subject are discrete in focus and intention, they are interdependently illuminating. Smith argues that the theatrical representation of male homoeroticism, shaped by patriarchal norms which both produce and deny it, finds full, transgressive expression only in the 'violent, political and male world' of tragedy. Traub, undertaking the formidable task of problematizing a female erotic dynamic which is absent in much patriarchal discourse, discovers this dynamic represented in the theatre, but frequently in an 'elegiac' mode that falls outside conventional categories of signification and political definition. In both papers, the social structuring of patriarchy is immanent in dramatic genre and rhetorical form.

Jean E. Howard's essay, focusing like Orgel's on *The Roaring Girl*, encapsulates many of the concerns that are fundamental to the volume as a whole. Howard pointedly contrasts the non-Shakespearean erotic landscape to that of Shakespeare, examining the complex inversion of hetero- and homosexual categories of representation that the play configures around the multi-dimensional Moll. Like Traub and Zimmerman, she also explores the problematic status of the female spectator and the possibilities of female erotic response to male productions in a male-dominated environment.

Notwithstanding the foregoing commentary, the collective significance of these essays does not lie in their areas of agreement or disagreement, however provocative and revealing. Rather, it lies in their attempt to foreground eroticism as a production of the English Renaissance theatre that is vitally linked to the construction of Renaissance sexuality and subjectivity; and to seek a theoretical framework for the study of eroticism that can accommodate these complex linkages. For such a compelling and ambitious task, this volume can be only a beginning.

Notes

1 For a fuller explanation of the relationship between eroticism and sexuality, see note 1 of my own essay in this volume, pp. 56–7.

2 I do not mean to suggest that these principles represent a comprehensive description of the cultural materialist position. The foremost concern of cultural materialism has of course been the *politics* of power, the relationship of government to ideologies of class, gender, race (see J. Dollimore [1984] and Dollimore and A. Sinfield [1985]). Indeed it may be said that the themes of political struggle and political expression have dominated postmodern cultural criticism in general, and for reasons that are themselves politically compelling (for example, for an analysis of the relationship of cultural materialism and the new historicism to politics and to each other, see J. E. Howard [1986], W. Cohen [1987] and D. E Wayne [1987]). My emphasis in this introduction is different because I wish to foreground eroticism as a category of analysis not wholly accommodated by contemporary critical paradigms and to indicate why this is so. This emphasis, however, should in no way compromise the centrality of politics to postmodern cultural criticism, including that represented in this volume.

3 Valerie Traub's *Desire and Anxiety: Circulations of Sexuality in Shakespearean Drama* (1992) represents another important effort to mediate psychoanalytic and materialist theory.

4 In a prefatory note to the latter essay, Althusser refers to the unconscious as Freud's 'revolutionary discovery', debased by revisionism and ideological exploitation and in need of rediscovery by means of Lacanian theory. In the essay itself he speaks of Lacan's 'basic proposal: to give Freud's discovery its measure in theoretical concepts by defining as rigorously as is possible today the *unconscious* and its "laws", its whole object' (1971b: 204).

5 Terry Eagleton challenges Althusser's interpretation of the Lacanian 'subject', his 'abolition of consciousness', and his equation of *all* lived experience with ideology (1991: 148–52). Dominick LaCapra provides incisive criticism of many aspects of Jameson's treatment of Lacan, particularly his equation of Lacan's Real with History, and his effort to convert the 'Lacanian thematic' to 'a totalizing understanding of narrative and dialectics holding forth a Utopian promise – something Lacan explicitly criticizes . . .' (1987: 249–51).

References

Althusser, L. (1971a) 'Ideology and ideological state apparatuses', in his *Lenin and Philosophy*, trans. B. Brewster, New York: Monthly Review Press, 127–86.

—— (1971b) 'Freud and Lacan', in *Lenin and Philosophy*, 189–219.

Belsey, C. (1985) *The Subject of Tragedy*, London and New York: Methuen.

—— (1992) 'Desire's excess and the English Renaissance theatre: *Edward II, Troilus and Cressida, Othello*', in Susan Zimmerman (ed.), *Erotic Politics: Desire on the Renaissance Stage*, New York and London: Routledge, 93.

Cohen, W. (1987) 'Political criticism of Shakespeare', in Jean E. Howard and Marion F. O'Connor (eds), *Shakespeare Reproduced*, New York and London: Methuen, 1–18.

Dollimore, J. (1984) *Radical Tragedy: Religion, Ideology and Power in the Drama of Shakespeare and his Contemporaries*, Chicago: University of Chicago Press.

—— (1991) *Sexual Dissidence: Augustine to Wilde, Freud to Foucault*, Oxford: Clarendon Press.

—— and Sinfield, A. (1985) *Political Shakespeare: New Essays in Cultural Materialism*, Ithaca and London: Cornell University Press.

Eagleton, T. (1991) *Ideology: An Introduction*, London and New York: Verso.

Howard, J. E. (1986) 'The new historicism in Renaissance studies', *English Literary Renaissance*, 16: 13–43.

Jameson, F. (1985) 'Imaginary and symbolic in Lacan: Marxism, psychoanalytic criticism and the problem of the subject', in Shoshana Felman (ed.), *Literature and Psychoanalysis: The Question of Reading: Otherwise*, Baltimore and London: The Johns Hopkins University Press, 338–95.

Kristeva, J. (1986) 'Semiotics: a critical science and/or a critique of science', in T. Moi (ed.), *The Kristeva Reader*, New York: Columbia University Press, 74–88.

LaCapra, D. (1987) *Rethinking Intellectual History: Texts, Contexts, Language*, Ithaca and London: Cornell University Press.

Traub, V. (1992) *Desire and Anxiety: Circulations of Sexuality in Shakespearean Drama*, London and New York: Routledge.

Wayne, D. E. (1987) 'Power, politics and the Shakespearean text: recent criticism in England and the United States', in Jean E. Howard and Marion F. O'Connor (eds), *Shakespeare Reproduced*, New York and London: Methuen, 47–67.

White, H. (1982) 'Method and ideology in intellectual history: the case of Henry Adams', in D. LaCapra and S. L. Kaplan (eds), *Modern European Intellectual History: Reappraisals and New Perspectives*, Ithaca: Cornell University Press, 280–310.

Williams, R. (1977) *Marxism and Literature*, Oxford and New York: Oxford University Press.

Chapter 2

The subtexts of *The Roaring Girl*

Stephen Orgel

i

In 1612 Mary Frith, alias Moll Cutpurse, the original of Middleton's and Dekker's *The Roaring Girl*, was brought before the ecclesiastical court to answer charges of public immorality,

> and then and there she voluntarily confessed that she had long frequented all or most of the disorderly and licentious places in this city, as namely she hath usually in the habit of a man resorted to alehouses, taverns, tobacco shops, and also to playhouses, there to see plays and prizes [i.e. matches]; and namely being at a play about three-quarters of a year since at the Fortune [Theater] in man's apparel, and in her boots, and with a sword by her side, she told the company there present that she thought many of them were of opinion that she was a man, but if any of them would come to her lodging they should find that she is a woman, and some other immodest and lascivious speeches she also used at that time. And also sat there upon the stage in the public view of all the people there present, in man's apparel, and played upon her lute and sang a song.

She confessed in addition to blasphemy, drunkenness, and consorting with bad company, but

> being pressed to declare whether she had not been dishonest of her body and hath not also drawn other women to lewdness by her persuasions and by carrying herself like a bawd, she absolutely denied that she was chargeable with either of these imputations.[1]

It is evident that for Mary Frith to dress as a man was in general inflammatory, in particular sexually, and that her habitual costume (hardly a disguise) formed a large element in the success of both her actionable theatrical performance and her continuing fascination for a variety of male inquisitors, formal and informal. The paradoxical element in the charges brought against her is worth stressing at the outset: her male dress outrages female modesty, but it is her assertion that she is really a woman, with its implied challenge to the male libido, that is taken to be 'immodest and lascivious'. Her masculine attire and comportment are, moreover, assumed to constitute licentious behaviour that is *specifically female*, implying that she is a whore and a bawd. The latter claims, relating to female sexuality, are the only ones she denies. Behind these particulars, and their curiously disarming representation in *The Roaring Girl*, is a much larger question: what is the relation between the construction of gender and its performance, whether on stage or in society at large; or, to put it more directly, what constitutes acting like a man or a woman?

Middeton's and Dekker's titular epithet was designed as an oxymoron, transgressing a variety of boundaries, not merely those of gender. As the term was initially used, roaring boys were characteristically upper class or gentry, their riotous behaviour an assertion of aristocratic privilege. It was behaviour that, though uncivil, was also conceived to be natural in men, as Sir Thomas Elyot testifies, defining the gender categories for Tudor readers:

> A man in his natural perfection is fierce, hardy, strong in opinion, covetous of glory, desirous of knowledge, appetiting by generation to bring forth his semblable [i.e. eager for offspring]. The good nature of a woman is to be mild, timorous, tractable, benign, of sure remembrance, and shamefast.
>
> (1531: 1. xxi)[2]

But even as the age defined its gender boundaries, it also continually – one might almost say compulsively – produced figures who overstepped or violated them. The hermaphrodite or androgyne appears as an ideal in various philosophical and poetic texts; the hero who plays the woman's role, modelled on the figure of Hercules with Omphale, reappears as an epic *topos* in Sidney and Spenser; the heroic woman is variously represented, sometimes (like Bradamant or Britomart) in male disguise, sometimes (like the Amazonian heroines through whom Jonson celebrated the Jacobean court in *The Masque of Queens*) overtly female, but in the military personae that declared their mastery of the male role as well. Indeed, as these examples suggest, in a Jacobean context the most striking aspect of Mary Frith was probably not her successful manipulation of the gender codes, but her ability to manipulate them from within her lower-middle-class status.

The virago is a cautionary *topos* throughout the popular literature of the age, but she is also a comic figure. If she is considered threatening, the threat is also regularly distanced and disarmed. But admiration too forms a significant component of the Renaissance response to women who are perceived as masculine. The legendary Long Meg of Westminster, whose stories provided a model for both Britomart and Moll Cutpurse, is invariably represented as an effective supporter of the social order, an

essentially conservative figure, whose intermittent transvestite exploits are
devoted to unmasking the pretensions of male upstarts in the interests of
confirming the patriarchal virtues. And unlike both the historical and fictive
Moll, she ultimately marries and renounces her pretensions to masculinity.

I want to focus first on the transvestism itself. Mary Frith's greatest
notoriety, at least in so far as the surviving sources convey it to us, coincided
with a growing public concern over what was seen as a significant masculini-
zation of feminine style. In 1620, according to John Chamberlain, King
James commanded the Bishop of London to instruct the clergy

> to inveigh vehemently and bitterly in their sermons against the insolency
> of our women, and their wearing of broad-brimmed hats, pointed doub-
> lets, their hair cut short or shorn, and some of them stilettos or
> poniards, . . . adding withall that if pulpit admonitions will not reform
> them he would proceed by another course.[3]

(McClure 1939: 2: 286–7)

This admonition was directed against the masculine fashion of women's
clothing, and it is to the point that the king had to be content with a
moral injunction. It was not illegal for women to dress as men; sumptuary
legislation concerned itself with violations of class, not violations of gender.
But the ministers did not invariably understand the point of the royal
injunction. 'The Dean of Westminster', Chamberlain reported in March,
'hath been very strict in his church against ladies and gentlewomen about
yellow ruffs, and would not suffer them to be admitted into any pew.'
Yellow ruffs being particularly stylish at the moment, the fashionable par-
ishioners appealed at once to the king, who was obliged to explain that 'his
meaning was not for yellow ruffs, but for other man-like and unseemly
apparel' (294). The slippage between sumptuary display and gender transgression was obviously not limited to the mind of the Dean of Westminster:
modern critics regularly do the same conflation when they assume that
Elizabethan sumptuary laws regulated cross-dressing. It is to the point
that in England, French and Italian fashionable male style is considered
effeminate: transvestism is, to a large degree, in the eye of the beholder.

It is not clear how far gender can even be said to be the central element
in such cases. For example, the cross-dressing represented in so much
Renaissance drama, the transvestism of Viola, Rosalind, Portia and Nerissa,
and Imogen, expresses a wide variety of patriarchal anxieties, but these have
more to do with the authority of the father within the family structure, with
issues relating to inheritance, the transfer of property and the contracting of
alliances, than with gender or sexuality – marriages are arranged for boys
as well as for girls, and the characteristic fantasy of freedom throughout
the drama of the period is one in which the children of both sexes can
elude the paternal arrangements and settle the question of their marriages
themselves. These anxieties are generational, a function of the patriarchal

structure itself, responding to those elements in society that are its essential currency. Women and children (and the society has an investment in representing women as perpetual children) become both a medium of exchange and the cultural metonyms for the working classes generally, all those elements that must be controlled if the patriarchy is to survive and prosper.

The masculine woman in such a context would be a singularly threatening symbol, or at least she should be if patriarchy is to account for her. How threatening in fact was she? There is no single answer, and the multiple ones are remarkably inconsistent. To begin with, we have seen that neither Elizabethan nor Jacobean society finds the most visible symbol of female masculinity, the transvestite woman, sufficiently threatening to enact any law enjoining her behaviour. On the other hand, witches, though epitomizing what was conceived as a specifically female propensity to wickedness, were also often accused of being either unfeminine or androgynous, as Banquo observes at his first sight of them in *Macbeth*:

> You should be women,
> And yet your beards forbid me to interpret
> That you are so.
>
> (1. 3. 45–7)

The specifically and dangerously female here, that is, expresses itself through inappropriate masculine attributes.

Four years after *Macbeth*, Ben Jonson employed a coven of witches to provide the antimasque for *The Masque of Queens*, his celebration of female heroism and virtue. So conceived, witches and queens are two sides of a single coin; the fearsome and the admirable share the same attributes of masculine vigour, strength and independence. Indeed, in the structure of the masque, the witches, defining themselves as 'faithful opposites / To fame and glory', *produce* their heroic antitheses. It is, moreover, precisely the masculinity of the queens that constitutes their virtue: they are not Elyot's 'mild, timorous, tractable' creatures, but military heroines, who appear and dance in the full armour Inigo Jones designed for them.

The famous image of Queen Elizabeth in full armour, as a later account put it, 'like some Amazonian empress' (Neale 1957: 308), rallying her troops at Tilbury when the attack of the Armada was imminent, indicates the degree to which the masculine woman could actually serve as an ideal. What is less easy to recognize is that it also indicates the changing nature of the ideological discourse of gender roles in the period: there is in fact no evidence that Elizabeth wore armour on this or any other occasion. The contemporary account says only that she was on horseback and carried a truncheon.[4] The claim that she was in military dress dates from decades later, and was invented as an argument against the pacifist tendencies of King James. The earliest depiction of her in armour at Tilbury is by the Caroline engraver Thomas Cecill;[5] this is the politics of nostalgia.

Elizabeth's speech to her troops is also a later confection; it survives in a variety of versions, but the earliest dates from shortly after the event and was approved, if not created, by her, and intended for publication. It is a characteristic performance, consciously playing against traditional gender roles. 'I know I have the body of a weak and feeble woman, but I have the heart and stomach of a king. . . . Rather than any dishonour shall grow by me, I myself will take up arms, I myself will be your general, judge, and rewarder of every one of your virtues in the field' (Ridley 1987: 286). This is not the rhetoric of an Amazon; Amazons do not present themselves as weak and feeble women. It combines the discourse Othello employs when he calls Desdemona his fair warrior with the Petrarchan, and more specifically Spenserian, ideology in which masculine heroism consists of service to a noble lady, and its rewards are not the spoils of war but the favour she dispenses. Indeed, the contemporary account of the event might be called proto-Spenserian: 'her presence and princely encouragement, Bellona-like, infused a second spirit of love, loyalty, and resolution into every souldier . . . , ravished with their Soveraygnes sight' (Nichols 1823: 2: 535).

General, judge, patron, war-goddess, love object and ravishing image: these are the roles played by this queen, this weak and feeble woman. The paradox is an essential part of the idealization. The elements of masculine clothing that constitute *haute couture* in the period – including weapons, stilettos and poniards – partake of the same ideology: 'O my fair warrior!' (figure). Here is Inigo Jones's version of the trope, the Countess of Bedford's costume for *The Masque of Queens*. Women dress not only for themselves and to impress other women, but also to be attractive to men. If masculine attire on women had been found generally repellent, it would not have been stylish, and we must conclude that there were Renaissance men who (not unlike many modern men) liked finding themselves in the women they admired. Transvestism is for us male to female. For the Renaissance it was – normatively, so to speak – female to male, and it took forms that ranged from the personal style exemplifed by Paulina in *The Winter's Tale*, whom Leontes accuses of being 'a mankind [i.e., mannish] witch', to those fashionable accessories of which King James complained to the Bishop of London, and on to outright gender crossing, where the transvestism is intended to deceive, and in a number of cases – the number grows significantly larger as the seventeenth century progresses – apparently succeeded in doing so for long periods.[6]

Linda Woodbridge has anatomized the developing disapproval of masculine fashion for women, culminating in two pamphlets published in 1620, *Hic Mulier*, an attack on women in male dress, and *Haec-Vir*, a reply attacking male effeminacy (1986: 139–51). It is clear, however, that the new cultural phenomenon was not the style of dress but the anxiety it provoked: Simon Shepherd cites a number of texts from the 1580s and 1590s that

Figure Inigo Jones, costume for the Countess of Bedford as Queen of the Amazons, 1609. (Devonshire Collection, Chatsworth. Reproduced by permission of the Trustees of the Chatsworth Settlement.)

similarly remark, with varying degrees of interest and disapproval, the popularity of masculine female clothing (1981, esp. chapter 6). That the anxiety has to do precisely with how much more sexually exciting the fashion renders women is clear from the costume as it is described. It is also clear that the excitement is intimately related to the crossing of gender boundaries. The costume consists of a 'ruffianly broad-brimmed hat and wanton feather . . . the loose, lascivious civil embracement of a French doublet, being all unbuttoned to entice [i.e. to reveal naked breasts] . . . most ruffianly short hair', and a sword (sig. A4; Rose 1984: 373). At times the woman is imagined in breeches, at others in skirts. Such women, the anonymous author argues, 'have laid by the bashfulnesse of [their] natures, to gather the impudence of Harlots' (Woodbridge 1986: 145). (Woodbridge artlessly wonders 'whether a doublet and broad-brimmed hat would be enough to make a woman look masculine, if her breasts were exposed' [ibid.]). Masculine dress is conceived here as empowering and liberating; it frees its wearers, however, not to be like men, but to be sexually active women – harlots.

It is easy to see why from the Jacobean royal perspective such behaviour would have seemed genuinely subversive, undermining both the structure of society and the norms of its microcosm in the family. Indeed, how close to home this may have hit is revealed in Paul van Somer's 1617 portrait of Anne of Denmark, James's queen, with broad-brimmed feathered hat and decolletage.[7] But, from another perspective, this courtly costume constitutes the same sort of idealization as representations of Elizabeth or the Countess of Bedford in armour. Contexts are everything: what was high style at court became subversive on the streets of London, and even this depended on where the critic stood to make the judgement. The proprieties of gender have everything to do with the proprieties of social class.

The idea that being a harlot constitutes masculine behaviour is no doubt paradoxical, but it shows precisely how much anxieties about women's sexuality, in this or any other period, are a projection of male sexual fantasies – being masculine meaning, in this context, being able to have constant and promiscuous sex. In the same way, Mary Frith's masculine attire was felt to be lewd and lascivious; and what was lewd and lascivious about it was precisely the provocation it offered to the masculine libido.

If we consider this in the context of Renaissance literature and drama, it is well worth pausing over. Literary heroines often disguise themselves as males, but the transvestism is invariably represented not as a provocation but as a protection, and, more strikingly, as an index to virtue, a way for women to live or travel in safety. The disguise is specifically a defence against male sexuality, which is conceived as the chief danger to female integrity – precisely the opposite of the assumptions behind the charges against Mary Frith. *The Golden Legend*, indeed, includes a number of transvestite saints' lives, in which female transvestism becomes the path to sanctity, a denial at once of both feminine frailty and masculine libido.[8]

ii

As a stratagem, the transvestite model might appear to be exclusively a literary one, but in fact there are at least two well-known cases in the period of women emulating Rosalind or Imogen, successfully disguising themselves as men to escape the dangers of court or patriarchy. In 1605, Elizabeth Southwell, one of Queen Anne's maids of honour, eloped with Sir Robert Dudley. Dudley was the illegitimate son of the Earl of Leicester, though he disputed the illegitimacy, claiming that his mother and Leicester had been legally married, and that Leicester's subsequent marriage to Lettice Knollys was bigamous. There appears, in fact, to have been good evidence to support his claim, though the courts decided otherwise, and declined to invalidate his father's marriage. The elopement was doubly scandalous since Dudley had a wife living, and had recently converted to Catholicism. The couple escaped to the continent with Elizabeth disguised as Dudley's page – we might compare Lorenzo's flight with Jessica from Shylock's house, or the travelling lovers of Donne's *Elegy 16*. They then lived openly in Lyons, and, despite the bigamy, received a papal dispensation to marry; they subsequently settled in Florence, and Dudley was rewarded by being made Duke of Northumberland and Earl of Warwick in the Holy Roman Empire – these were Leicester's titles, and the creation in effect legitimized Dudley within an alternative, Catholic aristocracy for Protestant England. Though his estates in England were impounded and sold, he was lucratively employed as a military and naval engineer by the Dukes of Tuscany. He built himself a palace in Florence (Lord Herbert of Cherbury, in his auto-biography, describes a visit to him there), and was honoured and given a villa by Duke Ferdinand II.[9] Few theatrical disguise plots conclude so happily.

A more tragic case was that of Lady Arbella Stuart, James I's cousin, the daughter of his uncle Charles Stuart Earl of Lennox and Lady Margaret Cavendish, the daughter of Bess of Hardwick – a marriage that itself had been arranged in defiance both of Queen Elizabeth's wishes and of English law.[10] Since Arbella was in the line of succession, and had, indeed, been implicated in at least one plot to depose James and put her on the throne, the king had a powerful interest in her marriage plans. Throughout her life, numerous candidates had been proposed by her and her family and rejected, first by Elizabeth and then by James. In 1610, ignoring the king's injunction, she secretly married William Seymour, to whom she had been engaged in 1603. When the marriage was revealed, the king's Council committed Seymour to the Tower, and placed Arbella under house arrest, initially in Lambeth. When it was found that this arrangement enabled her to communicate easily with her husband, she was ordered to be sent to Durham; but on the journey her health seemed to be affected, and she was allowed to stay in Barnet for some weeks. When the move to Durham once again seemed imminent, she took action. As P. M. Handover describes it, she

> pretended to her chaplain's wife, Mrs Adams, that she was stealing out to pay a last visit to her husband, but would be returning in the morning. Mrs Adams helped her to disguise herself by pulling a pair of French-fashioned hose over her petticoats, putting her feet into russet boots with red tops, and donning a doublet, black hat and black cloak. She wore a man's peruke with long locks that partly concealed her face and a rapier swung bravely at her side.
>
> (1957: 275)

In this disguise, she fled from house imprisonment to join the husband with whom James I had forbidden her to live. Seymour too escaped from the Tower, also in disguise. Arbella made the journey successfully, and actually managed to board a French vessel sailing for Calais, but she and Seymour missed their rendezvous, and she refused to disembark in France without him. She was arrested at sea and brought back, to be imprisoned in the Tower for the remaining four years of her life.

No doubt the Lady Arbella saw herself as a romantic heroine; but it is hardly hyperbole to say that the literary models offered her the only possible hope of release from the intolerable situation her paternity had placed her in. Her disguise confirms at least this much of the charge that male dress for women represents 'the impudence of harlots': it was adopted as the means to erotic satisfaction. It is to the point that both these cases involve the negotiation of forbidden marriages.

iii

The historical Mary Frith never married, but as Middleton and Dekker present her in *The Roaring Girl*, she is powerfully concerned with matrimony, both as the object of wooing and as the enabling figure for other marriages. If we consider the figure as she is manifest in contemporary accounts and in the very few historical records of her life, her presentation on the stage appears to be radically revisionist. Here, to begin with, is a summary of her career taken from the only contemporary biography, published in 1662, three years after her death. She was born around 1584,[11] a middle-class child, daughter of a shoemaker in the Barbican district of the City of London. She had a good education, but would not apply herself, and showed her masculine leanings early:

> A very *Tomrig* or *Rumpscuttle* she was, and delighted and sported only in Boys play and pastime, not minding or companying with the Girls:

many a bang and blow this Hoyting procured her, but she was not so to be tamed or taken off from her rude inclinations . . . , her Needle, Bodkin and Thimble, she could not think on quietly, wishing them changed into Sword and Dagger for a bout at Cudgels.

When she grew to be a 'lusty and sturdy wench' she was sent into domestic service, but she hated housework, nor would she marry, for 'above all she had a natural abhorrence to the tending of children' (Anon 1662: 6, 13) – that 'natural' is worth remarking. Leaving service, she adopted male dress, and became notorious as a bully, pickpurse, fortune-teller, receiver and forger.

In another source, Alexander Smith's *History of the Lives of the Most Notorious High-way Men, Foot-Pads, and Other Thieves* (1714), she appears as a more dangerous and powerful figure, who 'once robbed General Fairfax on Hounslow Heath, shot him through the arm, and killed two horses on which his servants were riding; . . . she was sent to Newgate, but procured her release by paying Fairfax two thousand pounds'.[12] If this story is correct, she must have been very prosperous or had very rich patrons; the amount of the indemnity was in the period an enormous sum.

Moll Frith was also, however, an attractive and popular figure, a London character. Her 1611 solo performance at the Fortune Theatre, wearing boots, breeches and a sword, singing and accompanying herself on the lute, was certainly not impromptu, since it is announced as forthcoming in the epilogue to *The Roaring Girl*; a large audience was obviously expected, no trouble was anticipated from the authorities, and both she and the theatre management must have assumed that they would do well out of it. We have seen that her brief stage career formed part of the charges against her when in 1612 she was called before the ecclesiastical court to answer accusations of immorality and immodest behaviour, including the wearing of men's clothes. That this was considered not dangerously masculine, but dangerously feminine, is clear from the evidence given against her, cited above: indeed, the feminine here, in a particularly clear way, is constructed out of the masculine.

The Moll Frith who appears in the biographical and documentary sources is dangerous, an outlaw, but also, partly as a function of her outlaw status, attractive and tempting. Even John Chamberlain's disapproving account of her management of the penance imposed on her by the court includes both rueful admiration and a genuine appreciation of her theatrical talents:

This last Sunday Moll Cutpurse, a notorious baggage (that used to go in man's apparel, and challenged the field of divers gallants), was brought to [Paul's Cross], where she wept bitterly and seemed very penitent, but it is since doubted she was maudlin drunk, being discovered to have tippled of three quarts of sack before she came to her penance: she had the daintiest preacher or ghostly father that ever I saw in pulpit, one

Ratcliffe of Brazenose in Oxford, a likelier man to have led the revels in some Inn of Court than to be where he was, but the best is he did extreme badly, and so wearied the audience that the best part went away, and the rest tarried rather to hear Moll Cutpurse than him.[13]

(1: 534)

Moll's manipulations are clear in this account. She necessarily underwent the penance in female dress, but her habitual usurpations of both gender and class conventions remain uppermost in the observer's mind – Chamberlain tells how she used to wear male clothing, and 'challenged the field of divers gallants', that is, dressed as well as many courtiers or dandies. Her tears initially appear to be the badge of her femininity; but they are revealed as having no more to do with her gender than has her costume -- they signify not repentance but defiance, and the intolerable deal of sack is yet another challenge to masculinity, a testimony to her ability to drink any man under the table. Chamberlain then proceeds to impugn the manliness of the one man in the scene, 'the daintiest preacher' he ever saw, fit only to be a dancing master to young law students wasting their time. If Chamberlain's moral feelings about this incident appear ambivalent, his account is a clear indication of the success of Moll's performance.

I want now to look at Middleton's and Dekker's version of her in *The Roaring Girl*, her use in the specifically theatrical context of cross-dressed boy/women and sumptuary transgressions. Moll the exciting scoundrel of the documents certainly constitutes an essential, if intermittent, allusion in the play. Her underworld credentials are clearly established; she has a circle of thieves and cutpurses with whom she speaks in canting language. But she serves essentially as an interpreter of that world to the middle-class world of the drama; she is an honourable, comic, sentimental peacemaker, who does not take purses, but recovers them.

The sexual challenge Mary Frith represented has a more complex vitality in the play. Refiguring an episode credited to Long Meg of Westminster,[14] she faces down and humiliates the odious Laxton, gallant and seducer, vowing

> To teach thy base thoughts manners! Thou'rt one of those
> That thinks each woman thy fond flexible whore;

(3. 1. 72–3)[15]

and takes on herself not only the defence of womankind, but the overturning of gender roles themselves:

>   What durst move you, sir,
> To think me whorish? . . .
> In thee I defy all men, their worst hates
> And their best flatteries, all their golden witchcrafts
> With which they entangle the poor spirits of fools:

Distressèd needlewomen and trade-fallen wives –
Fish that must needs bite, or themselves be bitten
    . . . Howe'er
Thou and the baser world censure my life,
I'll send 'em word by thee, and write so much
Upon thy breast, 'cause thou shalt bear't in mind:
Tell them 'twere base to yield where I have conquered.
I scorn to prostitute myself to a man,
I that can prostitute a man to me!

                                                    (3. 1. 88–112)

It is men here who practise witchcraft and seduction; women are 'fish that
must needs bite' (the fisherman, presumably, not the baited hook) to avoid
being bitten. The reversal of roles is in fact a reflection of the play's vision
of society, with its profound confusions of gender. Middleton and Dekker
spell out the cultural implications of Mary Frith's forthcoming indictment
for acting like a whore by dressing like a man.

Laxton has earlier been sexually excited by Moll, not only by her masculinity, but by her metamorphic quality as well. She appears wearing a male
jerkin over her woman's duster; the gallants offer her tobacco (smoking was
a male pastime, hence the ecclesiastical court's charge that Moll frequented
tobacco houses) and, though they know she is a woman, address her as
'sirrah'. To Laxton, she 'has the spirit of four great parishes, and a voice
that will drown all the city!' – if this sounds like ambivalent praise, it is
not represented as such. When Moll attacks and defeats a bully carrying a
rapier, Laxton swears he will love her forever for performing 'gallantly'
and 'manfully' (2. 1. 247–62). Laxton is captivated by her ability to be
everything to everyone, but his praise also has an obviously auto-erotic
element:

> She slips from one company to another like a fat eel between a Dutch-
> man's fingers.
>
>   (2. 1. 206–7)

He particularly admires Mistress Gallipot's characterization of Moll:

> Some will not stick to say she's a man, and some, both man and woman.
>   (2. 1. 209–10)

Laxton likes the polymorphous quality of this; but he clearly admires most
of all the double model it provides for his fantasy life:

> That were excellent: she might first cuckold the husband
> and then make him do as much for the wife!
>
>   (2. 1. 211–12)

Moll's male persona implies a universal sexual prowess; but Laxton also takes it as indicating how forthcoming she will be for him.

But Laxton's admiration, of course, constitutes the most dubious of tributes to the woman who plays the man's role. As Marjorie Garber points out, his name implies that he 'lacks stones', he is a man without balls (Barber 1991: 224). Moll is surrounded by men who are less than men; the play is full of references to impotence, castration, false phalluses, counter-tenors; it even includes a character named Sir Beauteous Ganymede, whose function in the plot is negligible, but who is, in the semiotic structure of the play, all but essential. If these are the men who admire and fear Moll, what is she to a 'real' man, a man who is as fully able and willing to play the man's role as she is?

The only man presented as admirable in the play is Sebastian Wengrave; the main plot concerns his attempt to marry his sweetheart Mary Fitzallard in defiance of his mercenary father's wishes. And in this plot, despite Moll's inflammatory behaviour, outrageous costume and underworld connections, she is revealed to be at heart a good bourgeoise. Her function is to facilitate Sebastian's marriage, to defeat the patriarchal menace in favour of the patriarchal virtues. These she also exemplifies: though she is committed to a single life, it is, she assures us, a life of chastity – she is, indeed, with the exception of Mary Fitzallard, the only unquestionably virtuous woman in the play. It is no accident that Sebastian's fiancée is also named Mary: the Roaring Girl declares herself, beneath her costume, a model of middle-class feminine behaviour. And by the same token, Mary, as part of the ruse to accomplish the marriage, disguises herself as a boy – and Sebastian finds that he prefers kissing her as a boy to kissing her as a girl.

MOLL: How strange this shows, one man to kiss another.
SEBASTIAN: I'd kiss such men to choose, Moll;
             Methinks a woman's lip tastes well in a doublet.

(4. 1. 45–7)

In this world, acting like a man is clearly better than acting like a woman, both more attractive and – the point is worth stressing – more likely to lead to an honourable and happy marriage. More than this, it is, in an important sense, a crucial element in acting like a woman. This is the lesson that Elizabeth Southwell and Arbella Stuart learned from drama and poetry, those indices to the culture's *topoi*. And though Moll Frith denies any interest in marriage, the play considers her eminently marriageable, and not merely by the likes of Laxton. Sebastian's father is brought to agree to his son's marriage to the perfectly suitable Mary through a ruse in which Sebastian claims to have transferred his affections to Moll. The ruse is outrageous, but though it has its grotesque aspects, it is not presented as inconceivable or even unlikely, and everyone takes it seriously: Moll is acknowledged to be an attractive and powerful figure, both on stage and off it. Theatre here holds the mirror up to nature – or, more precisely, to culture: this is a world in which masculinity is always in question. In the discourse of patriarchy, gender is the least certain of boundaries. Acting like a man is the most compelling way of acting like a woman.

Notes

1 From the *Consistory of London Correction Book*, fols 19–20. See Mulholland (1987: 262–3). The quotation is modernized.
2 The quotation has been modernized.
3 Quotations from Chamberlain have been modernized.
4 Susan Frye has traced the changing accounts of the incidents in 'The myth of Elizabeth at Tilbury', forthcoming in *Sixteenth-Century Journal*.
5 Reproduced in Corbett and Norton (1964: plate 19).
6 In fact, female transvestism as a style of life was evidently far more widespread than standard sources acknowledge. In upper-class women the practice is an occasional stratagem, but the majority of cases are of lower-class women, many of whom served as soldiers or even sailors, and took wives. Dekker and van de Pol (1989) map the territory; its evidence is mostly Dutch, and no earlier than the late seventeenth century, but it is clear that this represents only a very small sample. Surviving records, in any case, relate only to those women whose gender was ultimately revealed.
7 Now in the royal collection; the picture is reproduced in Millar (1977: 26).
8 The *topos* is authoritatively surveyed in Anson (1974).
9 Information about Elizabeth Southwell and Dudley is from the *Dictionary of National Biography* under Robert Dudley (1: 582–3), Handover (1957: 216–17); and Durant (1978: 151).
10 Since Lennox, through his father the Earl of Darnley, had a claim on the English throne, the royal assent was required for any marriage he might contract. For information about Arbella Stuart, in addition to the *DNB* (under Arbella), Handover (1957) and Durant (1978), see Steen (1988).
11 The date given in the *Life* is 1589, but this has been shown to be incorrect; see Gomme (1976: xiii).
12 Cited in the *DNB* under Mary Frith (1: 741).
13 A defiant version of the incident is recounted in the *Life* (Anon 1662: 69).
14 A similar incident is alluded to in the *Life* (Anon 1662: 87–8).
15 References to *The Roaring Girl* are to Mulholland (1987). I have corrected a misprint at 2. 1. 212.

References

Anon. (1662) *The Life and Death of Mrs. Mary Frith. Commonly Called Mal Cutpurse*, London: W. Gilbertson.
Anson, J. (1974) 'The female transvestite in early monasticism', *Viator* 5.
Corbett, M. and Norton, M. (1964) *Engraving in England in the Sixteenth and Seventeenth Centuries*, Part III, Cambridge: Cambridge University Press.
Dekker, R. and van de Pol, L. (1989) *The Tradition of Female Transvestism in Early Modern Europe*, London: Macmillan.

DNB (1975) *The Compact Edition of the Dictionary of National Biography*, Oxford: Oxford University Press.

Durant, D. (1978) *Arbella Stuart*, London: Weidenfeld & Nicolson.

Elyot, T. (1531) *The Boke Named the Governour*, London: T. Berthelet.

Garber, M. (1991) 'The logic of the transvestite: *The Roaring Girl*', in D. S. Kastan and P. Stallybrass (eds), *Staging the Renaissance: Reinterpretations of Elizabethan and Jacobean Drama*, New York and London: Routledge.

Gomme, A. (ed.) (1976) *The Roaring Girl*, London: Ernest Benn.

Handover, P. (1957) *Arbella Stuart*, London: Eyre & Spottiswoode.

McClure, N. (1939) *Letters of John Chamberlain*, Philadelphia: American Philosophical Society.

Millar, O. (1977) *The Queen's Pictures*, New York: Macmillan.

Mulholland, P. (ed.) (1987) *The Roaring Girl*, Manchester: Manchester University Press.

Neale, J. (1957) *Queen Elizabeth*, New York: Doubleday.

Nichols, J. (1823) *Progresses . . . of Queen Elizabeth*, London: John Nichols.

Ridley, J. (1987) *Elizabeth I*, London: Constable.

Rose, M. B. (1984) 'Women in men's clothing: apparel and social stability in *The Roaring Girl*', *English Literary Renaissance*, autumn (14, 3: 367–91).

Shepherd, S. (1981) *Amazons and Warrior Women*, Brighton: Harvester.

Steen, S. J. (1988) 'Fashioning an acceptable self: Arbella Stuart', *ELR* 18: 78–95.

Woodbridge, L. (1986) *Women and the English Renaissance*, Urbana: University of Illinois Press.

Chapter 3

Twins and travesties

Gender, dependency and sexual availability in *Twelfth Night*[1]

Lisa Jardine

VIOLA: He nam'd Sebastian. I my brother know
Yet living in my glass; even such and so
In favour was my brother, and he went
Still in this fashion, colour, ornament,
For him I imitate.

(3.4.389–93)[2]

[*Ingling Pyander*]
Walking the city, as my wonted use,
There was I subject to this foul abuse:
Troubled with many thoughts, pacing along,
It was my chance to shoulder in a throng;
Thrust to the channel I was, but crowding her,
I spied Pyander in a nymph's attire:
No nymph more fair than did Pyander seem,
Had not Pyander then Pyander been;
No Lady with a fairer face more grac'd,
But that Pyander's self himself defac'd;
Never was boy so pleasing to the heart
As was Pyander for a woman's part;
Never did woman foster such another,
As was Pyander, but Pyander's mother.
Fool that I was in my affection!
More happy I, had it been a vision;
So far entangled was my soul by love,
That force perforce I must Pyander move:
The issue of which proof did testify
Ingling Pyander's damnèd villainy.
. . .
O, so I was besotted by her words,
His words, that no part of a she affords!
For had he been a she, injurious boy,
I had not been so subject to annoy.[3]

This paper tries to accommodate some of the apparently contradictory currents stirred by these two cross-dressing passages, to provide a single, coherent version of the erotic possibilities contained under a kind of rubric of transvestism in the early modern period. For, in the current text-critical literature, we seem to be being told *both* that these are texts of sexual fantasy, disturbing and transgressive, *and* that these texts record some 'actual' possibility for individualized, subversive affirmation of sexuality.[4] I do not myself believe we shall ever know how many cross-dressed youths and young women were to be found on the streets of London around 1600, but I do believe that it is possible to show that the distinctive ways in which the textual imputation of their existence function in the various narratives which have come down to us can be resolved into a consistent positioning of dominant to dependent member of the early modern community.[5]

I have, of course, spoken about cross-dressing before, in *Still Harping on Daughters* (Jardine 1983). But that was in the context of an argument specifically focused on the *irrelevance* of any detectable emotional intensity associated with the cross-dressed boy-player to any reconstruction, on the basis of the drama of the age of Shakespeare, of a peculiarly *female* early modern intensity of feeling. Here my argument will be differently focused: upon the way in which, in the early modern period, erotic attention – an attention bound up with sexual availability and historically specific forms of economic dependency – is focused upon boys and upon women in the *same* way. So that, crucially, sexuality signifies as *absence of difference* as it is inscribed upon the bodies of those equivalently 'mastered' within the early modern household, and who are placed homologously in relation to that household's domestic economy. Inside the household, I shall argue, dependent youths and dependent women are expected to 'submit', under the order of familial authority, to those above them. And the strong ideological hold of the patriarchal household ensures that, in the space *outside* the household – in the newer market economy whose values govern the street and the public place – the tropes which produce structural dependency as vulnerability and *availability* are readily mobilized to police the circulation of young people.

Outside the household, the freely circulating woman is 'loose' (uncontained) – is strictly 'out of place',[6] and her very comeliness in conjunction with her unprotectedness (no male kin with her) signifies as availability (as it continues, residually, to do today). And outside the household the dependent boy (the 'youth') is also constructed, via the patriarchal household, as 'at risk' – more legitimately in transit on 'business', but also, in his transactional availability, sexually vulnerable.[7] In the street, the bodies of the boy and the unmarried woman elide as they carry the message of equivalent sexual availability – male and female prostitution is represented textually (and probably fantasized communally) as transvestism. The boy discovered as a girl reveals her availability for public intercourse; the girl dis-covered as a boy reveals that intention to sodomy for financial gain.[8] The boy who walks the street cross-dressed as that comely girl (whether in reality or in fantasy/grotesque fiction) does not, therefore, misrepresent himself – he conceals (and then reveals) the range of sexual possibilities available. The girl who enters the male preserve (ordinary, tavern or gaming-house) cross-dressed does not misrepresent herself, either. She is, in any case, 'loose', and eases the process of crossing the threshold into the male domain – controls the manner of presenting herself in a suitable location for paid sex.[9]

I suggest that the way in which *dependency* functions in relation to representations of the sexual in early modern English culture is vital to a suitably historicized reading of cross-dressing and gender confusion in Elizabethan and Jacobean drama.[10] Here I shall try to show this set of relations in operation in the complex gender doubling and twinning of Shakespeare's *Twelfth Night*.

'The household was the classic form of patriarchy', writes Alan Bray (1982: 51). In the period with which we are concerned, 'family' and 'house-hold', as descriptions of the ordered unit for communal living, designate groupings which include both close and distant kin, and a range of non-kin.[11] There is a constant 'drift of young persons' (as David Herlihy calls it), a flow of young adolescents into and out of the wealthier households – both of distant kin, and of non-kin in 'service'.[12] And, in addition to the body of young well-to-do dependents in the wealthy household, there were numbers of adolescent servants: 'The great majority of the adolescent population probably entered some form of service or apprenticeship', writes Ralph Houlbrooke. In Ealing, in 1599, about a quarter of the total population of 427 was in service of some kind (1984: 173).[13] Of the eighty-five households in Ealing, 'a staggering 34.2 per cent of them contained one or more servants' (Bray 1982: 50–1). Finally, 'in the upper and middle ranks of society children were commonly sent away from home to another house-hold' (Houlbrooke 1984: 150), as part of their education. (Whilst they resided in Calais, the Lisles placed two of their daughters with French families of a wealth and status corresponding to their own (St Clare Byrne 1985: 126–7). 'The patriarchal household with its servants was an institution that touched the lives of an immense number of people' (to quote Bray again); 'it was an institution that necessarily influenced the sexual lives of those who lived within it' (1982: 51). That patriarchal household exercised its considerable authority and wielded its extensive economic power pre-dominately over young men and women between the ages of 14 and 24.

It is against this kind of background that Susan Amussen locates patriar-chal authority at the most fundamental levels of consciousness-formation in the period:

[The catechism] asserted that the family was the fundamental social institution, and that order in families was both necessary for and parallel to, order in the state. In the catechism, this idea is developed in the discussion of the Fifth Commandment, to 'honour thy father and mother'. The 1559 Prayer Book's catechism . . . summarized . . .

> My duty towards my neighbour is to love him as myself, and to do to all men as I would they should do unto me: to love, honour, and succour my father and mother: to honour and obey the King and all that are put in authority under him: to submit myself to all my governors, teachers, spiritual pastors and masters: to order myself lowly and reverently to all my betters: . . . to learn and labour truly to get mine own living, and to do my duty in that state of life unto which it shall please God to call me.
>
> (1988: 35–6)[15]

In the middle to upper ranks of society, deference and submissiveness were internalized in the form of 'good manners':

> In a society in which service was the most important avenue to advancement at all levels, one of the most essential skills was the ability to make oneself acceptable to superiors. . . . Marks of respect to be shown in conversation with superiors included baring the head, dropping the right knee, keeping silence till spoken to, listening carefully and answering sensibly and shortly. Compliance with commands was to be immediate, response to praise heartily grateful.
>
> (Houlbrooke 1984: 147)[16]

For dependent youth, obedience was both a condition of their economic support, and an internalized state.

In 1630, Meredith Davy of Minehead, was prosecuted for sodomy at the Somerset Court of Quarter Sessions.

> According to the evidence of his master's apprentice, a boy 'aged twelve years or thereabouts' called John Vicary, with whom he shared a bed, Davy had been in the habit of having sexual relations with the boy on Sunday and holiday nights after he had been drinking; eventually the boy cried out and Davy ended up before the Justices.
>
> (Bray 1982: 48)

As Bray glosses this:

> The young apprentice would have had a lower standing in the household than Davy, who was an adult; and it was presumably this which encouraged him – wrongly as it turned out – to think that he could take advantage of the boy. It is an important point. In a household of any

substantial size the distinction in their status would have been only one of a series of such distinctions; it was part of the nature of the household itself. The household was a hierarchical institution, in which each of its members had a clearly defined position. It was also a patriarchal institution, in which the pre-eminent position was that of the master; and the distinction in status between master and servant was in some respects a model for distinctions between the servants themselves.

(ibid.)

And, if we stay with this case just a little longer, once the alleged social transgression *had* taken place, the outcome of the discovery and prosecution seems to support the view that such activity was regarded as only *slightly beyond the boundaries* set on allowable demands for 'submission' from one considerably lower in the social hierarchy of the household.[17]

> Richard Bryant, the servant who slept in the room with Davy and the boy . . . eventually took the matter to the mistress of the household, but it is striking as one reads his evidence how long it took him to realize what was going on and how reluctant he is likely to appear to us now to have been to draw the obvious conclusions.

(Bray 1982: 77)

Finally, at the end of the boy, John Vinlay's, evidence, he notes: 'since which time [Davy] hath layn quietly with him'. In other words, household life continued unchanged – the boy continued to share a bed with (hence, to be in a position of submission to) the alleged assaulter. Davy himself 'denieth that he ever used any unclean action with the said boy as they lay in bed together; and more he sayeth not' (Bray 1982: 69).[18]

In *Twelfth Night* the twin siblings, Viola and Sebastian, are of good family and fatherless.[19] They are, therefore, obliged to become dependent on households other than those of their own close kin. Indeed, one might argue that *finding a place* in the domestic economy of a household other than that of their family of birth is the initiation of the drama – they are shipwrecked on an unspecified voyage, and voyages are (in narrative) conventionally *quests* or searches.[20] In addition to the careful specification of their being orphaned before the age of majority ('when Viola from her birth / Had numbered thirteen years'), the audience are persistently reminded of the extreme youth of *both* twins (since each resembles the other so completely):

OLIVIA: Of what personage and years is he?
MAL: Not yet old enough for a man, nor young enough for a boy: as a squash is before 'tis a peascod, or a codling when 'tis almost an apple. 'Tis with him as standing water, between boy and man. He

is very well-favoured, and he speaks very shrewishly. One would think his mother's milk were scarce out of him.

(1.5.157–64)[21]

After the shipwreck, the first objective of the siblings is to transform their state from vagrancy to service (or, possibly, from wage-labour to service – Sebastian's 'gets' Antonio's purse, while Viola's relationship with the captain is constructed as a cash-transaction).[22] Both twins make immediately for the court of the Duke who 'governs here'. Both exchange their non-renewable cash assets (Viola's purse; Sebastian's borrowed purse) for the security of 'service' within a wealthy household ('I'll serve this duke' (1.3.55); 'I am bound to the Count Orsino's court' (2.2.41–2)). Viola's cross-dressing eases her way into Orsino's service.[23] Sebastian, mis-taken for Cesario, takes Olivia to be spontaneously offering an invitation to enter her *service* – an invitation he accepts as the very 'dream' he wished for: 'Go with me to my house . . . would thou'dst be rul'd by me!' (4.1.53,63).[24]

The *eroticization* of Viola/Cesario and of Sebastian is dramatically constructed in terms of their relationship to the domestic economy, and the place they occupy in relation to the heads of their adopted households. In the case of both Cesario's and Sebastian's 'place', this is fraught with erotic possibility in the very process of being established as 'service' (something which by now we might expect, in the light of the discussion of the early modern household at the beginning of this paper). The audience is entirely aware of the ambiguity in Sebastian's 'retention' by Olivia – he reads it as an invitation to enter her service, she offers it as a profession of passionate, sexual love and a marriage proposal. But Orsino's attachment to his new 'young gentleman', Cesario, is no less charged with erotic possibilities:

> VAL.:   If the Duke continue these favours towards you, Cesario, you are like to be much advanced. . . .
> VIOLA: You either fear his humour, or my negligence, that you call in question the continuance of his love. Is he inconstant, sir, in his favours?

(1.4.1–8)

'Love' here hovers dangerously between the mutual bond of service and passionate emotional attachment.[25] And the confusions possible in the Orsino/Viola service relationship are clinched shortly thereafter:

> DUKE: O then unfold the passion of my love,
>   Surprise her with discourse of my dear faith;
>   It shall become thee well to act my woes:
>   She will attend it better in thy youth,
>   Than in a nuncio's of more grave aspect.

VIOLA: I think not so, my lord.

DUKE: Dear lad, believe it;
For they shall yet belie thy happy years,
That say thou art a man; Diana's lip
Is not more smooth and rubious: thy small pipe
Is as the maiden's organ, shrill and sound,
And all is semblative a woman's part.
I know thy constellation is right apt
For this affair . . . .
     . . . Prosper well in this,
And thou shalt live as freely as thy lord,
To call his fortunes thine.

VIOLA: I'll do my best
To woo your lady: [*Aside*] yet, a barful strife!
Who'er I woo, myself would be his wife.

(1.5.24–42)

As Orsino eroticizes Viola in relation to Olivia he specifies the possibilities for eroticizing his own attention to the 'small pipe' and the 'maiden's organ' of the preferred youth in his service. As 'pipe' and 'organ' are 'semblative a woman's part' they position Cesario as desired dependant of Orsino – as available for his own sexual pleasure. So that when Orsino takes the hand of Cesario, at the close of the play, and claims her as his sexual partner, he does no more than confirm the terms of his original engagement with his 'young gentleman':

DUKE: Boy, thou hast said to me a thousand times
Thou never should'st love woman like to me.

VIOLA: And all those sayings will I over-swear,
And all those swearings keep as true in soul
As doth that orbed continent the fire
That severs day from night.

DUKE: Give me thy hand,
And let me see thee in thy woman's weeds.

(15.1.265–71)[26]

Of course, the erotic twist in *Twelfth Night* is achieved by the irony that it is *Olivia* – the lady of significant independent means and a disinclination to submit herself and her lands to any 'master'[27] – whose eroticized relationship of 'service' with Cesario is most socially and sexually transgressive. I think critics are right in seeing this as Olivia's 'come-uppance' – patriarchy's retribution for mis-taking the conventions both of service and of marriage as a *female* head of household in an order explicitly designated male in its defining relationships.[28]

In the resolution of the play, however, the easy redeployment of the erotic possibilities of Viola's and Sebastian's service to the households of Orsino and Olivia, respectively, literally *resolves* the union of the two lines. At the end of the play, the marriages of the twin siblings to Olivia and Orsino effect what Orsino's courtship of Olivia was originally designed to achieve – the Orsino and Olivia households enter into a kin relationship with one another:

> OLIVIA: My lord, so please you, these things further thought on,
>   To think me as well a sister, as a wife,
>   One day shall crown th'alliance on't so please you,
>   Here at my house, and at my proper cost.
> DUKE: Madam, I am most apt t'embrace your offer.
>   [*To Viola*] Your master quits you; and for your
>   service done him,
>   So much against the mettle of your sex,
>   So far beneath your soft and tender breeding,
>   And since you call'd me master for so long,
>   Here is my hand; you shall from this time be
>   Your master's mistress.
> OLIVIA: A sister! you are she.
>
> (5.1.315–25)

The happy ending is one in which the erotic potential of service is appropriately contained within the admissible boundaries of the patriarchal household – dependent women 'mastered' by husbands or brothers; dependent boys elevated by marriage into masters and heads of households themselves (even desired dependent girls regulated into dependent younger sisters). But, to return to my opening remarks, this is romance – a fictional resolution in which insuperable problems are superable, convenient twinning can iron out the crumpled social fabric of early modern life. In the street, the problem remains – the troubling possibility, 'in a throng', that those who appear to be available in the market place, gender-wise, are not what they seem (either are not available, but in transit between households, or are cross-dressed and marketing sodomy for female prostitution, female prostitution for boy-playing). In the market place, the disreputable sexual favours sought from passing, available 'youth' blatantly fail to comply with the procreative requirements of reputable, marital intercourse. And the very confusion which hovers around desirability surely points to the historic specificity of early modern eroticism. Eroticism, in the early modern period, is not gender-specific, is not grounded in the sex of the possibly 'submissive' partner, but is an expectation of that very submissiveness. As twentieth-century readers we recognize the eroticism of gender *confusion*, and reintroduce that confusion as a feature of the dramatic narrative. Whereas, for the

Elizabethan theatre audience, it may be the very *clarity* of the mistakenness – the very indifference to gendering – which is designed to elicit the pleasurable response from the audience.[29]

Notes

1 Since I wrote this paper, Alan Bray published his crucial article on homosexuality and male friendship in Elizabethan England (1990: 1–19). I have also benefited from discussion of a draft of this paper with Alan Bray, and wish to express my gratitude to him.

2 All references to *Twelfth Night* are to the Arden edition.

3 Thomas Middleton, 'Micro-Cynicon' (1599), in Bullen 8, 1886: 131–3. I am grateful to Bray (1982), in whose work I first found reference to this poem.

4 For the transgressive version see, most recently and convincingly, Dollimore (1986: 53–81). For the 'actual' affirmation version see Rose (1984: 367–91); and Howard (1988: 418–40).

5 Most of the textual accounts of cross-dressing (whether on the stage or in the street), like the 'Ingling' verse just cited and the Rainolds poem I use in *Still Harping on Daughters*, are clearly already adjusted to the fictional tropes of cross-dressing/illicit desire. Even sumptuary rules (as cited by Howard and others) aspire to control *excesses* which threaten good order – which is to say, dress which *signifies*, on which disorder is inscribed. The deposition relating to Mary Frith is a good example of the textual difficulties: in the record (whose narrative shape is controlled by the recording clerk and 'his Lordship', the bishop (?) who interrogates), the 'immodest and lascivious speeches', and 'shame of her sexe' collides with the slender textual traces of her refusal to accept the charge 'being pressed', 'whether she had not byn dishonest of her body & hath not also drawne other women to lewdnes by her perswasions & by carrying her self lyke a bawde'. To cross-dress is to signify as (to 'carry oneself' as) a bawd (deposition transcribed in full in Mulholland 1987: 262–3). The spate of 'Moll Frith' plays which accompanied her court appearance seize upon the event's bawdy potential (Mulholland 1987: 13) – for example, by suggesting she might 'take her own part' in the play (which 'part', and how related to *stage* cross-dressing?) and that she would play the viol on stage (the lewd possibilities of viol playing are considerable, as Howard points out in her essay for this volume). In a paper for the 1989 meeting of the Shakespeare Association of America, Stallybrass quoted Augustin Philips's will in which he left his apprentice various specified desirable items of clothing, and his 'bass viol'. Here too it seems possible that the legacy has been adjusted to the tropes of (intimate) devoted service – the bass viol and the shared items of dress connoting the closeness of the master-servant relationship.

6 It is fascinating that this exactly corresponds to Mary Douglas's 'dirt is matter out of place' (1966).

7 See R. Ascham, *The Scholemaster*, and its 'morals' source, Xenophon's *Cyropaedia*. I am extremely grateful to Lorna Hutson for making the vulnerability of the 'youth' clear to me, and for all the helpful discussion we had on this paper.

8 Throughout this paper I use the contemporary term 'sodomy' rather than the nineteenth-century 'homosexuality', or any of its cognates. In this I follow Bray (1982: 13–14), and Bullough in Bullough and Brundage (1982: 55–71).

9 To see how far back this goes as a fictionalizing of 'loose' women transgressively

entering the male preserve see Knighton's *Chronicon* (1348), quoted in Rickert (1949: 217). I am grateful to Rob Pope for bringing this passage to my attention.

10 This, I now think, is a more correct version of what I wrote earlier: 'The dependent role of the boy player doubles for the dependency which is women's lot, creating a sensuality which is independent of the sex of the desired figure, and which is particularly erotic when the sex is confused' (1983: 24).

11 For a clear account of the consistent use of the terms 'family' and 'household' to designate those who cohabit under a single roof, as dependants of one adult male in the eighteenth century see Tadmor (1989). In Bray (1982), see especially the clear account on pp. 44–6.

12 'The overall pattern in the circulation of members between [households of specified levels of wealth, in fifteenth-century Florence] was similar for men and for women, but there are also some significant differences in the movements of the two sexes. The richest households tend to gather in both boys and girls as they age, from birth up to their middle teens. At exact age 15, the 25 per cent of wealthy households contain 45 per cent of the boys and 43.5 per cent of the girls (as opposed to 39 per cent and 35 per cent respectively of the cohort of babies, age 0–2). This drift of children primarily means that wealthy households were taking in orphaned relatives. The incoming children probably also included many young relatives who had lost their fathers, and whose mothers had remarried and deserted them [*sic*]. The mother joined the household of her new husband, but usually did not take her children with her. The kindred of her late husband had to look to their care. . . . If we had data on servants and apprentices [registered with their household of birth in the Florentine census] we would undoubtedly observe an even more massive drift of young persons into and out of the homes of the wealthy. We know from other sources that "life-cycle" servants were numerous at Florence, as widely in traditional society. These young people, girls especially, spent their years of late childhood in service; they thereby earned their keep and accumulated from their earnings the dowry they needed for marriage' (Herlihy 1985: 153).

13 See Laslett in Laslett and Wall (1972: 125–58, table, 130). See also Wall (1978).

14 Data from Laslett and Wall. See also Beier (1985: 22–6); and Laslett's introduction, *passim*, for the complexity of the early modern household or family.

15 See also Bray (1982: 45), and the work in progress on early modern adolescence and service by Paul Griffiths (Clare College, Cambridge), especially his unpublished paper, 1990.

16 For the classic statement see Laslett (1972: 10): 'The seventeenth century patriarchal family had many of the characteristics of the patriarchal household. It included not only wife and children, but often younger brothers, sisters, nephews and nieces: male superiority and primogeniture were unquestioned. Most striking was the presence of very large numbers of servants, whose subjection to the head of household was absolute.'

17 For a brilliant account of the ambiguities concerning the relationship between service and sexual favours contained within the early modern patriarchal household, see Cynthia Herrup's paper on the trial of the Earl of Castlehaven. I read this paper while I was working on my own, and Herrup's argument was tremendously helpful in sharpening my own perception of the relationship between household dependency and the construction of sexuality.

18 On sexual exploitation of servants in general see, most recently, Amussen (1988: 159). In *Othello*, the shared bed in service, used by Iago to enflame Othello's jealousy, fully exploits the sexual availability of the bedfellow: 'I lay with Cassio lately, . . . In sleep I heard him say "Sweet Desdemona, / Let us be wary, let us

hide our loves;" / And then, sir, would he ... kiss me hard, / As if he pluck'd up kisses by the roots, / That grew upon my lips, then laid his leg / Over my thigh, and sigh'd, and kiss'd' (3.3. 419–31).

19 There is a steady, interesting insistence in the text on the good birth of the twins, *and* on their having full purses at their disposal. This seems to place them pivotally between the household economy and that of the market place. Although employment in the former was, historically, as precarious as that in the latter (wage-labour), there is no question that in the play-text only the household is seen as a suitable 'place' for Viola and Sebastian. On wage-labour versus service see Beier (1985).

20 'My father was that Sebastian of Messaline whom I know you have heard of. He left behind him myself and a sister, both born in an hour' (2.1.16–19); 'My father ... died that day when Viola from her birth / Had numbered thirteen years'; 'O, that record is lively in my soul! / He finished indeed his mortal act / That day that made my sister thirteen years' (5.1.240–6).

21 See also the Duke's emphasis on the extreme youth of Cesario when he cautions him against marrying an older woman (2.4.24–39). In the same passage the Duke calls Viola 'boy'. Sebastian (mirror-image of the cross-dressed Viola) is consistently referred to as 'youth' (for example 3.4.368).

22 See Beier (1985) for a gloss on the security of service versus the insecurity of waged labour (the temporarily full purse).

23 It perfectly fulfils the trope of serving devotion, as represented in saints' lives and romance. See Jardine (1983).

24 In terms of tropes, here is the moralizers' trope of the vulnerable boy captured in service by dominating female householders. See Ascham, and of course, Plautus's *Menaechmi* and Secchi's *Gl'Ingannati* (both of which link this play with *A Comedy of Errors*). In *Two Gentlemen of Verona* the two tropes are run into one, when Julia takes the name Sebastian (a straightforward signifier of male dependency and vulnerability) in order to pursue her fickle lover in faithful service. See Beier (1985: 22): 'Regarding [living-in service] we are told that the master/servant relationship was the lynch-pin of a patriarchal society in which "every relationship could be seen as a love-relationship".'

25 In the source story the heroine, dressed as a boy, fears she may be asked by her master for 'bedroom favours'. For a related discussion of the ambiguities of 'love' in the context of patronage see Barrell (1988: 18–43) on 'love' and patronage in Shakespeare's sonnet 29.

26 I think the 'woman's weeds' line is quite close in its possibilities to the seductively transgressive Pyander.

27 John Manningham's diary (1602) records a performance he saw of the play: 'A good practise in it to make the steward beleeue his Lady widdowe was in Loue wth him by counterfayting a lett^r / as from his Lady in generall tearmes telling him what shee liked best in him / and p[re]scribing his gesture in smiling his apparraile / &c./. And then when he came to practise making him beleeue they tooke him to be mad' (Arden *Twelfth Night*, xxvi). Manningham's mistaken memory ('widow' when Olivia in fact mourns the deaths of her father and brother) confirms the fact that as a figure she is recognizably the independent woman of means whose own will and desires figure troublingly strongly in choice of husband (and thus, continuation of the paternal line).

28 Olivia's femaleness is also the cause of her steward Malvolio's mis-taking *their* service relationship as passionate 'love'.

29 So, my final note addresses the vexed question of Middleton's *The Roaring Girl*. On this reading, Moll is neither male nor female, or *both* male and female,

confusing the several traditions which represent economic dependency via cross-dressing in private and in public. So the joke about the promise that Moll herself would come and play her own part in the play, *in place of* the boy who 'actually' takes it, is that it simply makes no difference to the 'performance'. Either way, that figure is replete with erotic potential.

References

Amussen, S. (1988) *An Ordered Society: Gender and Class in Early Modern England*, Oxford: Blackwell.

Barrell, J. (1988) 'Editing out: the discourse of patronage and Shakespeare's twenty-ninth sonnet', in J. Barrell, *Poetry, Language and Politics*, Manchester: Manchester University Press, 18–43.

Beier, A. L. (1985) *Masterless Men: The Vagrancy Problem in England 1560–1640*, London: Methuen.

Bray, A. (1982) *Homosexuality in Renaissance England*, 2nd edn 1988, London: Gay Men's Press.

—— (1990) 'Homosexuality and the signs of male friendship in Elizabethan England', *History Workshop Journal* 29: 1–19.

Bullough, V. L. (1982) 'The sin against nature and homosexuality', in V. L. Bullough and J. Brundage (eds), *Sexual Practices and the Medieval Church*, Buffalo, New York: Prometheus, 55–71.

Dollimore, J. (1986) 'Subjectivity, sexuality, and transgression: the Jacobean connection', *Renaissance Drama*, n.s. 17: 53–81.

Douglas, M. (1966) *Purity and Danger*, London: Routledge & Kegan Paul.

Griffiths, P. (1990) ' "At their own hande" and "out of service": residual lumps of young people in early modern England', paper given to the Cambridge Early Modernists, April.

Herlihy, D. (1985) *Medieval Households*, Cambridge, Mass.: Harvard University Press.

Houlbrooke, R. A. (1984) *The English Family, 1450–1700*, London: Longman.

Howard, J. E. (1988) 'Crossdressing, the theatre, and gender struggle in early modern England', *Shakespeare Quarterly* 39, 4: 418–40.

Jardine, L. (1983) *Still Harping on Daughters*, 2nd edn 1989, Brighton: Harvester.

Laslett, P. (1972) 'Mean household size in England since the sixteenth century', in P. Laslett and R. Wall (eds), *Household and Family in Past Time*, Cambridge: Cambridge University Press, 125–58.

Middleton, T. 'Micro-Cynicon' (1599), in A. H. Bullen (ed.) (1886) *The Works of Thomas Middleton*, repr. 1964, New York: AMS Press 8: 130–5.

Mulholland, P. (ed.) (1987) *The Roaring Girl*, Manchester: Manchester University Press.

Quaife G. R. (1979) *Wanton Wenches and Wayward Wives: Peasants and Illicit Sex in Early Seventeenth Century England*, London: Croom Helm.

Rickert, E. (1949) *Chaucer's World*, London: Oxford University Press.

Rose, M. B. (1984) 'Women in men's clothing: apparel and social stability in *The Roaring Girl*', *English Literary Renaissance* 14, 3: 367–91.

St Clare Byrne, M. (ed.) (1985) *The Lisle Letters: An Abridgement*, Harmondsworth: Penguin.

Tadmor, T. (1989) ' "Family" and "friend" in *Pamela*: a case study in the history of the family in eighteenth-century England', *Social History* 14: 289–306.

Wall, R. (1978) 'The age at leaving home', *Journal of Family History* 3.

Chapter 4

Disruptive desire
Artifice and indeterminacy in Jacobean comedy

Susan Zimmerman

Recent scholarly examinations of the English Renaissance theatre as a site for sexual production, focusing primarily on Shakespeare, have addressed the erotic dynamic of the transvestite stage only obliquely. Their preoccupation has been with the function of cross-dressing within dramatic fictions as socially liberating role inversion (as exemplified, for example, by Rosalind, Viola, Portia), and thus, more fundamentally, with sexuality as gender oppression.[1] In such a critical paradigm, the eroticism implicit in transvestism is theatrically incidental; subsumed into the *gestalt* of the fiction, it serves a larger (and of course subversive) design.[2]

In order to reposition eroticism in our historicizing of the Renaissance theatre we need to shift attention to the flatter, more formulaic terrain of much non-Shakespearean Jacobean drama, and eventually to reconsider Shakespeare in terms of it. In these dramatic works, the erotic potential of transvestism is foregrounded – particularly the convention's power to disrupt fictional constructs and call attention to its own artifice. Indeed, by directly violating the audience's presumed suspension of disbelief, Jacobean playwrights seemed to have deliberately and self-consciously privileged transvestism for purposes of erotic titillation and, in so doing, to have invited audience participation in the erotic transgression of culturally inscribed sexual categories.

The responses of individual Jacobean spectators to erotic stimuli originating on the stage are of course unknowable. But by focusing on opportunities provided in the plays for stage–spectator interaction, the structure of the theatrical dynamic may be problematized according to a conceptual model that combines material analysis of stage practice with psychoanalytic theory of erotic desire. Accordingly, if one assumes with Freud that sexual categories are culturally inscribed, that they overlie a polymorphously perverse sexual disposition and are subject to destabilization, one may argue that such destabilization inhered in Jacobean transvestite performance; that the dynamic of this destabilization was erotically charged; and that Jacobean theatre-goers (including, most problematically, female spectators) would have been implicated in it. Within the context of this paradigm, Jacobean drama functioned as a distinctive erotic discourse in a multi-vocal culture, and the theatre as a privileged site for the instantiation of that discourse.

i

Julia Kristeva has reminded us that monotheistic, patrilinear societies require the radical separation and incompatability of the sexes, the demonization of women, and the centralizing of eroticism in the reproductive function (1986).[3] These are familiar themes in those canonical discourses of the English Renaissance – theology, law and social doctrine – that defined the hegemony. Such discourses inscribed difference onto a hierarchy of cultural practices necessarily oppressive to women, whose position as 'other' was essential to the partriarchal social construct. But in privileging oppositional structures, these discourses invite deconstruction informed by psychoanalytic theory, which insists on the impossiblity of mutually exclusive categories. Especially pertinent in this regard is the principle that binary opposites are inescapably implicated in each other; thus arbitrary fixity has at best a tenuous hold on the internal contradictions it attempts to suppress. Accordingly, ostensibly patriarchal, hierarchically ordered discourses, because of the very rigidity with which they are constituted, paradoxically undermine the oppositions they seek to valorize.

Among Renaissance exemplars, the medical treatises of early modern England, fundamentally implicated in the society's production of sexuality, including that of the theatre, are acutely revealing in this regard. Put simply, many – probably most – of these accounts contain a male-dominated, unisexual model for sexual differentiation.[4] Based on Galen, this model sought to account for female sexual anatomy as an inversion of male anatomy: turned inside out, a woman's sexual organs would be identical to those of a man. Moreover, heat, the determining factor in conception, was generated with greatest intensity in the male. Thus men and women were arranged 'along an axis whose telos [was] male' (Laqueur 1986: 2); sexual design and life itself originated in the male principle.

None the less, despite its explicit insistence on male supremacy, the unisexual model simultaneously served to unfix the body, to free it of categorial restraints. The male principle was not completely ascendant because boys passed through a 'female' developmental phase (and were cross-dressed accordingly); under certain stimuli, a woman's homologous sex organs could descend and externalize, rendering her male (a phenomenon occurring in reverse only rarely); and cases of hermaphroditism tried by the courts were adjudicated according to behavioural rather than anatomical criteria ('an external or internal penis was only the diagnostic sign'). In short, the absence of biological difference in the unisexual model precluded a stable system of sexual dimorphism in the Renaissance: 'Maleness and femaleness did not reside in anything particular' (Laqueur 1990: 135).

The image of the hermaphrodite in the celebrated cases that circulated in social discourse – the inside-out made manifest – encapsulated the paradox of Renaissance sexual homologies. But from the standpoint of medical theory such creatures were more rightly termed androgynes: that is, their condition resulted not from the joining together of complementary halves (as in the Ovidian myth of Hermaphroditus and Salmacis), but from the unsuccessful division of a problematically unified entity (as in the myth of the sexes which Aristophanes relates in Plato's *Symposium*). Not surprisingly, the Aristophanic myth resonates in Freud, whose theory of sexuality is grounded in the idea of an originally indeterminate sexual disposition subject to restrictive, formative stimuli which ultimately divide, or genderize the subject.[5]

According to Freud, the sexual instinct in very early infancy is polymorphously perverse, which signifies that it has no *natural* object, animate or inanimate.

> It seems probable that the sexual instinct is in the first instance independent of its object;. . . . the sexual instinct and the sexual object are merely soldered together.
>
> (*SE* 7: 148)

> The object of an instinct is the thing in regard to which or through which the instinct is able to achieve its aim. It is what is most variable about an instinct and is not originally connected with it. . . .
>
> (*SE* 14: 122)

In choosing objects of desire throughout pre-genital stages of development, the subject remains impervious to gender distinctions, and also desires that which pertains to both sexes:

> all human beings are capable of making a homosexual object-choice and have in fact made one in their unconscious . . . a choice of an object independently of its sex – freedom to range equally over male and female objects – as it is found in childhood . . . is the original basis from which both the normal and the inverted types develop.
>
> (*SE* 7: 145–6)

The imposition of gender, a culturally induced division,[6] is never wholly successful; even in so-called normal adulthood, 'no individual is limited to the modes of reaction of a single sex' (*SE* 23: 188). Moreover, the polymorphous sexual disposition with which every human being begins life, subsumed in the unconscious in the course of sexual development, may become manifest in a variety of sexual perversions:

> the sexual instinct itself must be something put together from various factors, and. . . . in the perversions it falls apart, as it were, into its components.
>
> (*SE* 7: 231)

These perversions are defined *as such* in terms of the repressive process that constitutes sexual maturation; that is, they are culturally coded, products of the imposition of hegemonic norms on the sexual development of the subject.[7]

The central metaphor of Renaissance medical discourse, that of homology, foregrounds two concepts: the making of sexes through divisions from common beginnings, and the instability of the resulting construct. What is culturally significant about this metaphor from a Freudian perspective is that it suggests slippages in the sexually repressive mechanisms constituted by Renaissance society – that is, a society that has found no mode for *clearly* demarcating the sexes (as biology claimed to do in the eighteenth century) is likely to be a less successful repressive force than one that believes in a biologically validated two-sex system. Or, to put it another way, a society which even indirectly acknowledges the impossibility of sexual fixity may on certain levels be less threatened by manifestations of sexual indeterminacy. In any case, its codes for sexual perversion will be difficult of access.

In a provocative statement (which bears a Freudian stamp) at the outset of his book, Laqueur implies that early modern sexual ideology, as opposed to its successors, masked wisdom in confusion:

> The record on which I have relied bears witness to the fundamental incoherence of stable, fixed categories of sexual dimorphism, of male and/or female. . . . Indeed, if structuralism has taught us anything it is that humans impose their sense of opposition onto a world of continuous shades of difference and similarity.
>
> (1990: 22, 19)

However male-dominant the Renaissance unisexual model purported to be, it ended up contesting, via its own internal contradictions, the oppositional structure that undergirds patriarchal societies. And in betraying a fascination for the deviant – for that which *unsettles* sexual difference – this discourse may well have negotiated a transaction between imagination and the unconscious: that is, it may have provided some measure of access to what Lacanian psychoanalytic theory terms pre-symbolic modes of sexual activity.

ii

As a primary locus for the interrogation of subjectivity, the English Renaissance theatre would also have served as a medium for the release of transgressive erotic impulses. A commercial enterprise heavily inscribed with communal traditions of popular culture, it offered 'an escape from supervision and from surveillance of attitude, feeling and expression' (Bristol 1985: 112). More fundamentally, its signifying practice was the represen-

tation of male and female subjects through the medium of acting, or disguise. Polyphonic and dialogic in the Bakhtinian sense, Renaissance theatre
called attention to its own textuality, its artifice, in the figuration of gendered subjects.

Artifice was undisguised on the Renaissance stage, an essential part of
the theatrical construct. The conventions of continuous staging, natural
lighting, unlocalized settings and anachronistic costuming framed the fiction; those of soliloquies, asides, prologues and epilogues interrupted or
discontinued it. The artifice of acting – the pre-condition for any theatre –
was underscored by transvestism. If the dialogic text of the Renaissance
theatre disrupted causality and logic, cross-dressing complicated that disruption by simultaneously interrogating sexual difference. Eroticism was inescapably implicated in these disruptions.

Cross-dressing on the Renaissance stage had, of course, a culturally specific meaning in terms of its centuries-old tradition in England. Despite the
pervasiveness of boy actors in the Middle Ages, and the liturgical cast of
much medieval drama,[8] theatrical transvestism was a continual cause for
concern among the custodians of social order. Theologically problematic
(it violated the Deuteronomic prohibition) and socially transgressive (particularly as appropriated for popular rituals of misrule, such as the celebration of the Boy Bishop), cross-dressing – and by implication sexuality
– had a disturbing, anarchic potential.[9]

During the Renaissance the case against it, based on well-established
scriptural exegesis, was most forcefully argued by the distinguished theo-
logian John Rainolds in correspondence conducted between 1591 and 1594
with two Oxford scholars: William Gager, the leading writer of academic
drama at Oxford, and Alberico Gentili, Professor of Civil Law.[10] With the
rapidly emerging public theatre as a backdrop for this rehearsal of traditional
argument, Gentili, by far the worthier opponent for Rainolds, took great
pains to restrict his defence of cross-dressed boys to amateur productions
such as those at Oxford. The sub-text that distinguishes this correspondence
as Renaissance is the mutual abhorrence with which Rainolds and Gentili
viewed the exploitation of cross-dressing for sexual purposes in the newly
commercialized theatre.

To be sure, English theatrical practice had undergone significant change
during the two decades preceding this dispute. The development of the
Children of the Chapel and the Children of St Paul's into companies
which played to aristocratic audiences in private theatres as well as at court
represented a new professional positioning for boy actors. The expansion
of early itinerant acting troupes to full-fledged adult companies with aristocratic sponsorship had revitalized the profession; and the construction of
large-scale, public, extra-mural theatres, ambiguously positioned in relation
to mechanisms of social control, was unprecedented.

In this expansive climate, the sexual transgressiveness of the boy actor became, to judge by contemporary accounts, impudent and explicit. For example, *Damon and Pythias*, performed by the Children of the Chapel in about 1564, includes a scene in which boys strut in big breeches, satirizing the disparity between their undeveloped organs and their outsized clothes: 'Yea, sir; are we not pretie men?. . . . I haue but for one lining in one hose, but vii els of Rug' (Malone Soceity Reprints 1957: TLN 1405, 1410). The same unabashed parodic style is reported in a 1569 royal performance:

> Plaies will neuer be supprest, while her maiesties unfledged minions flaunt it in silkes and sattens. . . . Even in her maiesties chappel doe these pretty vpstart youthes profane the Lordes Day by the lascivious writhing of their tender limbs, and gorgeous decking of their apparell, in feigning bawdie fables gathered from the idolatrous heathen poets.[11]

Both performances link sexual innuendo with exotic and inappropriate apparel, which conflates (and confuses) violations of sumptuary and sexual norms. The high artifice of these disparities became the trademark style of the boys' companies in the 1570s and 1580s.

Rainolds' attack on transvestite acting, fuelled by alarm at the burgeoning influence of the theatre, fully recognized the threat represented by transgressive boy actors. Relentlessly hierarchical and doctrinaire, he admitted no exception to the Deuteronomic injunction. Ironically, Rainolds' dogmatism was necessary as a counterforce to his empathic understanding of the temptations he excoriated. In assailing the erotic appeal of the cross-dressed boy actor, he unwittingly served up an incisively sensitive account of the psycho-dynamics of male spectatorship.

According to Rainolds, the initial danger for the male spectator in viewing a cross-dressed boy was the incitement to lust for a woman. He cites Dionysius Carthusianus:

> *For the apparell of wemen . . . is a great provocation of men to lust and leacherie: because a womans garment being put on a man doeth vehemently touch and moue him with the remembrance and imagination of a woman; and the imagination of a thing desirable doth stirr up the desire.*

(Binns 1974: 103)

When cross-dressed boys danced, the impulse to lust was greatly intensified, again, by triggering in the viewer's mind a train of erotic associations. To illustrate the consummate appeal of the dancing boy, Rainolds borrowed from Propertius a description of his mistress:

> How much lesse seemely then is it for young men to danse like wemen . . . whereby what a flame of lust may bee kindled in the hearts of men . . . a Heathen Poet [has shown] more fullie by his owne experience; affirming that hee was not ravished so much with his mistresses face

though marvellous faire and beautifull, nor with her heare hanging downe loose after the facion about here smooth necke; nor with her radiant eyes, like starres; nor with her silkes, and outlandish braverie; as hee was with her galant dansing.

(102)

Rainolds assumed the credibility of the theatrical impersonation; Propertius' mistress conflates with the boy impersonator. Moreover, the language of Rainolds' paraphrase, with its sensual detail, romantic images and series of rhythmic repetitions, reinforces his notion of erotic irresistibility. In Rainolds' construction, the male spectator was seduced by the beauty of the female fiction.

But, as Stephen Orgel has recently argued, the erotic appeal of the boy actor was *also* that of a boy. Male spectators not only lusted after the woman in the drama 'but after the boy beneath the woman's costume, thereby playing the woman's role themselves' (1989: 16). Rainolds, subtly tuned to this dual dynamic, offered a powerfully wrought description of homoerotic kissing:

certaine spiders, if they doe but touch men onely with their mouth, they put them to wonderfull paine and make them madde: so beautifull boyes by kissing doe sting and powre secretly in a kinde of poyson, the poyson of incontinencie, as Clemens Alexandrinus speaking of vnholy and amatorie kisses, saieth: Amatorie embracing goeth in the same line with amatorie kissing, if not a line beyond it.

(102)

In his interesting shift from a specific instance of homoeroticism to a general statement on all amatory kissing and embracing, Rainolds did not distinguish between male and female as unholy erotic object(s). As in the description of Propertius' mistress, he suggested the simultaneity of dual attractions.

Since Rainolds was at best an infrequent theatre-goer, these descriptions are projections or fantasies of what the theatre – particularly a libertine, commercial theatre – made possible. His concerns were shared by other anti-theatrical polemicists who betrayed a similar conviction that the theatre was powerfully enabled to effect sexual disruption.[12] Moreover, writing to Gentili in the early 1590s, Rainolds was yet to witness the consolidation of the major adult companies, a phenomenon which greatly strengthened this disruptive potential.

At their apogee in the 1580s, the boys' companies brought polish, audacity and verbal agility to the stage, exploiting, as Heywood put it, the privilege of juniority (1612: G3v), and attracting most of the leading playwrights of the period. Although some adults performed in these groups, for the most part boys played against one another. Thus the impersonation of women, generally assigned to boys under fifteen, complemented the impersonation of men: the disparity between juveniles and the adults they imitated was a form of masquerade or mockery. When the boys returned to the stage after a ten-year hiatus, companies of primarily adult actors, well-established and hugely popular, offered a different tonality of perform-ance.[13]

The contrast in styles would have been most evident in the sexual sphere. Notwithstanding the fact that throughout the early 1600s, boys' and adult companies shared playwrights and theatrical practices, and sometimes per-formed the same plays, they could not have created the same erotic reson-ances in performance. Scenes featuring two boys playing women might have resonated similarly, but not those featuring impersonations of men and women, especially in sexual contexts. When an actor in a male role did not need to impersonate adult-ness, his interaction with a cross-dressed actor, particularly a cross-dressed boy, changed. Presumably, the adult actor, by virtue of age, voice, physical appearance and interpretive range, lent credence to the (usually) heterosexual dramatic fiction. He also could put a pederastic gloss on the homosexual valences of cross-dressing within that fiction. Thus the temptations of transvestism assailed by Rainolds were rendered explicit in this dynamic.[14] The dual lens on the dramatic action that the adult male actor provided was in all likelihood angled most directly at adult male spectators.

The erotic responses of women spectators to the Renaissance stage, public or private, were not, of course, anatomized in contemporary accounts. The theatre was a male preserve, the transvestite acting convention a confir-mation of it. At least in the public theatres, women, particularly aristocratic women, occupied marginal positions as spectators; contrary to common assumption, their presence in large numbers up to about 1614 has not been established.[15] Paradoxically, however, this marginality probably did not affect the participation of women spectators in the interactive dynamic between drama and audience, especially in terms of erotic valances.

As we have seen, on the transvestite stage, particularly that of the mature adult companies in the Jacobean period, hetero- and homoerotic stimuli for male spectators were mutually dependent. The heterosexual fiction may actually have mediated the underlying homosexual appeal of the transvestite actor; in any case it was a mixture of erotic stimuli that distinguished the theatrical dynamic. The androgynous beauty of the cross-dressed boy actor blurred socially inscribed sexual categories, thereby fusing or overlapping disparate erotic impulses in the experience of the male spectator.

As a form of sexual deconstruction, this dynamic must have made room for that category of spectator – woman – who represents one term of the deconstructed duality. This is not to say that women and men would have responded similarly to the same theatrical stimuli (or, of course, that all men and all women would have shared essentialist responses). However much sexual categories were blurred on stage, they could not be collapsed completely because spectators were culturally constituted by these categories and brought heavily inscribed sexual predispositions to the theatre. Therefore the erotic appeal of heterosexual fiction, androgynous beauty and explicitly male homosexual exchange – theatrical phenomena that contemporary polemics castigated in terms of male responses – would have resonated differently for the demonized 'other' in a dualistic culture. But by participating in a drama which interrogated this dualism, women would have had access to a similar *range* of erotic experience, as well as to the erotically charged confusion that accompanies the displacement of sexual boundaries.[16]

Jonathan Dollimore once posed a question pertinent to this study: 'Which, or how many, of the several gender identities embodied in any one figure [on the transvestite stage] are in play at any one time?' (1986: 65). The question assumes a fluid movement among an actor's dramatic personae, complemented by the spectator's capacity for – to paraphrase Catherine Belsey – a multiplicity of possible identifications.[17] The erotic distinction of the Jacobean transvestite theatre was that it permitted the deconstruction of the symbolic androgyne and the concomitant release of repressed sexual energies. Through the blurring of oppositional categories, the reaching back toward indeterminacy, it empowered its audience to explore, in some measure, the polymorphous disposition that underlies all sexuality.

iii

The Jacobean comedies which I will now examine exemplify the deconstructive process which I have been describing. In them, the convention of transvestite acting was self-consciously exploited in the interests of manipulating erotic audience response. Spectators of these plays were not permitted wholly to suspend their disbelief in the dramatic fiction; instead, they were made to shift continually between perspectives within and without this fiction. In thus foregrounding the sexual artifice of the transvestite tradition, playwrights constituted that artifice as part of a distinctive and erotically charged dramatic form.

Strategies for interrupting and displacing dramatic fictions include references, implicit or explicit, to the body beneath that of the actor's impersonation (including scenes of broad, bawdy humour); excessive attention to the age, beauty and apparel of the cross-dressed boy, and especially to the complex sexual appeal of boy actors twice cross-dressed; ostentatious kissing and embracing; attenuated scenes of primarily sexual interest (such as bedroom scenes); and meta-theatric commentary on theatrical artifice, particularly 'send-ups' of the transvestite convention itself.

In selecting plays I have focused primarily on those with cross-dressed heroines because erotic strategies dependent on transvestism are easiest to illustrate through such figures. Two, possibily three, of the plays were probably written by Thomas Middleton and all were presumably performed between 1610 and 1623 by adult acting companies whose erotic range in performance, as described earlier, was extensive.[18]

In dealing with selected features of these comedies, I will not be distorting their tonality. Illicit sexual intrigue unfolds on mutually reinforcing levels in each of them: it is the obsessional centre of dramatic action and audience response. Social and economic concerns, although heavily implicated in such intrigue, are subordinated to it. For example, in Middleton's *No Wit, No Help Like a Woman's* (c. 1611),[19] Kate Low-water, ruined tenant of the widowed Lady Goldenfleece, denounces the avaricious practices of her patron and, through a strategem of cross-dressing, administers the widow's reform. But this ethical orientation serves only to frame and partially displace Kate's chief function, which is to orchestrate the erotic responses inspired by her cross-dressed status. Moreover, the Low-water plot (Middleton's invention) is connected – feebly – to an elaborate incest theme adapted from Italian prose comedy. What pervades the entirety of the play, as well as others to be examined here, is a preoccupation with sexual deviance.

In *No Wit, No Help*, Lady Goldenfleece is wooed by several suitors, chiefly Weather-wise, an eccentric, and Lambston, the main contender. Early in the play, Kate-in-disguise (whom I am calling MaleKate, since the play provides no name for this persona), attends a banquet hosted by Weather-wise for the widow and his rivals. Lady Goldenfleece, engaged in a flirtation with Lambston, is quickly compelled by the youthful beauty and confident demeanour of MaleKate ('The more I look on him, the more I thirst for't' [2.1.207]), inspiring Kate to dupe the widow by entering the competition for her hand. But Weather-wise is similarly attracted to MaleKate: 'A proper woman turn'd gallant! If the widow refuse me, I care not if I be a suitor to him. I have known those who have been as mad, and given half their living for a male companion' (180–3).

In the fiction, Weather-wise does not know that Kate is cross-dressed. His reference to her as 'a proper woman turn'd gallant' underscores Male-Kate's androgynous appeal, made possible by the indeterminate sexuality of the boy actor who projects this appeal: the 'male companion' that Weather-wise covets does indeed exist outside the fiction, beneath the double mask. On the transvestite stage, Weather-wise's freely acknowledged pederastic attraction to MaleKate is an inescapable *double entendre*. Moreover, it is Weather-wise and his associates who throughout the play call attention to MaleKate's androgyny, ironically, by jealously denouncing Lady Goldenfleece's desire to marry him as sexually deviant: 'They marry now but the third part of husbands / Boys, smooth-fac'd catamites, to fulfill their bed, / As if a woman should a woman wed' (4.3.68–70); 'And at night with a boy tossed in a blanket' (90); 'a boy keeps her under' (100); 'This 'tis to marry beardless domineering boys!' (5.1.261).

To be sure, Lady Goldenfleece responds to MaleKate's androgyny, his less-than-manly beauty, with the same lustful directness as does Weather-wise. But she also admires his intelligence, wit and air of command, and these are qualities which the audience associates with the persona of the resourceful Kate, fine-tuner of seductive schemes. Thus in the fiction Lady Goldenfleece is simultaneously attracted to an unfinished youth, a womanly boy (as Weather-wise contends), *and* (unknowingly) to the more mature aspects of a self-sufficient woman – not unlike Lady Goldenfleece herself. That the distinguishing qualities of both Kate and the widow defy conventional criteria for the 'feminine' adds yet another transgressive layer to this homoerotic dynamic.

However, *outside* the fiction Lady Goldenfleece and her suitor are male actors, and this complication is *also* operative in the play. When in the wooing scenes, MaleKate's passion is tested in an exchange of kisses, the fiction is deliberately, if temporarily abrogated. Presumably, the supererogatory explicitness of kissing on a transvestite stage (sexual intrigue can easily do without it, as we see in most of Shakespeare) reminds the audience of the body beneath the sexual disguise and shifts the erotic ambience. During the banquet scene, in one such suspended moment, Lambston kisses Lady Goldenfleece in an ostentatious display designed to quell his envious rivals. When MaleKate takes Lambston's place, that is, when one of the kissing actors is cross-dressed twice, playing a woman dressed as a man seducing another woman, the erotic resonances are confusingly multi-valent.

That the play consistently attenuates these resonances is most evident in the culminating bedroom scene, where Lady Goldenfleece's impatience to make love is played against MaleKate's coy dalliance and pretended anger:

LADY G.:   Now, like a greedy usurer alone,
   I sum up all the wealth this day has brought me,
   And thus I hug it.
MIST. L-W.: Prithee!
LADY G.:   Thus, I kiss it.
MIST. L-W.: I can't abide these kissings.
LADY G.:   How, sir? Not!
   I'll try that sure, I'll kiss you out of that humor.

(5.1.1–5)

And so on. When after a protracted delay, during which the audience luxuriates in a erotically charged comic confusion, Kate finally reveals herself, she does so with a wonderfully redolent irony that unmasks more than the fiction of MaleKate. Proclaiming 'And I've my neck-verse perfect, here and here' (5.1.344), she points to her breasts, effectively destabilizing the dramatic resolution of the sexual intrigue by means of reference to the boy actor.[20]

The unstable sexual identities of *No Wit, No Help*, the multi-dimensional confusions of the play, allow ample space for spectator responses attuned to the erotic possibilities of such confusion. In *The Widow* (c. 1616, probably by Middleton),[21] the same deliberate undermining of sexual certainties is apparent, although the mode of manipulating erotic response is different.

This comedy also uses a cross-dressed heroine, Martia, as the focal point for erotic titillation, but, rather than being the initiator of a sexual intrigue, she is the victim of a series of mischances from which she must extricate herself. Her cross-dressed status seems arbitrary; the rationale for it, that she has fled her father's command that she marry an old man, is alluded to only briefly. Martia's shifts in fortune entail multiple cross-dressings: she first appears as a woman disguised as a man (Ansaldo), undergoes several changes of male attire, and finally allows herself to be disguised as a woman. These visually compelling shifts of personae, coupled with the situational humour, focus audience attention on Martia/Ansaldo's *body* – as erotic object(s), as playground for comic deception.

The first scene featuring cross-dressing is a scopophilic tease. Ansaldo appears, posing as a comely 'younger son', singing in a delicate, underdeveloped voice and keeping time ('Pretty and handsomely with your little hand there' [3.1.13]) for the entertainment of a male travelling companion who turns out to be the leader of a gang of thieves. Threatened with search and seizure ('if I take you in hand, / You'll find me rough' [57]), Ansaldo tries to ward off his assailants with an unloaded pistol, but they bawdily deride this ruse: 'The pistol cannot speak. / He was too young. / I ever thought he could not' (99–101). Fearing full discovery, and worse, Ansaldo submits to his captors (one of whom commands, '. . . bear him into th' next copse and strip him' [104]), but he escapes (in offstage action) before they remove his underclothes. In the multiple mockeries of this scene, audience awareness of the boy actor mediates the shifts between Ansaldo the male and Martia the woman. Obviously, the much-touted strip can only be conducted off-stage.

The erotic allure of Ansaldo's androgynous body is underscored emphatically when, without sumptuary support for sexual identity, wearing only a shirt, he stumbles into the sexual domain of Phillippa, an older, married woman. Ansaldo is discovered in deshabille by Violetta, Phillippa's maid, who brings him to her mistress' bedchamber: 'a sweet young gentleman, / Robb'd even to nothing, but what first he brought with him: / The slaves had stript him to the very shirt, mistress; / I think it was a shirt; I know not well / For gallants wear both now-a-days' (3.3.24–8). Phillippa, captivated and lustful, is moved to embellish Ansaldo's beauty by dressing him in an old suit of her elderly husband, which heightens her desire. The neutrality of Martia/Ansaldo's body, its function as a kind of mannikin which may be outfitted with sex-defining adornment, is further emphasized in a later stratagem, when Phillippa transforms Ansaldo once again with her own gown and head-tire: 'What think you now sirs, / Is't not a goodly, manly gentlewoman?' (5.1.157–8). Ansaldo's female dress adds homoerotic spice to Phillippa's fantasies of sexual consummation: she imagines him/her as maidservant by day, lover by night.

Martia/Ansaldo in disguise as Phillippa's female creation also appears desirable to Francisco, a gallant who has rebuffed Phillippa's earlier sexual advances. In a scheme to spite Francisco, Phillippa urges a match between – as she sees it – Francisco and Ansaldo-in-disguise. Francisco, easily ensnared, woos the proffered lady, kissing and embracing her at Phillippa's gleeful urging ('Give her a lip-taste, / That she herself may praise it' [5.1.267]). When the couple marries, Phillippa's maid announces triumphantly: 'Here they come, / Here they come, one man married to another!' (5.1.400–1). The audience knows that Ansaldo is Martia and that Phillippa is bound to be foiled, but on another level which the play has consistently foregrounded, it also knows that the changeling actor is a boy. Phillippa is both right and wrong, and so is Francisco: the erotic currents of this play criss-cross in many directions.

Like *No Wit, No Help*, *The Widow* has more than one sexual intrigue. In another action, a young widow, Valeria, is courted by two superannuated suitors and an impudent gallant, Ricardo. The bawdiness of the wooing scenes makes much of the sexual limitations of the old men, and of Ricardo's sprightliness. But the most arresting feature of the courtship intrigue is a meta-theatric tour de force in which Ricardo and Francisco (who also functions as Ricardo's friend) mock the business of courting women as well as the practice of transvestite acting.

Early in the play the two gallants play-act a wooing scene. Ricardo takes up the woman's role ('Come, come make me your woman' [1.2.79]) despite Francisco's protest that he would laugh if his friend were to don a farthingale. When Ricardo proves much too easy to woo, Francisco plays the woman:

RIC.   Tell me, as you're a woman, lady, what serve kisses for but to stop all your mouths?

FRAN.   Hold, hold, Ricardo!

RIC.   Disgrace me, widow?

FRAN.   Art mad? I'm Francisco.

(ATT.) Signor Ricardo, up, up!

RIC.   Who is't? Francisco?

FRAN.   Francisco, quotha! what, are you mad, sir?

RIC.   . . . I was i' the fairest dream.

FRAN.   'Tis a strange way methinks.

RIC.   Learn you to play a woman not so scornfully then;
For I am like the actor that you spoke on:
I must have the part that overcomes the lady
I never like the play else.

(135–48)

Without benefit of costume, and outside the prevailing fiction of the play, Ricardo demonstrates how easy it is to switch genders – to get lost in a fiction of his own. Francisco may call this 'strange', but it is no stranger than Francisco's own position at the end of the play when he successfully kisses a woman presumed by some in the fiction to be a man, and recognized by the audience to be a man/woman/boy actor. Ricardo as a woman may seem laughable in one avatar, but in the end everyone gets lost in the fiction.

Although *More Dissemblers Besides Women* (1516?),[22] is also a play about erotic power, it features a cross-dressed female figure not in a central but in a subsidiary role, as one of several comic devices reinforcing dominant sexual motifs. The chief female figure is the Duchess of Milan, committed to perpetual chastity since the death of her husband and due for an erotic come-uppance. Not surprisingly, it takes only one strong temptation to shatter the Duchess's resolve and redirect her energies to the satisfaction of sexual desire. Her intrigue for achieving this purpose involves Lactantio, a gallant whose pregnant mistress is disguised at court as the page Antonio. The device of the cross-dressed page functions as the occasion for gratuitous scenes of bawdy humour with a male homoerotic orientation.

Unlike Kate and Martia, Lactantio's mistress is a reluctant transgressor, shunning the implications of male disguise, modest and fearful – in short, a conventionally feminine creation. In the fiction, this disposition circum-scribes her/his androgyny: Antonio's erotic appeal is always described by males. His diminutive stature and delicate sensibilities – his 'girlishness' – are key elements in this appeal, repeatedly emphasized in the play:

But you can keep a little tit-mouse page there,
That's good for nothing but to carry toothpicks.

(3.1.77–8)

[if] you chance to fall and hazard the breaking of your little buttocks

(1.4.25–6)

'tis pity that thou wert ever bred to be thrust through a pair of canions; thou wouldst have made a pretty foolish waiting-woman but for one thing.

(1.4.59–66)

He's too little for any woman's love i' th' town
By three handfuls:

(5.1.145–6)

He is so soft, th'unkindness of a word
Melts him into a woman.

(3.1.134–5)

Antonio's femininity inspires the bawdy imagination of Dondolo, the scabrous servant with whom Antonio lodges. It is Dondolo who ridicules Antonio's size as well as his distaste for indelicate chores: 'are you not big enough to air a shirt? were it a smock now, you liquorish page, you'd be hanged ere you'd part from't' (1.4.47). The ease with which Antonio may wear either shirt or smock, either male or female persona, titillates Dondolo, and his ribald commentary on Antonio's androgyny generalizes Antonio's condition. Gallants are indistinguishable from their mistresses ('All your young gallants here of late wear smocks, / Those without beards especially' [68–9]; 'being both in smocks [in bed], they'd be taken for sisters' [73–4]); and young girls play the role of homosexual boys:

DON.   . . . you've many daughters so well brought up, they speak French naturally at fifteen, and they are turned to the Spanish and Italian half a year after.

PAGE: That's like learning the grammar first, and the accidence after, they go backward so.

DON.   The fitter for th' Italian.

(80–6)

When a frustrated Dondolo later complains to Lactantio of Antonio's aloofness, his own homosexual desire is explicit:

when all the lodgings
Were taken up with strangers th'other night
He would not suffer me to come to bed to him
But kick'd, and prick'd, and pinch'd like an urchin. . . .
There's no good fellowship in this dandiprat,
This dive-dapper, as in other pages:
They'd go a-swimming with me familiarly
I' th' heat of summer, and clap what-you-call-'ems;
But I could never get that little monkey yet
To put off his breeches:
A tender, puling, nice, chitty-fac'd squall 'tis.

(3.1.82–5, 91–7)

In effect, the page Antonio represents the boy actor with the girlish attributes that Rainolds so feared. His submissive female persona as Lactantio's mistress, barely masked in his disguise as page, is an erotic come-on to a male homosexual alliance: Antonio and the boy actor are the same. The absence of female figures within the fiction who are attracted to the page is significant; without this overlay, the erotic potential of the cross-dressed figure is not fully explored.[23]

Antonio-like pages appear frequently in Jacobean drama, as do their counterparts, the spunky, resourceful cross-dressed women of wit. These types are variable (for example, the page sometimes serves as erotic object for women as well as men), and may to some degree be combined. Moreover, a female figure in a comedy need not cross-dress in all instances to serve the purposes of that dramatic device.[24] For example, in *The Spanish Gypsy* (c. 1623, probably by Ford and Dekker),[25] Costanza, 'twelve and upwards', is a child–woman posing as a gypsy who combines the physical attributes of the diminutive page with the swagger and confidence of the reprobate. Although she is not cross-dressed. the carnivalesque atmosphere of the outlaw gypsy camp (another kind of meta-theatre) is equally effective as a licensing device for the disruption of sexual norms.[26]

Despite her dubious circumstances and tender age, Costanza's beauty, widely touted, has captivated many men: 'the sweetest, / The wittiest rogue'; 'the prettiest toy'; 'This little ape'; 'that little fairy' (1.5. *passim*); 'Thy pretty little body'; 'I must . . . marry this cherry-lipped, sweet-mouthed villain' (2.1.205, 244–5). She repudiates their overtures: 'Marry me! . . . I'll wear no shackles; liberty is sweet; that I have, that I'll hold' (250–2). Wary of the disturbing duality of her attractiveness, Costanza's father cautions restraint: 'a many dons / Will not believe but that thou art a boy / In woman's clothes . . . be to thyself / Thyself, and not a changeling' (2.1.97–9, 103–4). But in a retort that could stand as the definitive credo of the boy actor, the intrepid Costanza revels in the manipulative power of her indeterminate condition:

How, not a changeling?
Yes, father, I will play the changeling;
I'll change myself into a thousand shapes,
To court our brave spectators; I'll change my postures
Into a thousand different variations,
To draw even ladies' eyes to follow mine;
I'll change my voice into a thousand tones,
To chain attention: not a changeling, father?
None but myself shall play the changeling.

(2.1.104–12)

Costanza might be described as an improbable cross between Lactantio's mistress and the Roaring Girl.[27] Her homoerotic appeal is partially tied to her delicacy, but this time it cuts both ways: Costanza the self-proclaimed changeling can draw the gazes of men *and* women. Her Moll Frith-like behaviour seems to contradict this delicacy, but the contradiction is itself enticing. There is an improbable element in Costanza's bawdy raillery with the gypsies, her arrogant defiances, her derring-do. The child–woman as outlaw is in fact a close match to the transgressive boy actor, particularly in terms of his erotic potential in playing off adult actors, as the changeling speech makes clear. Not only are Costanza's suitors captivated by her chameleon variations, so also are the 'brave spectators'. Once again the veil between the fiction and the dramatic convention that constitutes it is thinly drawn.

iv

In arguing that Jacobean playwrights deliberately manipulated the transvestite acting convention for erotic effect, and that spectators of both sexes were inescapably drawn into the resulting confusions, I have focused on a genre which invites such manipulation. Jacobean comedy could hardly fail to take advantage of the most obvious comic device at hand, and the actor cross-dressed twice, as we have seen, was especially rich in erotic potential. That audiences were receptive to such game-playing, that they brought to the theatre a culturally inscribed fascination with sexual indeterminacy, may be assumed from the alacrity with which Jacobean playwrights exploited this predisposition. Their comedy offered a range of transgressive opportunities – hetero- and homoerotic fantasies to be customized by the individual spectator. Moreover, it privileged a kind of democratic eroticism, accessible to all, emanating from the *process* of creating sexual confusions, from the jumbling of overlapping sexual nuances.

But if comedy openly exploited the transvestite convention, tragedy and tragi-comedy seemed to have privileged continuity of dramatic fiction and emotional effect, thereby rendering the erotic function of transvestism in these plays much more difficult to problematize. A common critical assumption, often unconscious, is that Jacobean spectators essentially blocked awareness of transvestism while viewing serious drama, much as modern audiences inscribed with the tradition of theatrical realism ignore other kinds of theatrical artifice.

My own suspicion is that the singular pervasiveness of sexual themes in Jacobean drama implicated transvestism to some degree in every dramatic structure, and that in all probability viewer sensitivity to multi-layered eroticism was never wholly suspended. This is a large supposition that cannot be adequately argued here. But the theoretical choices are clear. We can credit Jacobean spectators with a compartmentalized mental programming that shut out transvestite nuances in serious drama; or we can credit them with an ability to sustain dual levels of erotic awareness without rendering serious fictions ridiculous.

Two brief examples taken from tragi-comedies of the period illustrate the complexity of the problem. *The Humorous Lieutenant*, by Fletcher (*c.* 1619) and *A King and No King*, by Beaumont and Fletcher (*c.* 1611) dramatize obsessive, incestuous desire.[28] In *The Humorous Lieutenant*, the role of Celia ('a very pretty wench'; 'she is very young, sure' [1.1.84; 3.4.20]), object of an Oedipal rivalry, is a tour de force for a boy actor. Celia ranges from timorous to devious to defiant, combining a 'male spirit' and a 'man's mind' with compelling sexual attractiveness, showcased by rich apparel, frequently changed, and by scenes featuring kissing and embracing. In *A King and No King*, a brother's consuming, destructive desire for his sister, orchestrated in careful gradations, culminates in a highly erotic meeting in which the would-be lovers fall to passionate embraces, barely broken off.[29]

Because these plays foreground male heterosexual obsessiveness, they are presumably concerned with sustaining the fiction of female impersonation. Yet the representation of Celia, linchpin of the action in *The Humorous Lieutenant*, borrows from the familiar arsenal used by comedic heroines to suggest sexual ambiguity, and it is difficult to imagine that these devices passed by the audience wholly unheeded. *A King and No King* is even more problematic. Here, the intensity of the fateful confrontation between brother and sister depends entirely on their touching and kissing, which in the comedies serves to *de-intensify* the fiction, to disrupt it with erotic counter-valences. Thus the moment of greatest dramatic tension in the play would seem to be compromised, even subverted.[30]

I submit that our difficulty in understanding the multi-dimensionality of Jacobean theatrical transvestism, and audience response to it, has much to do with our own alien gaze. The signifying practice of Jacobean theatre was dialogic, unlike that of theatrical realism; and the erotic dynamic of the Jacobean stage was linked to a theory of sexuality at a great remove from ours. In the context of these differences, the gaze of modern theatrical spectators is more restricted, less supple than was that of our Jacobean counterparts. Thus it seems dangerous to assume that Jacobean spectators could *not* have accommodated the erotic disruption of serious fiction, even at moments most critical to the effectiveness of that fiction.

I have argued that the Jacobean theatre was the privileged site for the instantiation of a discourse that gave voice to Renaissance fascination with sexual indeterminacy and that appropriated transvestism as its signifier. Because this discourse seemed to delight in what might be called the pluralities of perversion, it challenged symbolic formations of its time *and* ours. Perhaps it is suitably ironic that in attempting to understand the sexual production of the Jacobean transvestite stage, we are caught in an historical trajectory that anticipates the repressions of our own future.

Notes

1 Although the terms 'gender' and 'sexuality' are used interchangeably in much of the scholarship, such critics as Gayle Rubin, Eve Kosofsky Sedgwick, and Valerie Traub argue the importance of distinguishing between them. Sedgwick

views gender in an historical context to mean 'a structuring force for axes of cultural discrimination whose thematic subject isn't explicitly gendered at all' – that is, for such oppositions as mind/body, active/passive. In practice, gender distinctions operate as mechanisms for social control and oppression. Sexuality is in an oblique relationship to gender, but not co-extensive with it because 'sexuality extends along so many dimensions that aren't well described in terms of the gender of object choice at all' – for example, public/private, singular/plural (1989: 55–6). Rubin succinctly isolates the central issue: 'Feminism is the theory of gender oppression. To automatically assume that this makes it the theory of sexual oppression is to fail to distinguish between gender, on the one hand, and erotic desire, on the other' (1989: 307). In her recent book (1992), Traub deals with such distinctions at length and with clarifying incisiveness.

2 For a review and evaluation of cross-dressing literature dealing primarily with gender issues, see Howard (1988).

3 In Kristeva's anatomization of the Judaeo-Christian tradition, the 'polymorphic, orgasmic body [of the woman], desiring and laughing' (1986: 141) represents the repressed desire of the male and must be isolated by the Law, and excluded from knowledge and power. As a consequence, only two modes of identification with the symbolic order are open to woman: as virgin, the sadistic model, in which she identifies with the father, renouncing *jouissance* and the mother; or as mother, the masochistic model, in which she engages in 'an endless struggle between the orgasmic maternal body and the symbolic prohibition' (147). Both models mediate the needs of the male community.

4 My summary of Renaissance medical theory derives from Thomas Laqueur (1986, 1990). His argument for the hegemonic pervasiveness of the male model is currently being contested by feminist scholars, including Janet Adelman, Heather Dubrow and Patricia Parker, among others. The argument here rests not on the exclusivity of the model but on its existence and currency in the English Renaissance.

5 In *Three Essays on the Theory of Sexuality*, Freud appropriates one image from the myth, that of the splitting of the male/female androgyne, to introduce his discussion of the sexual instinct (*Standard Edition of the Complete Psychological Works* [hereafter *SE*] 7: 136). Much later, in *Beyond the Pleasure Principle*, Freud invokes the entire myth (the splitting of male/male, male/female and female/female androgynes) to adumbrate a theory which opposes Eros (sexual instinct, self-preservation) to Thanatos (death instinct), although as instincts both signify 'an urge . . . to restore an earlier state of things' (*SE* 18: 36). His hypothesis that 'living substance at the time of its coming to life was torn apart into small particles which ever since have endeavoured to reunite through the sexual instincts' (*SE* 18: 58), an attempt to relate psychic process to principles of physics, was repudiated in *An Outline of Psychoanalysis*, published posthumously in 1940. All references to Freud in the text are taken from *The Standard Edition of the Complete Psychological Works of Sigmund Freud*, ed. James Strachey 1953–74.

6 I do not mean to imply that the genderizing of the subject (the highly problematic 'Oedipal phase') represents the first instance of psychic division, nor that the Aristophanic myth as employed by Freud affirms any original unity of the subject other than that which Lacan terms Imaginary. My chief concern here is with the relation of the polymorphously perverse sexual instinct to the structure of desire, and not with the alienation of the divided subject within that structure.

7 Jonathan Dollimore's concept of the 'perverse dynamic', an incisive elucidation of these Freudian themes, argues that perversion 'originates internally to just

those things it threatens'. Because the unnatural is a displacement of the natural, 'the most terrifying fear may be not of the other but of the same' (1990: 182, 192). Dollimore's *Sexual Dissidence* (1991) provides an extensive analysis of this concept.

8 For evidence of the virtually exclusive use of men and boys in medieval plays, pageants and processions, see Tydeman (1978, esp. chap. 7); and Wickham (1987). The most extensive treatment of the 500-year tradition of boy actors in England is Hillebrand (1964).

9 Several medieval documents from England and the continent emphasize the importance of locating beautiful boys with androgynous appeal to perform, for example, 'a very handsome young man about twenty years old, without a beard and . . . with the most beautiful hair of a woman extending over his shoulders' (Meredith and Tailby [eds] 1983: 209); and 'qui estoit ung tres beaul fitz et ressembloit une belle jonne fille' (Twycross 1983: 134). Although the symbolic framework of medieval drama implies iconic or stylized acting in which sexual valences were circumscribed, the eroticism of boy actors on the medieval stage has only recently become a subject of study (Twycross: 123–80).

10 Gager offended Rainolds by including what Rainolds believed to be a caricature of his views in a 1591–2 student production of Seneca's *Hippolytus*, for which Gager wrote additional scenes. Gager parried with Rainolds until May 1593, when Gentili took up the defence. Two of Rainolds' letters to Gager and the first four Latin letters exchanged between Gentili and Rainolds were printed in 1599 as *Th' Overthrow of Stage-Playes*. See J. W. Binns (1974: 95–120). Further references to the Rainolds–Gentili correspondence are taken from Binns and included in the text.

11 This description is quoted by Thomas Warton from a lost pamphlet entitled *The Children of the Chapel Stript and Whipt*. The pamphlet was once in the possession of the Bodleian. See Chambers (1923, 2: 34–5).

12 In her study of the major English polemical tracts, Laura Levine (1986) argues that the disruption fundamentally feared was that of sexual identity itself.

13 It is interesting that boy actors were probably not members of pre-Elizabethan adult troupes, so that men played the female roles. As these troupes developed in size and appeal, they gradually incorporated boys, who then adjusted to a pre-existing structure dominated by adults. See Bevington (1962: esp. 73–9). For changes in the status and styles of boys' companies in the Jacobean period, see Hillebrand (1964); Shapiro (1977); and Gair (1982).

14 Based on her experiment with all-male student productions of mystery plays, Twycross opined that casting a boy actor in the role of Mary Magdalene in the saint's play of that name would have triggered a subconscious feeling in the audience 'that a boy was being corrupted by the man, thus bringing into play all the confusions and revulsions revealed by Rainolds' (1983: 159).

15 This is a large issue that merits independent analysis. However, a single example will demonstrate the methological problems implicit in recent research on the subject. In *Playgoing in Shakespeare's London* (1987), Andrew Gurr concludes that ladies (as opposed to citizens' wives and prostitutes) 'went relatively rarely to common playhouses before 1600, but were in numbers at the Globe from 1599 to 1614' (63). Gurr derives his evidence from records given in two appendices: contemporary references to playgoers and to playgoing, respectively. Appendix 1 contains no reference to any woman at a public theatre before 1614, when Elizabeth Williams, sister-in-law of Sir Dudley Carleton, went to the Globe (I have excluded the appearance of Moll Frith at a 1611 performance of *The Roaring Girl*). In Appendix 2, there are 28 references (among 140 playgoing citations) to

women in the theatres between 1574 and 1625: 9 concern ladies, only one of which clearly alludes to a public theatre (the Globe in 1624). The frequently quoted statement of Horatio Busino in 1617 supposedly alludes to the Fortune, but this is an interpolation of an anonymous writer commenting on Rawdon Brown's translation of Busino's letter: see Anon, 'Diaries and dispatches of the Venetian Embassy at the Court of King James I, in the years 1617, 1618', *Quarterly Review* 102 (1857), 398–438, esp. 416; and G. E. Bentley, who identifies the error and tracks its dessemination up to 1968 in *The Jacobean and Caroline Stage* (1968) 6: 151–2. (The Busino error also appears in Cook 1981: 160). Similar problems of interpretation arise with other entries in Appendix 2. Thus these documents provide virtually no evidence for aristocratic women in the popular playhouses between 1599 and 1614, although they do support Gurr's claim that they were rarely present in the 1590s.

16 Teresa de Lauretis (1984) attempts to define 'positionalities of identification' (107) for female spectators of the contemporary film that are not dictated by the culturally coded male gaze of the camera. Twentieth-century film and Jacobean drama are hardly analogous, but in referring to 'the scopic drive [deriving from scopophilia, Freud's word for visual pleasure] that maps desire into representation' (67), and to Freud's concept of masculine and feminine as 'positions occupied by the subject in relation to desire' (143), de Lauretis does suggest the reformative power of female desire in relation to male representations. Ironically, it appears to me that the Jacobean theatre probably provided more room for the play of this power than does the modern movie theatre.

17 Catherine Belsey (1985) defines subjectivity as 'the point of intersection of a range of discourses', rather than 'a single, unified presence'. While deconstructing the notion of metaphysical identity, Belsey gives eloquent expression to the principle under scrutiny here: 'The point is . . . to define through the internalization of difference a plurality of places, of possible beings, for each person in the margins of sexual difference, those margins which a metaphysical sexual polarity obliterates' (188–9).

18 In featuring Middleton I do not mean to endorse the concept of authorial intentionality but rather am using him as representative of a kind of Jacobean theatrical production.

19 *No Wit, No Help* was first printed for Humphrey Moseley in 1657 (SR entry, 1653). Its date of composition is conjectural, based on Middleton's use of Thomas Bretnor's 1611 almanac, which the play seems to use extensively. Middleton's authorship (his name appears on the title page) has not been disputed. Although there is no record of the play's Jacobean production, Middleton wrote for adult companies after 1608. All references are to Lowell E. Johnson (ed.) 1976.

20 If the shifting levels of the erotic dynamic in *No Wit, No Help* move the audience in and out of the sexual fiction, so does the meta-theatric mockery of the masque that Weather-wise and his friends rehearse for the wedding feast (3.1). In this side-play, the group resists impersonating two of the four elements, earth and water, as females. Their bawdy exchange with the writer of the masque makes reference to theatrical practice and to temperamental actors who refuse the direction of the playtext.

21 The title page of *The Widow*, printed for Moseley in 1652, reads 'As it was acted at the private House in Black-Fryers, with great Applause, by His late Majesties Servants. Written by Ben: Johnson/John Fletcher/Tho: Middleton'. Stylistic arguments have been made for Middleton's sole authorship (for a summary of this debate, see Lake 1975: 38–43); however, attribution is still uncertain. Bentley (1956, 4: 902) places the date of composition about 1616. The Prologue of the

1652 quarto provides strong suggestion of a performance at court, although there is no indication of when this may have occurred. All references are to Bullen (ed.), vol. 5, 1885a.

22 *More Dissemblers Besides Women* was printed for Humphrey Moseley in 1657 and issued together with *Women Beware Women* in an octavo volume entitled *Two New Plays*. Moseley's SR entry of 1653 attributes the play to Middleton, and most scholars consider it to be his alone, composed *c.* 1615 (see Bentley 1956, 4: 888–9; Lake 1975:20). Lake cites 1619 as the date of first performance (1976: 219–21); Sir Henry Herbert's Diary refers to a performance at court by the King's Men on Twelfth Night, 1623/4 (Bentley 1956, 4: 888). All references are to Bullen (ed.) vol. 6.

23 Another scene in the play, a lesson in pricksong and dancing which coincides hilariously with the onset of labour, exploits Antonio's dual persona in blatant physical comedy, again with a male homosexual slant. The scene is full of bawdy innuendo ('he is one / Must have it put into him'; 'Enter him, Nicholao, / For the fool's bashful, as they're all at first, / 'Till they be once well enter'd' (5.1.164–5). When Antonio proves an impossibly maladroit dancer, the dancing master wrenches his limbs into obscene positions. The humour here depends on Antonio giving birth, that is, on the exposure of his female persona, but the explicitly homoerotic puns simultaneously refer to the 'real' sex of the page.

24 In one variation, cross-dressed female figures are not perceived by the audience to be cross-dressed for much of the play. For examples, see Fletcher's *Philaster* (1610), Middleton's (and Webster's?) *Anything for a Quiet Life* (*c.* 1621), and of course Jonson's *Epicoene* (1609), although the latter, as a play performed by a boys' company, falls outside the purview of this study. More rarely, male figures within the fiction are cross-dressed as females. In Heywood's *The Golden Age* (1611), Jupiter infiltrates Diana's company of virgins (who are also lesbian lovers), as a virago in order to seduce Calisto. Their love-making is explicitly enacted in 2.1 ('you kiss too wantonly'; 'by thy soft paps let my hand descend'; 'let your skirt be raised', etc.). See Heywood (1851) ed. Collier, vol. 2: 31–5.

25 *The Spanish Gypsy* was printed in 1653 for Richard Marriott; Middleton and Rowley appear on the title page. Although accepted with reservations by Bentley (1956, 4: 892–5), this attribution has been discredited. Lake believes Dekker and Ford to be the original authors (1975: 215–28); MacD. P. Jackson finds evidence for Ford, and 'perhaps Dekker or Rowley or Brome' (1979: 131–6, especially 134). The play was allowed by Sir Henry Herbert in 1623 and performed at court by the Lady Elizabeth's Men in the same year (1623/4). All references are to Bullen (ed.), vol. 6.

26 The association of radical transgression with gypsies seems to be a cultural stereotype. In *More Dissemblers Besides Women*, for example, the noblewoman Aurelia, thwarted in love, defies social prohibitions by escaping in disguise to a gypsy camp. Here, Aurelia's reckless behaviour acts as a foil for the rigidly chaste stance of the Duchess; in *The Spanish Gypsy* the outlaw motif complements a more sinister plot, that of a nobleman's rape of his betrothed.

27 Dekker and Middleton's *The Roaring Girl* (*c.* 1611) may be the most complex example of the Jacobean theatre's proclivity for transgressive eroticism. Therefore the recent critical emphasis on Moll as a proto-feminist, and the association of the play with the later *Hic Mulier, Haec Vir* controversy have somewhat distorted the primacy of her figure as symbolic centre of a fiction that is almost wholly preoccupied with varieties of sexual perversion. Jean E. Howard's essay in this volume not only provides a provocative analysis of this missing perspective but for the first time conjoins issues of eroticism with those of gender.

28 Raph Crane's 1625 manuscript of *Demetrius and Enanthe*, although imperfect, is the most authoritative text for *The Humorous Lieutenant*; editors usually make use of the 1647 Beaumont and Fletcher Folio as well. The date of composition, conjectured from a list of actors in the King's Men at the time of first performance, found in the second folio, is presumed to be between 1619 and 1625, which positions the play after the death of Beaumont. There is no record of the Jacobean production (see Bentley 1956, 3: 343–7). *A King and No King* was entered in the SR in 1618; the first quarto, with Beaumont and Fletcher on the title page, was published in 1619. However, a note by Henry Herbert in 1662 refers to its original licensing in 1611; and it was acted at court by the King's Men in 1611 and 1612/13 (see Chambers 1923, 3: 225). References to *The Humorous Lieutenant* are taken from the Variorum Edition of *The Works of Francis Beaumont and John Fletcher*, vol. 2, 1905; and to *A King and No King* from vol. 1, 1904, of the same edition. Both plays were edited by R. Warwick Bond.

29 ARB.   brothers and sisters may
     Walk hand in hand together; so will we.
     Come nearer: is there any hurt in this?
                . . .
   PAN. Methinks
     Brothers and sisters lawfully may kiss.
   ARB. And so they may, Panthea; so will we;
     And kiss again too: we were scrupulous
     And foolish, but we will be so no more.
   PAN. If you have any mercy, let me go
     To prison, to my death, to anything:
     I feel a sin growing upon my blood,
     Worse than all these, hotter, I fear, than yours.

                                        (4.4.142–3; 152–60)

30 In an original and illuminating essay for this volume, Peter Stallybrass focuses on just such moments in Renaissance tragedy, and, further, develops a theory for gender in the Renaissance that accommodates the concept of indeterminacy.

References

Anon. (1857) 'Diaries and dispatches of the Venetian Embassy at the Court of King James I, in the Years 1617, 1618', *Quarterly Review* 102: 398–438.

Beaumont, F. and Fletcher, J. (1904) *A King and No King*, in R. W. Bond (ed.), *The Works of Francis Beaumont and John Fletcher*, vol. 1, London: George Bell & Sons and A. H. Bullen.

Belsey, C. (1985) 'Disrupting sexual difference: meaning and gender in the comedies', in John Drakakis (ed.), *Alternative Shakespeares*, London: Methuen, 166–90.

Bentley, G. E. (1956 [3 and 4]; 1968 [6]) *The Jacobean and Caroline Stage*, Oxford: Clarendon Press.

Bevington, D. (1962) *Children of the Revels: The Boy Companies of Shakespeare's Time and Their Plays*, New York: Columbia University Press.

Binns, J. W. (1974) 'Women or transvestites on the English stage?: an Oxford controversy', *Sixteenth Century Journal*, 5, 2: 95–120.

Bristol, M. (1985) *Carnival and Theatre*, New York and London: Routledge.

Chambers, E. K. (1923) *The Elizabethan Stage*, vols 2, 3, Oxford: Clarendon Press.

Cook, A. J. (1981) *The Privileged Playgoers of Shakespeare's London 1576–1642*, Princeton: Princeton University Press.

de Lauretis, T. (1984) *Alice Doesn't: Feminism, Semiotics, Cinema*, Bloomington: Indiana University Press.

Dollimore, J. (1986) 'Subjectivity, sexuality, and transgression: the Jacobean connection', *Renaissance Drama* n.s. 17: 53–81.

——(1990) 'The cultural politics of perversion: Augustine, Shakespeare, Freud, Foucault', *Textual Practice* 4, 2: 179–96.

——(1991) *Sexual Dissidence: Augustine to Wilde, Freud to Foucault*, Oxford: Clarendon Press.

Edwards, R. (1957) *Damon and Pythias*, Malone Society Reprints, Oxford: Oxford University Press.

Fletcher, J. (1905) *The Humorous Lieutenant*, in R. W. Bond (ed.), *The Works of Francis Beaumont and John Fletcher*, vol. 2, London: George Bell & Sons and A. H. Bullen.

Freud, S. (1953–74) *The Standard Edition of the Complete Psychological Works of Sigmund Freud*, J. Strachey (ed.), vols 7, 14, 18, 23, London: The Hogarth Press.

Gair, R. (1982) *The Children of St. Paul's: The Story of a Theatre Company 1553–1608*, Cambridge and New York: Cambridge University Press.

Gurr, A. (1987) *Playgoing in Shakespeare's London*, Cambridge: Cambridge University Press.

Heywood, T. (1851) *The Golden Age*, in J. P. Collier (ed.), *Dramatic Works of Thomas Heywood*, vol. 2, London: Shakespeare Society.

——(1612, repr. 1941) *An Apology for Actors*, New York: Scholars' Facsimiles and Reprints.

Hillebrand, H. N. (1964) *The Child Actors: A Chapter in Elizabethan Stage History*, New York: Russell & Russell.

Howard, J. (1988) 'Crossdressing, the theatre, and gender struggle in early modern England', *Shakespeare Quarterly* 39, 4: 418–40.

Jackson, MacD. P. (1979) *Studies in Attribution: Middleton and Shakespeare*, Salzburg: Institut für Anglistik und Amerikanistik, Universität Salzburg.

Kristeva, J. (1986) 'About Chinese women', in Toril Moi (ed.), *The Kristeva Reader*, New York: Columbia University Press, 138–59.

Lake, D. (1975) *The Canon of Thomas Middleton's Plays*, Cambridge: Cambridge University Press.

——(1976) 'The date of *More Dissemblers Besides Woman*', *Notes and Queries* 221: 219–21.

Laqueur, T. (1986) 'Orgasm, generation and the politics of reproductive biology', *Representations* 14: 1–41.

——(1990) *Making Sex: Body and Gender from the Greeks to Freud*, Cambridge, Mass., and London: Harvard University Press.

Levine, L. (1986) 'Men in women's clothing: anti-theatricality and effeminization from 1579 to 1642', *Criticism* 28: 121–43.

Meredith, P. and Tailby, J. (eds) (1983) *The Staging of Religious Drama in Europe in the Later Middle Ages: Texts and Documents in Translation*, EDAM Monograph Series 4, Kalamazoo: Medieval Institute Publications.

Middleton, T. (1885a) *The Widow*, in A. H. Bullen (ed.), *The Works of Thomas Middleton*, vol. 5, Boston: Houghton, Mifflin & Co.

——(1885b) *More Dissemblers Besides Women*, in Bullen (ed.), vol. 6.

——(1885c) *The Spanish Gypsy*, in Bullen (ed.), vol. 6.

——(1976) *No Wit, No Help Like a Woman's*, L. E. Johnson (ed.), Lincoln: University of Nebraska Press.

Orgel, S. (1989) 'Nobody's perfect: or why did the English stage take boys for women?', *South Atlantic Quarterly* 88, 1: 7–29.

Rubin, G. (1989) 'Thinking sex: notes for a radical theory of the politics of sexuality', in Carole S. Vance (ed.), *Pleasure and Danger: Exploring Female Sexuality*, New York: 267–319.

Sedgwick, E. (1989) 'Across gender, across sexuality: Willa Cather and others', *South Atlantic Quarterly* 88, 1: 53–72.

Shapiro, M. (1977) *Children of the Revels: The Boy Companies of Shakespeare's Time and Their Plays*, New York: Columbia University Press.

Traub, Valerie (1992) *Desire and Anxiety: Circulations of Sexuality in Shakespearean Drama*, London and New York: Routledge.

Twycross, M. (1983) ' "Transvestism" in the Mystery Plays', *Medieval English Theatre* 5, 2: 123–80.

Tydeman, W. (1978) *The Theatre in the Middle Ages: Western European Stage Conditions c. 800–1576*, Cambridge: Cambridge University Press.

Wickham, G. (1987) *The Medieval Theatre*, 3rd edn, Cambridge: Cambridge University Press.

Chapter 5

Transvestism and the 'body beneath'
Speculating on the boy actor[1]

Peter Stallybrass

My paper starts from a puzzle: what did a Renaissance audience *see* when boy actors undressed on stage? The puzzle could, of course, be resolved by a simple (and, for my argument, damaging) move. The boy actor doesn't undress, or, at least, doesn't undress to the point of disturbing the illusion; the audience *sees* nothing. Against such a move, I want on the one hand to think quite bluntly about the prosthetic devices through which gender is rendered visible upon the stage. In that sense, the visible is an empirical question (although a question to which we seem to have surprisingly few answers). But, on the other hand, I want to suggest the degree to which the Renaissance spectator is required to *speculate* upon a boy actor who undresses, and thus to speculate upon the relation between the boy actor and the woman he plays. This speculation depends upon a cultural fantasy of sight, but a fantasy, I shall argue, that plays back and forth between sexual difference as a site of indeterminacy (the undoing of any stable or given difference) and sexual difference (and sexuality itself) as the production of contradictory fixations (fixations articulated through a fetishistic attention to particular items of clothing, particular parts of the body of an imagined woman, particular parts of an actual boy actor). I want to suggest that on the Renaissance stage the demand that the spectator *sees* is at its most intense in the undressing of the boy actor, at the very moment when *what* is seen is most vexed, being the point of intersection between spectatorship, the specular, and the speculative.

The prosthetic body

Perhaps the most substantial theatrical property of many Renaissance companies was a bed. It is a property which is called for in play after play, mainly in tragedy, but also in history and comedy. *Volpone* revolves around the bed in which Volpone simulates death, the bed from which he rises in his attempted rape of Celia; *Cymbeline* hinges upon Iachimo spying upon Imogen while she lies asleep in bed; in *The Maid's Tragedy*, Evadne ties the king to the bed in which they have made love before she kills him; in

Othello, the bed bears the bodies of Desdemona, Emilia and Othello in the final scene. One becomes accustomed to stage directions like: 'King a bed' (Beaumont and Fletcher 1610: 5.1.12); 'Enter Othello, and Desdemona in her bed' (Shakespeare 1623b: 5.12); 'Enter Imogen in her Bed, and a Lady' (Shakespeare 1623d: 2.2). The bed becomes a focal point of scenes of sleep, of sex, of death. But bed scenes also focus upon facts so obvious that they resist interpretation as we hasten on to find out what these scenes are *about*: they draw attention to undressing or being undressed, to the process of shedding those garments through which class and gender were made visible and staged. They stage clothes as signs which can be put on and off, outward signs which can be assumed or shed.

At the same time, bed scenes foreground the body: the body which is either literally or symbolically about to be exposed. And here we come to a peculiar problem. The consensus of recent scholars on Renaissance transvestism has been that it is self-consciously staged mainly, or only, in comedy. Lisa Jardine, in her important work on the boy actor to which I am deeply indebted, states what has now become a commonplace:[2]

> the eroticism of the boy player is invoked in the drama whenever it is openly alluded to: on the whole this means in comedy, where role-playing and disguise is part of the genre. In tragedy, the willing suspension of disbelief does customarily extend, I think, to the taking of the female parts by boy players; taken for granted, it is not alluded to.
>
> (Jardine 1983: 23)

But in bed scene after bed scene in Renaissance tragedy, we begin to witness an undressing or we are asked to see or to imagine an undressed (or partially undressed) body within the bed. What is it we are being asked to see?

If we take *Othello* as our starting point, we may reach some puzzling conclusions. As Lynda Boose has finely argued, the 'ocular proof' that Othello demands is reworked in the play as the audience's voyeuristic desire to *see*, to grossly gape (Boose 1987). But what are we to gape *at*? From the beginning of the eighteenth century, as Michael Neill has shown, illustrators of *Othello* were obsessively concerned with the depiction of the final bed scene. Even as Desdemona's 'Will you come to bed, my Lord?' (5.2.24) was cut from theatrical productions, illustrators focused upon the dead Desdemona lying in bed (Neill 1989: 35 fn.). And what the illustrators above all reveal (requiring that the spectator grossly gape) are the bedclothes and clothing pulled back to show a single exposed breast (see the illustrations by Boitard (1709), Loutherbourg (1785), Metz (1789), and Leney (1799) in Neill 1989: 386–9). The bed scene, then, is taken by the illustrators as an opportunity for the display of the female body, and in particular of a woman's breast.

Although we cannot take such illustrations as reflecting eighteenth-century stage productions, we do, in fact, find the exposure of the female breast recurrently called for by stage directions after the introduction of women actors to the stage in the previous century. On the Renaissance stage, actual boys played seeming 'boys' who were 'revealed' to be women – Ganymede as Rosalind, Cesario as Viola.[3] But on the Restoration stage, women played boys who were revealed to be women. And they were often revealed as women by the exposure of their breasts.

In fact, the commonest technique for the revelation of the 'woman beneath' after the Restoration was the removal of a wig, whereupon the female actor's 'true' hair would be seen. In Boyle's *Guzman* (1669), for instance, a woman disguised as a priest is exposed when 'Francisco pulls off her Peruque, and her Womans Hair falls about her ears' (quoted in Wilson 1958: 84). Now this, of course, can depend upon the interplay of prostheses, an interplay which would have been perfectly possible on the Renaissance stage. The audience would have no means of knowing (any more than we do today) whether the hair beneath the wig was the hair of the actor or another wig. The play of difference (male wig/female hair) had no necessary relation to the anatomical specificities of the actor's body. If, then, the distinction of the sexes is staged as a distinction of hair (and above all of hair length), it will be constantly transformed by changes in hair styles. Sexual difference may, in this case, seem essentially prosthetic: the addition (or subtraction) of detachable (or growable/cuttable) parts.

It is precisely such a prosthetic view which William Prynne had denounced in *The Unlovelinesse of Lovelockes* (1628). There, he elaborates at length on St Paul: 'Doth not even nature itself teach you, that, if a man have long hair, it is a shame unto him? But if a woman have long hair it is a glory to her' (*I Corinthians* 11.14–15). From Prynne's perspective, the problem is precisely that 'nature' doesn't seem to have taught its lesson thoroughly enough. Cavalier men flaunt their long hair (and, from 1641, were to ridicule their opponents as 'Roundheads', in reference to their close-cropped hair). Prynne asserts that gender is defined by 'the outward Culture of [our] Heads, and Bodies' (Prynne 1628: A3v), and that the long hair of men and the short hair of women erase sexual difference. We live, he claims, in 'Unnaturall, and Unmanly times: wherein . . . sundry of our Mannish, Impudent, and inconstant Female sexe, are Hermaphrodited, and transformed into men' because they 'unnaturally clip, and cut their Haire' (ibid.: A3, G2). Asserting hair as a sign of *natural* difference, Prynne is particularly fierce in his denunciation of wigs: 'the wearing of counterfeite, false, and suppositious Haire, is *utterly unlawfull*' (ibid.: C4v, original emphasis). In using the putting on and the taking off of wigs as the mark of gender difference, the Restoration stage turned Prynne on his head. 'Natural' signs became the artifices of malleable gender.

But, as I noted above, the Restoration theatre used a second, overlapping method of revealing the 'woman beneath': the exposure of the female actor's breasts. The methods are overlapping because they could be used together:

in Wycherley's *The Plain Dealer* (1676), when Fidelia, in disguise, confesses that she is a woman, Vernish 'Pulls off her peruke and feels her breasts'; and in Hopkins' *Friendship Improv'd* (1699), Locris, refusing to fight with her lover, says: 'Here's my bare Breast, now if thou dar'st, strike here. (*She loosens her robe a little, her Helmet drops off, and her Hair appears*)' (Wilson 1958: 84–5). Here, the stage directions are ambiguous: if Vernish feels Fidelia's breast and Locris 'loosens her robe', we cannot be sure what it was that an audience was supposed actually to *see*.

The revelation of the female actor's breasts, though, is central to the staging of Aphra Behn's *The Younger Brother; Or, the Amorous Jilt* (1696). In that play, there is an elaborate bed scene in which Mirtilla, in love with the cross-dressed Olivia, says 'Come to my Bed' (stage direction: '*She leading him [sic] to her Bed*), while the Prince, who is in love with Mirtilla, breaks in upon the scene. The prince grabs hold of the cross-dressed Olivia, and the stage direction reads: '*The* Prince *holding* Olivia *by the Bosom of her Coat, her Breast appears to* Mirtilla.' Mirtilla: 'Ha! what do I see? – Two Female rising Breasts. / By heav'n, a Woman.' The Prince, however, has not seen these signs of Olivia's gender, and so the revelation is repeated by Mirtilla who, as a later stage direction reads, '*Opens* Olivia's *Bosom, shows her Breasts*' (Behn 1696: 5.2. 390). It is worth remarking that Aphra Behn uses the revelation convention to play with the relation between woman and woman (it is Mirtilla who first sees Olivia's breasts, it is she who opens Olivia's bosom).[4]

But there can be little doubt that such stagings of the female actor's breasts were usually constituted for the arousal of the heterosexual male spectator. (A more extended discussion of this point would look at the significant position of the Restoration theatre in the *construction* of the 'heterosexual male spectator'.) According to Colley Cibber, the very presence of female actors upon the stage helped to constitute a new audience (or rather new spectators): 'The additional Objects then of real, beautiful Women, could not but draw a portion of new Admirers to the Theatre' (Cibber 1968: 55). In the Epilogue to Nathaniel Lee's *The Rival Queens* (1677), the actors protest that if their male spectators continue to lure female actors away from the stage, they will return to using boy actors:

For we have vow'd to find a sort of Toys
Known to black Fryars, a Tribe of choopping Boys.
If once they come, they'l quickly spoil your sport;
There's not one Lady will receive your Court:
But for the Youth in Petticoats run wild,
With oh the archest Wagg, the sweetest Child.
The panting Breasts, white Hands and little Feet
No more shall your pall'd thoughts with pleasure meet.

The Woman in Boys Cloaths, all Boy shall be,
And never raise your thoughts above the Knee.

(Lee 1677: 282)

There are several interesting features about this epilogue: first, the threat to replace women with boy actors is not imagined as a *general* loss but as a loss to the male spectator alone. The female spectator, on the contrary, is imagined as running wild after the 'Youth in Petticoats'. The boy actor is thus depicted as particularly alluring to women, a possibility that has been addressed by Stephen Orgel (1989b: 8).

But the grammar of the Epilogue is strangely playful about the crucial question: the difference between a boy actor and a female actor. 'The panting Breasts, white Hands and little Feet' seem at first to follow directly on from, and thus to be the attributes of, the archest wags, the sweetest children, but this possibility is retracted in the next line: 'No more' shall such breasts, hands and feet be seen when boy actors return. Yet the *feet* of the boy actor would seem to be adequate enough for his female role, if we are to take literally that he will 'never raise your thoughts above the Knee'. The crucial point of that latter line, of course, is what the boy actor does *not* have: implicitly a vagina; explicitly breasts.

It is that explicit absence upon which I want to dwell here. For recent criticism has been particularly concerned with the 'part' that the boy actor has which is not in his part. (I would want to suggest, incidentally, that that part has been peculiarly distorted [and enlarged] by being thought of as a 'phallus', as if a boy's small parts weren't peculiarly – and interestingly – at variance with the symbolic weight of THE phallus.) Criticism has thus been concerned with what Shakespeare calls the 'addition' which the boy actor brings to a female role. But in bed scene after bed scene, what is staged is a tableau in which we are about to witness the female body (and most particularly the female breast), even as it is a boy who is undressing. Indeed, there seems to be something so odd about this fact that it has simply been overlooked (an important exception, to which I am deeply indebted, is Shapiro 1990; for an earlier attempt to touch on this subject, see Rosenberg 1971: 17, 19).

So let me declare first of all what the puzzles are to which I have no solution. Did boy actors wear false breasts? There seem to be no records of such a practice, but the female fury at the beginning of *Salmacida Spolia* was presumably played by a professional actor and his/her '*breasts hung bagging down to her waist*' (quoted in Gossett 1988: 112). Or did boys use tight lacing to gather up their flesh so as to create a cleavage, or were they simply flat-chested, or . . . ? While John Rainolds denounces Achilles' transvestism, which William Gager had used in defence of the academic stage, he notes that Achilles had learned from Deidamia 'howe *he must hold his naked brest*' (Rainolds 1599: 17). A further question: in undressing scenes, how far did the boy actor go in actually removing his clothes or, if he was in bed, how much of his flesh was revealed? These are the questions I shall *not* be attempting to resolve.

Indeed, I want less to suggest a resolution than to express the dimensions of the problem. Lisa Jardine, whom I quoted above, assumes that the significance of the boy actor is virtually erased in tragedy (although her argument as a whole finely attends to the crucial importance of the cross-dressed boy). And Kathleen McLuskie (in what I take to be an implicit critique of Jardine) pushes for a *generally* conventional view of the boy actor (McLuskie 1987). To support her argument, she draws upon R. A. Foakes' *Illustrations of the English Stage*, which reproduces title pages and illustrations to play quartos in which women are represented with their breasts fully or partially exposed. McLuskie appears to conclude that this is how we are meant to think of the boy actors: within the convention, we can imagine them fully as women. But Foakes' *Illustrations* are themselves puzzling when we try to relate them to the practices of the English Renaissance stage and to the boy actor. (Only one of the illustrations to which I will refer can, in my view, be thought of as in any way an illustration *of* the stage; the others are illustrations (some presumably re-uses of woodcuts made for other purposes) *for a reader* of play quartos, a very different matter.)

How do these illustrations depict the female body, and, in particular, women's breasts? There is no one answer to this. To start with the three different title pages to *If You Know Not Me, You Know Nobody* in 1605, 1623, and 1639. All depict Elizabeth I, conventionally enough, in an elaborate gown with a low cut bodice (Foakes 1985: 91–3). But there is no suggestion of a cleavage, and only in the 1605 woodcut do two loops of pearls suggest the shape of her breasts. If a boy actor should want to imitate such an appearance, he would have no difficulty in doing so with the help of costume alone. And the same is true for the women represented on the title pages of *The Fair Maid of the West* (1631) and of *Englishmen for my Money* (1616) in which the attributes of gender depend upon hair and costume, and the bodices in these cases extend up to the neck (Foakes 1985: 130, 166). But the title page of William Alabaster's *Roxana* (1632) is more complicated. It is famous for the fact that in one of its panels it shows actors upon a stage (Foakes 1985: 73). The woman on the stage is clearly depicted as having swelling breasts. Another panel of the title page shows a couple in classical clothes, the man touching the woman's breasts, which are clearly depicted, as is her right nipple. At the furthest extreme, there are the title pages of Beaumont and Fletcher's *Philaster* (1620) and Sir William Lower's *The Enchanted Lovers* (1658), both of which depict women with fully exposed breasts (Foakes 1985: 118, 146). (On 30 May 1668, Pepys went to see *Philaster*, 'where it is pretty to see how I could remember almost all along, ever since I was a boy, Arethusa, the part which

I was to have acted at Sir Robert Cookes's; and it was very pleasant to me, but more to think what a ridiculous thing it would have been for me to have acted a beautiful woman' [Pepys 1916: 94–5].) Some play quartos, then, draw attention to the specifications of women's bodies in ways which would be extremely difficult (if not impossible) to represent upon the stage.

Now this whole discussion would be irrelevant if we assumed that the convention of the boy actor meant that the physical body of the boy was subsumed by the conventions of femininity signified by costume and gesture. That such subsumptions are, indeed, one feature of Renaissance theatrical and non-theatrical texts is a point to which I shall return. But what I want to emphasize here is the extent to which such subsumptions were also played with to the point of their undoing. That they *could* be played with has something to do with systematic dislocations between visual and linguistic systems of representation in the Renaissance. I noted above the extent to which visual representations of women in play quartos move between representations which depend upon costume/hair/gesture and those which also depend upon a display of the naked body, and in particular of the naked breast. The displayed breast is a metonymy for woman. Since for us, both 'breast' and 'bosom' are always already gendered, this comes as little surprise. But in the Renaissance, both 'breast' and 'bosom' are used interchangeably for men and women. ('Pap', on the other hand, was usually applied only to women.) 'Bosom', indeed, seems to be more frequently gendered as *masculine*. For instance, after the 1611 translation of the Bible which introduced the Hebraic 'wife of thy bosome' and 'husband of her bosome', it was only the *former* expression which became current, thus re-emphasizing the bosom as male (see *OED*). In Ford's *'Tis Pity She's a Whore*, Giovanni offers his dagger to his sister, Annabella, and says: 'And here's my breast; strike home! / Rip up my bosom' (1633a, 1.3) The language of breasts and bosoms tended to be either ungendered or absorbed into the power of the patriarch. To 'toy' with breasts verbally, then, had no obvious implications for the relation of the boy actor to his female role.

But this indeterminacy of gender at the verbal level (an indeterminacy which, I would argue, was determined by a motivated absorption of the female body) was opposed by the visual codes in which the breast was insistently gendered as female. What remains extraordinary is the extent to which this female-gendered breast is staged by the boy actor. In Jonson's *The Devil is an Ass*, for instance, as Wittipol approaches '[t]hese sister-swelling brests' of Frances Fitz-Dottrell, the stage direction reads: '*he growes more familiar in his Courtship, plays with her paps, kisseth her hands, &*' (1631: 2.6.71). (Michael Shapiro gives other striking examples [1990: 1–2].) But the boy actor's 'female body' is most commonly the object of attention in tragedy and tragi-comedy. There, we are asked not to *imagine* the boy actor as he is dressed *up*, but literally to *gaze* at him whilst he *undresses*.

This staging of the undressing boy is particularly striking in death scenes and bed scenes which draw attention to the boy actor's 'breast'. In Ford's *Love's Sacrifice*, the Duke says to Bianca 'Prepare to die', and she responds:

> I do; and to the point
> Of thy sharp sword with open breast I'll run
> Half way thus naked.
>
> (1633b, 5.1)

But even more striking is the way in which Shakespeare in both *Antony and Cleopatra* and *Cymbeline* changes his sources so as to stage the boy's breast. In Plutarch, Cleopatra attaches an asp to her *arm*. Shakespeare retains this, but only after she has already placed an asp upon her *breast*. And Cleopatra/the boy actor, who has already imagined seeing '[s]ome squeaking *Cleopatra* Boy my greatnesse', focuses upon the contradictory vision of Cleopatra's nursing breast/the boy actor's breast: 'Dost thou not see my Baby at my breast, / That suckes the Nurse asleepe' (1623c, 5.2.218, 308–9).[5] An audience seems to be required to observe the splitting apart of what later critics assumed to be a stable 'convention'. More than that, critics have appealed to the presence of the boy actor to 'explain' that certain stagings would have been 'impossible'. Enobarbus's description of Cleopatra is thus taken as a technique of avoidance, by which the audience is spared the embarrassment of gazing at a transvestite boy. But what becomes of such explanations when, again and again, we find Renaissance dramatists going beyond their sources to demand that we witness the boy actor at the very point which a later audience has ruled unimaginable?

In *Cymbeline*, for instance, as Iachimo observes Imogen asleep in bed, he fetishizes both the chamber, the bracelet which will represent her lost honour, and a 'mole Cinque-spotted' upon 'her left brest' (1623d, 2.2.37–8). This last detail, like the asp on Cleopatra'a breast, is truly remarkable. It has been argued that Shakespeare used *Frederyke of Jennen* as a source for *Cymbeline*, and in that pamphlet John of Florence notes *not* a mole on the *breast*, but a wart on the *arm* of Ambrose's wife: 'it fortuned that her lefte arme lay on the bed; and on that arme she had a blacke warte' (Anon. 1560: 197). But Shakespeare replaces the wart with a mole (thus following Boccaccio's version of the story), a mole which is given a *precise* but *imaginary* location upon the body of the boy actor. To make the left breast the object of this voyeuristic scene is to focus our attention on one of the sites of the cultural differentiation of gender. But that site produces antithetical readings: Imogen's swelling breast; the breast of a boy actor. It is as if within the dramatic fiction, the fetishistic signs of presence are forced to confront the absences which mark the actor's body. Or perhaps we might rather say that two contradictory realities are forced to peer into each other's faces. In *Cymbeline*, at the very moment where a later audience would expect a discrete effacement of the theatrical means by which gender is produced, those means are verbally and visually staged.

The specifically erotic charge of such bed scenes is suggested by Aphra Behn, even as she attempts to defend herself against the supposed indecency of her plays. Accused of staging lewd revelations of the actor's body ('they cry, *That Mr.* Leigh *opens his Night Gown, when he comes into the Bride chamber*'), she responds that the best plays are full of such things:

> *Valentinian* all loose and ruffld a Moment after the Rape . . . , the *Moor of Venice* in many places. The *Maids Tragedy* – see the Scene of undressing the Bride, and between the *King* and *Amintor*, and after between the *King* and *Evadne* . . .
>
> (Behn 1687: 186)

It is striking that Behn, in thinking of the erotics of the theatre, thinks of Rochester's *Valentinian*, a Restoration play which explicitly stages homoeroticism,[6] and Renaissance plays in which the undressing of the bride was performed by a boy. Behn, of course, would have seen the plays performed with female actors, but she nevertheless emphasizes the extent to which these plays reveal the body.

To be aware of the fetishistic staging of the boy actor, of the insistence that we see what is not there to see, is to conceptualize the erotics of Renaissance drama in totally unfamiliar ways. Think, for instance, of the end of *Othello* (1623b: 4.3). 'Prithee, tonight / Lay on my bed our weddingsheets', Desdemona says to Emilia. But interpolated between the command and the on-stage arrival of the bed itself, we are asked to witness the boy actor prepare for bed. In one sense, the scene suggests that this preparation is itself a kind of transvestism – a crossing from day to night, from the clothes of a Venetian noble to a shift. And it is curious to note how such 'closet' scenes are frequently – and strangely – marked by an explicit movement from formal to informal dress. Even ghosts obey this convention, if we are to believe the first quarto of *Hamlet*, where Hamlet Senior, appearing to his son in Gertrude's closet, has put off his armour and put on his nightgown. Both in *Othello* and *Hamlet*, the body seems to be simultaneously sexualized and made vulnerable. But in *Othello*, the movement from one set of clothes to another is curiously truncated. Desdemona's command to Emilia, 'Give me my nightly wearing', is followed some twenty lines later by Emilia's enquiry, 'Shall I go fetch your nightgown?' to which Desdemona answers 'No'. In fact, the absence of the nightgown makes all the more insistent the fact that we are witnessing Desdemona/a boy actor undress. The undressing is the more *present* as a strip-tease for the *absence* of any substitute clothing. 'Prithee unpin me', Desdemona says, and later, rejecting the nightgown, 'No, unpin me here.'[7]

Before I return to this moment of voyeuristic suspense where the staged body prepares to split into the unpinned clothes and the 'body beneath', I want to note how the scene as a whole stages a series of splittings or – to put it another way – a series of radical crossings of perspective. First, there is the presentation to the audience of Emilia's impressively relativistic view of sexual morality, a view which threatens to re-present the whole play as grotesque farce, the absurd magnification of 'a *small* vice'. Curiously, and to the disturbance of many critics, the 'sport' which Emilia commends seems to migrate into the language of Desdemona:

DES.   unpin me here;
     This Lodovico is a proper man.
EMIL.   A very handsome man.
DES.   He speaks well.
EMIL.   I know a lady in Venice would have walk'd
     barefoot to Palestine for a touch of his nether lip.

As Desdemona is unpinned, Othello is displaced by that 'proper man', Lodovico. At the same time, Desdemona herself takes on the voice of a maidservant called Barbary. (I am here indebted to Raima Evans's work on this scene.) The willow song is the song of that maid, whose name is itself a curious transposing of Iago's slur against Othello as he goads Brabantio: 'you'll have your daughter cover'd with a Barbary horse; you'll have your nephews neigh to you'. Barbary: the name for bestial male sexuality; the name for a maid betrayed in love – 'poor Barbary'. A single signifier slides between male and female, animal and human, betrayer and betrayed, and at the same time between opposed notions of the 'barbarian' as oppressor and as victim. And it is the song of a poor maid which the Venetian noble will reiterate.

I want to draw attention to these slippages within the signifier because they provide one possible model through which we could read the undressing of Desdemona. On such a reading, the closure of the play would be unsettled by a startling moment of indeterminacy when we are held in suspension between cultural antitheses and, at the same time, between the fiction of Desdemona and the staging of the boy actor. But I do not believe that 'indeterminacy' is an adequate way of thinking about these moments. Rather, we are forced into contradictory attitudes about both sexuality and gender: on the one hand, gender as a set of prosthetic devices (in which case, the *object* of sexual attention is absorbed into the play of those devices); on the other, gender as the 'given' marks of the body (the breast, the vagina, the penis) which (however analogous in Galenic medicine) are read as the signs of an absolute difference (in which case, sexuality, whether between man and woman, woman and woman, or man and man, tends to be organized through a fixation upon the supposedly 'essential' features of gender). But on the Renaissance stage, even those 'essential' features are located – whether prosthetically or at the level of the imaginary – upon *another body*.

In comedy, the relation between the boy's body, the female role and erotic play is at times explicitly articulated. In *The Taming of a Shrew*, the Lord says to the boy in the first scene:

> And dresse yourselfe like some lovelie ladie,
> And when I call see that you come to me.
> For I will say to him thou art his wife,
> Dallie with him and hug him in thine armes,
> And if he desire to goe to bed with thee,
> Then faine some scuse and say thou wilt anon.

(Anon. 1594: 71)

And Sly puts '*The boy in Woman's attire*' on his knee and says that 'she and I will go to bed anon' (72). In Shakespeare's *The Taming of the Shrew*, the Lord requires of the boy that he greet Sly not only with 'kinde embracements' but with 'tempting kisses' (Shakespeare 1623a: Ind. 1.116), and there is an expanded invocation of the pleasures of the bed:

> Wee'l have thee to a Couch,
> Softer and sweeter then the lustfull bed
> On purpose trim'd up for Semiramis.

(Ind. 2.38–40)

Sly's invitation to bed is also amplified: 'Madam undresse you, and come now to bed' (Ind. 2.118). In both plays, any undressing or bed scene is explicitly circumvented, and this draws attention to the fact that in bed scenes (such as the ones I have looked at above) female clothes and boy actor are separated out.

But even here, I think, we can note a radical oscillation between a sense of the absolute difference of the boy from his role and the total absorption of the boy into the role. In other words, if Renaissance theatre constructs an eroticism that depends upon a play of differences (the boy's breast / the woman's breast), it also equally conjures up an eroticism which depends upon the total absorption of male into female, female into male. In the printed text of Shakespeare's *The Shrew* in 1623, the boy is named as 'Bartholomew my Page' (Ind. I. 103) and yet, in changing into the clothes of a woman, he is entirely subsumed into her role. When in *A Shrew*, a stage direction reads '*Enter the boy in Woman's attire*', in *The Shrew* it reads: '*Enter Lady with Attendants*' (Ind. 2. 99). Moreover, the speech prefixes are all for '*Lady*' or '*La*'. The text thus accomplishes what John Rainolds warns against in *Th' Overthrow of Stage-Playes*: 'beware the beautifull boyes *transformed into women* by putting on their raiment, their feature, lookes and facions' (1599: 34, my emphasis). This transformation is carefully erased by a modern editor like Brian Morris, who emends the stage direction to read '*Enter [PAGE as a] lady*' and changes the speech prefixes to read '*Page*' (Morris 1981: 168). In the Folio *The Shrew*, we are thus presented with a wild oscillation between contradictory positions: the plot of the induction demands that we remain aware of Bartholomew *as* Bartholomew, while the language of the text simply cuts Bartholomew, replacing him with 'Lady'.

Such wild oscillations are peculiarly resonant upon the stage, precisely because of the boy actor. But comparable shifts are also characteristic of non-dramatic texts. In *Frederyke of Jennen*, as soon as 'Ambroses wyfe' takes on the name of 'Frederyke' she becomes 'he'. Where a modern text would want to register the 'body beneath' (that is, 'she dressed as he'), *Frederyke* inscribes the transformation of female into male through name and clothes. But, on the other hand, the transformation of Frederick back into Ambrose's wife *does* depend upon the revelation of the body beneath:

> in the meane whyle went the lorde Frederyke secretly away, and came into the chamber, where she did unclothe her al naked saving a clothe before her membres, and than came into the hall before the kyng and al his lordes . . .
>
> (Anon. 1560: 202)

Yet this 'revelation' itself suggests no simple hierarchical relation of 'reality' between what would later be read as 'disguise' and the 'true' body: clothed, he is 'lorde Frederyke'; naked, she is 'the woman' and then 'his [Ambrose's] wyfe'.

This oscillation of gender within a single sentence is even more striking in Barnabe Rich's tale 'Of Apolonius and Silla': Silla dresses in men's clothes and assumes the name of her brother, Silvio. When accused by Julina of impregnating her, Silvio/Silla reveals 'his' body:

> here with all loosing his garmentes doune to his stomacke, and shewed *Iulina* his breastes and pretie teates, surmountyng farre the whitenesse of Snowe it self, saiying: . . . see I am a woman the daughter of a noble Duke . . .
>
> (Rich 1581: 177)

Silvio shows '*his*' breasts which show that he is a woman (but also, curiously, that he is a nobleman's daughter). The phrase 'his breastes and pretie teates' thus enacts the very cross-gendering at the grammatical level which the sentence is undoing at the level of narrative. The garments which are 'his' – the social inscriptions of masculinity – retain, however briefly, their power to name a body which is equally powerfully asserted as *hers* ('I am a woman'). And the body which is 'hers' is in turn reinscribed as 'his' through the name of father and husband ('the daughter of a noble Duke', 'Ambroses wyfe').

The power of clothes, like language, to *do* things to the body is suggested in both these romances, and it is this power of clothes which is so insistently asserted by anti-theatricalists. Calvin, in his sermons on Deuteronomy, if he sometimes thinks of clothes as *manifesting* sexual difference, equally thinks of them as *creating* difference: 'God intended to shew us that every bodies attyring of themselves ought to be such, *as there may be difference betweene men and women*' (1583: 773, my emphasis). Similarly, Prynne thinks of women who 'mimic' masculinity as 'hermaphrodited and trans-formed into men' (1628: A3) and of male actors 'metamorphosed into women on the Stage' (1633: 171). And he follows Calvin in arguing that 'a mans attyring himselfe in womans array . . . perverts one principall use of garments, *to difference men from women*' (1633: 207, original emphasis).

The anti-theatricalists thus feared the power of clothes to *produce* new subjects, to metamorphose boy into woman, commoner into aristocrat. John Rainolds' powerful attack upon the academic stage (and, by extension, upon all theatrical activity) was provoked in the first instance by the almost magical properties of transvestism (Boas 1914: 231–4; Young 1916: 593–604; Binns 1974: 95–101; Jardine 1983: 14–17). Rainolds, one of the greatest scholars of his day, had himself cross-dressed in his youth (Boas 1914: 105–6) and in *Th' Overthrow of Stage-Playes* he admits that 'he did play a womans part upon the same stage, the part of Hippolyta' (Rainolds 1599: 45). But what exactly *is* the danger of transvestism? Here, Rainolds' citations are frequently opaque, as, for instance, the following from Dionysius Car-thusianus:

> *the apparell of wemen* (saith he) *is a great provocation of men to lust and leacherie: because a womans garment being put on a man doeth vehemently touch and move him with the remembrance and imagination of a woman: and the imagination of a thing desirable doth stirr up the desire.*
>
> (Rainolds 1599: 96)

What does Rainolds' translation imply? That the woman's body is imprinted upon or within the clothes? That women's clothes, when they touch and move the male wearer, will awaken the desire *for* women (whom he will remember and imagine) or the desire *to be* a woman? Will the desire be homo- or heteroerotic and will it be directed towards another or towards the self?

The Renaissance theatre was thus the site for the prosthetic production of the sexualized body through the clothing of the body and the mimed gestures of love. But it was also the site where the prosthetic production was dramatically staged and speculated upon, as the boy actor undressed, as the fixations of spectators were drawn back and forth between the clothes which embodied and determined a particular sexual identity and contradictory fantasies of the 'body beneath' – the body of a woman, the body of a boy; a body with and without breasts.

The transvestite body[8]

The interplay between clothing and undressing on the Renaissance stage organized gender around a process of fetishizing, which is conceived *both* as a process of fixation *and* as indeterminable. If the Renaissance stage demands that we '*see*' particular body parts (the breast, the penis, the naked body), it also reveals that such fixations are inevitably unstable. The actor is both boy and woman, and he/she embodies the fact that sexual fixations are not the product of any categorical fixity of gender. Indeed, all attempts to fix gender are necessarily *prosthetic:* that is, they suggest the attempt to supply an imagined deficiency by the exchange of male clothes for female clothes or of female clothes for male clothes; by displacement from male to female space or from female to male space; by the replacement of male with female tasks or of female with male tasks. But all elaborations of the prosthesis which will supply the 'deficiency' can secure no essence. On the contrary, they suggest that gender itself is a fetish, the production of an identity through the fixation upon specific 'parts'. The imagined 'truth' of gender which a post-Renaissance culture would later construct is dependent upon the disavowal of the fetishism of gender, the disavowal of gender as fetish. In its place, it would put a fantasized biology of the 'real'.

But it is this notion of the 'real' which seems to be dramatically undone in undressing scenes, as in *Othello* when Desdemona/the boy actor is unpinned. Lynda Boose has demonstrated how the play itself demands both concealment (of the sexual scene, of the bed and its burden which 'poisons sight') and exposure (the stimulated desire that we should *see*, should 'grossly gape'). But, as I have argued, *what* we should see is radically uncertain. It is not so much a moment of indeterminacy as of contradictory fixations. On the one hand, the clothes themselves – the marks of Desdemona's gender and status – are held up to our attention; on the other, we teeter on the brink of seeing the boy's breastless but 'pinned' body revealed. It is as if, at the moments of greatest dramatic tension, the Renaissance theatre stages its own transvestism.

Contradictory fixations, though, are precisely what mobilize *Othello*. Think, for instance, of how Iago constructs the narrative of Desdemona's betrayal so that Othello can approach the 'grossly gaping' of her being 'topp'd'. He does it by casting *himself* in the role of Desdemona:

> I lay with *Cassio* lately . . .
> In sleepe I heard him say, sweet *Desdemona*,
> Let us be wary, let us hide our Loves,
> And then (Sir) would he gripe, and wring my hand:
> Cry, oh sweet Creature: then kisse me hard,
> As if he pluckt up kisses by the rootes,

That grew upon my lippes, laid his Leg ore my Thigh,
And sigh, and kisse . . .

(1623b: 3.3.419–31)

It is these contradictory fixations (Desdemona and/as the boy actor, Desdemona and/as Iago) which a later theatre would attempt to erase, precisely because the *site* of the audience's sexual fixation is so uncertain.

This uncertainty is, paradoxically, most powerfully felt by anti-theatrical writers. They oscillate between seeing the boy actor as woman, as neither woman nor man, as alluring boy, as male prostitute (or 'dogge', to use Rainolds' term). Prynne, for instance, incorporates Cyprian's account of how the theatre taught 'how a man might be effeminated into a female, how their sex might be changed by Art' (1633: 169). But he can also think of actors as those who, 'by unchaste infections of their members, effeminate their manly nature, being both effeminate men and women, yea, being neither men nor women' (ibid.). Yet the uncertainty of *what* anti-theatricalists saw in no way inhibited the fascinated fixity of their (imaginary) gaze. What they gazed at was a theatre imagined *as a bedroom*, a bedroom which spills off the stage and into the lives of players and audience alike:

> O . . . that thou couldest in that sublime watch-tower insinuate thine eyes into these Players secrets; or set open the closed dores of their bed-chambers, and bring all their innermost hidden Cels unto the conscience of thine eyes. . . . [M]en rush on men with outragious lusts.

(Prynne 1633: 135)

So writes Prynne, translating Cyprian. And Phillip Stubbes sees the actors as contaminating the spectators so that, 'these goodly pageants being done, every mate sorts to his mate . . . and in their secret conclaves (covertly) they play *the Sodomits*, or worse' (Stubbes 1583: 144–5). But *what* anti-theatricalists saw in the 'secret conclaves' of the theatrical bedroom constantly shifted, thus mimicking the shifting perspectives of the Renaissance stage itself.

For the bed scenes and undressing scenes with which I have been concerned produce moments of dizzying indeterminacy. It was such moments that Freud attempted to describe in his essay on 'Fetishism', where the fetish stands in for and mediates between the marks of sexual difference.[9] Freud writes:

> In very subtle instances both the disavowal and the affirmation of the castration (of woman) have found their way into the construction of the fetish itself. This was so in the case of a man whose fetish was an athletic support-belt which could also be worn as bathing drawers. This piece of clothing covered up the genitals entirely and concealed the distinction between them. Analysis showed that it signified that women were castrated *and* that they were not castrated; and it also allowed of the hypo-

thesis that men were castrated, for all these possibilities could equally well be concealed under the belt. . . .

The athletic support-belt, through its concealments, supports contradictory hypotheses. But for Freud, all those hypotheses must be grounded in the fantasy of castration. Why? Because Freud needs to find a fixed point (and a *male* point) outside the play of fetishism, a point to which all other fetishes will teleologically point. The fetishist is, Freud suggests, someone whose interest *'comes to a halt half-way, as it were'* (my emphasis). 'Thus the foot or shoe owes its preference as a fetish – or a part of it – to the circumstance that the inquisitive boy peered at the woman's genitals from below, from her legs up.' The fetish is, for Freud, but part of the larger category of perversions. 'Perversions', he writes in the 'Three essays on the theory of sexuality':

> are sexual activities which either a) *extend*, in an anatomical sense, beyond the regions of the body that are designed for sexual union, or b) *linger*, over the intermediate relations to the sexual object which should normally be traversed rapidly on the path towards the sexual aim.
>
> (Freud 1905: 62)

The very notion of the perverse, like that of the fetish, can only emerge in relation to a) the parts of the body which are 'naturally' sexual and b) a teleological path towards the genitals. The transvestite theatre of the Renaissance, though, does not allow for any such distinction between the 'perverse' and the normal teleological path.

From a Freudian perspective, it 'comes to a halt half-way, as it were'. It does so because it resists the sexual and narrative teleologies which would be developed in the eighteenth and nineteenth centuries. But that resistance is, I believe, less a matter of indeterminacy than of the production of contradictory fixations: the imagined body of a woman, the staged body of a boy actor, the material presence of clothes. Freud's brilliant insight was to see that the 'real person' was itself a displacement of fetishism:

> The progressive concealment of the body which goes along with civiliz-ation keeps sexual curiosity awake. This curiosity seeks to complete the sexual object by revealing its hidden parts. It can, however, be diverted ('sublimated') in the direction of art, if its interest can be shifted away from the genitals on to the shape of the body as a whole.
>
> (Freud 1905: 69)

'The body as a whole', then, is itself a fantasy, a sublimation. But for Freud, the real tends to reappear *behind* or *beneath* that fantasy, a real which always tends towards the formation of sexual difference. In the 'mingle-mangle', the 'hodge-podge', the 'gallimaufry' of Renaissance tragedy, though, contradictory fetishisms (body parts, costumes, handkerchiefs, sheets) are staged not in the play of pure difference but in the play between indeterminacy and fixation.

Notes

1 I am deeply indebted for ideas, references and challenges to Lynda Boose, Greg Bredbeck, Linda Charnes, Lisa Jardine, David Kastan, Michael Shapiro, and Valerie Traub; and I couldn't even have begun without the stimulus of Jonathan Dollimore, Marjorie Garber, Ann Rosalind Jones, Stephen Orgel, Phyllis Rackin and Susan Zimmerman.

2 For important revisions to Lisa Jardine's earlier work, see her 'Twins and travesties' in this volume.

3 On the occasional presence of women on English stages prior to the Restoration, see for instance Stokes (1985–6: 335–6); Bentley (1941: 25); and Gossett (1988).

4 Interestingly, it seems that it was for the revelation of the *male* body that Behn was most virulently criticized: taxing her with indecency, her critics, she writes, claim '*That Mr.* Leigh *opens his Night Gown, when he comes into the Bride-Chamber;* if he do, which is a Jest of his own making, and which I never saw, I hope he has his Cloaths on underneath. And if so, where is the Indecency?' Behn goes on to imply that the charge of indecency is specifically levelled against her as a woman writer: 'had the Plays I have writ come forth under any Mans Name, and never known to have been mine; I appeal to all unbyast Judges of Sense, if they had not said that Person had made as many good Comedies, as any one Man that has writ in our Age; but a Devil on't the Woman damns the Poet' (Behn 1687: 186, 184).

5 For other accounts of Cleopatra and the boy actor, see Rackin (1972), Shapiro (1982), and Gruber (1985).

6 *Valentinian* 5.5 opens with 'Valentinian *and the* Eunuch *discovered on a Couch*'. Valentinian says:

> Oh let me press these balmy Lips all day,
> And bath my Love scorch'd Soul in thy moist Kisses.
> Now by my Joys thou art all sweet And soft,
> And thou shalt be the Altar of my love;
> Upon thy Beauties hourly will I offer,
> And pour out Pleasure and blest Sacrifice,
> To the dear Memory of my Lucina . . .

> (Rochester 1696: 215)

7 John Russell Brown has pointed out to me that, in the dominant theatrical tradition, the 'unpinning' refers to Desdemona's *hair*. That there is no Renaissance warrant for this is suggested by the *OED*, which actually quotes Desdemona's lines as referring to the unpinning of *clothes*, and also gives further examples.

8 My account of transvestism, and of the boy actor in general, is deeply indebted to Jonathan Dollimore's brilliant essay on 'Subjectivity, sexuality and transgression' (1986).

9 My account of fetishism is deeply indebted to Marjorie Garber (1989). See also her fine, wide-ranging study, *Vested Interests*.

Bibliography

Agnew, J.-C. (1986) *Worlds Apart: The Market and the Theater in Anglo-American Thought, 1550–1750*, Cambridge: Cambridge University Press.

Anon. (1560) *Frederyke of Jennen*, in J. M. Nosworthy (ed.) *Cymbeline*, the Arden Shakespeare, London and New York: Methuen, 1955, 191–204.

Anon. (1594) *The Taming of a Shrew*, in G. Bullough (ed.) *Narrative and Dramatic Sources of Shakespeare*, vol. 1, London: Routledge & Kegan Paul, 1957.

Appadurai, A. (1986) 'Introduction: Commodities and the politics of value', in A. Appadurai (ed.) *The Social Life of Things: Commodities in Cultural Perspective*, Cambridge: Cambridge University Press, 3–63.

Beaumont, F. and Fletcher, J. (1610) *The Maid's Tragedy*, ed. A. Gurr, Berkeley: University of California Press, 1969.

Behn, A. (1687) *The Lucky Chance; Or, An Alderman's Bargain*, in M. Summers (ed.) *The Works of Aphra Behn*, vol. 3, New York: Phaeton, 1967 (1915).

—— (1696) *The Younger Brother; Or, the Amorous Jilt*, in M. Summers (ed.) *The Works of Aphra Behn*, vol. 4, New York: Phaeton, 1967 (1915), 311–99.

Bentley, G. E. (1941) *The Jacobean and Caroline Stage*, vol. 1, Oxford: Clarendon Press.

——(1984) *The Profession of Player in Shakespeare's Time*, Princeton: Princeton University Press.

Binns, J. W. (1974) 'Women or transvestites on the Elizabethan stage?: an Oxford controversy', *Sixteenth Century Journal*, 5, 2: 95–120.

Boas, F. S. (1914) *University Drama in the Tudor Age*, Oxford: Oxford University Press.

Boose, L. (1987) ' "Let it be Hid": Iago, Renaissance pornography, and *Othello's* "grossly gaping" audience', unpublished ms.

Calvin, J. (1583) *The Sermons of M. John Calvin Upon . . . Deuteronomie*, trans. A. Golding, London.

Chambers, E. K. (1923) *The Elizabethan Stage*, vol. 4, Oxford: Clarendon Press.

Cibber, C. (1968) *An Apology for the Life of Colley Cibber*, ed. B. R. S. Fone, Ann Arbor: University of Michigan Press.

Dollimore, J. (1986) 'Subjectivity, sexuality and transgression: the Jacobean connection', *Renaissance Drama*, n.s. 17: 53–81.

—— (1990) 'The cultural politics of perversion: Augustine, Shakespeare, Freud, Foucault', *Genders*, 8: 1–16.

Foakes, R. A. (1985) *Illustrations of the English Stage 1580–1642*, London: Scolar Press.

Ford, J. (1633a) *'Tis Pity She's a Whore*, in H. Ellis (ed.) *John Ford*, New York: Hill & Wang (1957), 5–163.

—— (1633b) *Love's Sacrifice*, in H. Ellis (ed.) *John Ford*, New York: Hill & Wang (1957), 257–340.

Freeburg, V. O. (1915) *Disguise Plots in Elizabethan Drama: A Study in Stage Tradition*, New York: Columbia University Press.

Freud, S. (1905) 'Three essays on the theory of sexuality', in James Strachey and Angela Richards (eds) *On Sexuality*, trans. James Strachey, Harmondsworth: Penguin, 1977, 33–204.

Garber, M. (1989) 'Fetish envy', paper given at the Modern Languages Association, New Orleans.

—— (1991a) 'The logic of the transvestite: *The Roaring Girl*', in D. S. Kastan and P. Stallybrass (eds) *Staging the Renaissance: Reinterpretations of Elizabethan and Jacobean Drama*, London and New York: Routledge, 221–34.

—— (1991b) *Vested Interests: Cross-Dressing and Cultural Anxiety*, New York and London: Routledge.

Gossett, S. (1988) ' "Man-maid, begone!": Women in masques', *English Literary Renaissance* 18: 96–113.

Gruber, W. (1985) 'The actor in the script: affective strategies in Shakespeare's *Antony and Cleopatra*', *Comparative Drama* 19, 1:30–48.

Hillebrand, H. N. (1926) *The Child Actors: A Chapter in Elizabethan Stage History*, New York: Russell & Russell, 1964.

Howard, J. (1988) 'Crossdressing, the theatre, and gender struggle in early modern England', *Shakespeare Quarterly* 39, 4:418–40.

Jamieson, M. (1968) 'Shakespeare's celibate stage', in G. E. Bentley (ed.) *The Seventeenth-Century Stage: A Collection of Critical Essays*, Chicago: University of Chicago Press, 70–93.

Jardine, L. (1983) *Still Harping on Daughters: Women and Drama in the Age of Shakespeare*, Brighton: Harvester.

Jonson, B. (1607) *Volpone, or the Foxe*, in C. H. H. Percy and E. Simpson (eds) *Ben Jonson*, vol. 5, Oxford: Clarendon Press, 1938.

—— (1631) *The Devil is an Ass*, in C. H. H. Percy and E. Simpson (eds) *Ben Jonson*, vol. 6, Oxford: Clarendon Press, 1938.

Lee, N. (1677) *The Rival Queens*, in T. B. Stroup and A. L. Cooke (eds) *The Works of Nathaniel Lee*, New Brunswick: Scarecrow, 1954, 211–13.

McLuskie, K. (1987) 'The act, the role, and the actor: Boy actresses on the Elizabethan stage', *New Theatre Quarterly* 3, 10: 120–30.

Marston, J. (1906) *John Marston's The Wonder of Women or The Tragedy of Sophonisba*, ed. W. Kemp, New York and London: Garland, 1979.

Maus, K. E. (1979) ' "Playhouse flesh and blood": Sexual ideology and the Restoration actress', *ELH* 46, 4: 595–617.

Morris, B. (ed.) (1981) *The Taming of the Shrew*, the Arden Shakespeare, London and New York: Methuen.

Neill, M. (1989) 'Unproper beds: Race, adultery, and the hideous in *Othello*', *Shakespeare Quarterly* 40, 4: 383–412.

Orgel, S. (1985) 'Making greatness familiar', in D. M. Bergeron (ed.) *Pageantry in the Shakespearean Theatre*, Athens: University of Georgia Press, 19–25.

—— (1989a) 'Nobody's perfect: or why did the English stage take boys for women?' *South Atlantic Quarterly* 88, 1: 7–29.

—— (1989b) 'The boys in the back room: Shakespeare's apprentices and the economics of theatre', paper given at the Modern Languages Association, New Orleans.

Pepys, S. (1916) *Pepys on the Restoration Stage*, ed. H. McAfee, New Haven: Yale University Press.

Prynne, W. (1628) *The Unlovelinesse of Lovelockes*, London.

—— (1633) *Histrio-Mastix*, London.

Rackin, P. (1972) 'Shakespeare's boy Cleopatra, the decorum of nature, and the golden world of poetry', *PMLA* 87: 201–12.

—— (1987) 'Androgyny, mimesis, and the marriage of the boy heroine on the English Renaissance stage', *PMLA* 102: 29–41.

Rainolds, J. (1599) *Th' Overthrow of Stage-Playes*, London.

Rich, B. (1581) 'Of Apolonius and Silla' in J. M. Lothian and T. W. Craik (eds) *Twelfth Night*, the Arden Shakespeare, London and New York: Methuen, 1975, 157–79.

Rochester, J., Earl of (1696) *Poems On Several Occasions with Valentinian*, London.

Rosenburg, M. (1971) *The Masks of Othello*, Berkeley: University of California Press.

—— (1978) *The Masks of Macbeth*, Berkeley: University of California Press.

Shakespeare, W. (1623a) *The Taming of the Shrew*, in C. Hinman (ed.) *The First Folio of Shakespeare: The Norton Facsimile*, New York: Norton, 1968.

—— (1623b) *Othello*, in C. Hinman (ed.) *The First Folio of Shakespeare: The Norton Facsimile*, New York: Norton, 1968.

—— (1623c) *Antony and Cleopatra*, in C. Hinman (ed.) *The First Folio of Shakespeare: The Norton Facsimile*, New York: Norton, 1968.

—— (1623d) *Cymbeline*, in C. Hinman (ed.) *The First Folio of Shakespeare: The Norton Facsimile*, New York: Norton, 1968.

Shapiro, M. (1977) *Children of the Revels: The Boy Companies of Shakespeare's Time and Their Plays*, New York: Columbia University Press.

—— (1982) 'Boying her greatness: Shakespeare's use of coterie drama in *Antony and Cleopatra*', *Modern Language Review* 77, 1: 1–15.

—— (1990) 'Crossgender casting, crossgender disguise, and anxieties of intimacy in *Twelfth Night* and other plays', paper given at the Shakespeare Association of America, Philadelphia.

Stokes, J. (1985–6) 'The Wells Cordwainers show: New evidence concerning guild entertainments in Somerset', *Comparative Drama* 19, 4: 332–46.

Stubbes, P. (1583) *The Anatomie of Abuses*, F. J. Furnivall (ed.), New Shakespeare Society, London: Trübner, 1877–9.

Styan, J. L. (1986) *Restoration Comedy in Performance*, Cambridge: Cambridge University Press.

Traub, V. (1991) 'Getting hot: Female erotic pleasure and the early modern theatre', paper given at the Shakespeare Association of America, Vancouver.

Wilson, J. H. (1958) *All the King's Ladies: Actresses of the Restoration*, Chicago: University of Chicago Press.

Young, K. (1916) 'William Gager's defence of the academic stage', *Transactions of the Wisconsin Academy of Sciences, Arts, and Letters* 18: 593–638.

Chapter 6

Desire's excess and the English Renaissance theatre

Edward II, Troilus and Cressida, Othello

Catherine Belsey

i

Marlowe's *Edward II* is a play about desire – and about desire's excess. There is not a great deal of love poetry in this textually austere tragedy. Instead, Edward's desire for Gaveston is dramatically represented, made palpable for the audience, in terms of a succession of separations. His lover's absence constitutes both the occasion and also the figure of Edward's longing. Gaveston is exiled, recalled, banished, brought back, parted from the king; they are reunited and then separated again. The first half of this divided play[1] repeatedly shows the king either mourning Gaveston's banishment (*Edward II* 1.4.305–18)[2], or anxiously asking for his absent favourite. This indeed is how the play begins, as Gaveston reads the king's letter recalling him from exile: '*My father is deceast, come* Gaveston,*/And share the kingdom with thy deerest friend*' (1.1.1–2). At Edward's own first appearance, he insists more defiantly that he must have Gaveston as his companion: 'Ile bandie with the Barons and the Earles,/And eyther die, or live with *Gaveston*' (1.1.137–8). In Act 2, after Gaveston's second banishment is repealed, 'The winde is good, I wonder why he stayes,/I feare me he is wrackt upon the sea' (2.2.1–2). The Royal Shakespeare Company production in 1990 showed Edward here staring longingly into the distance, shading his eyes with his hand. 'How now, what newes, is *Gaveston* arrivde?' (2.2.6). And again after their brief secret reunion at Tynemouth, 'O tell me *Spencer*, where is *Gaveston*?' (2.4.1). His lover's absences give material form to Edward's passion, endow with dramatic substance the lack which motivates desire, and thus enable a condition which is quintessentially negative to find a mode of representation.

Judging by the number of absence poems, farewells and valedictions in the period, English Renaissance lovers seem to have been exceptionally given (textually, at least) to parting. Absence in the lyric poetry of the period is like a winter, even in spring;[3] it is darkness,[4] heaviness, a desert;[5] it commonly resembles death;[6] and exceptionally it is 'trepidation of the spheares'.[7] The many aubades, appeals to the sun to delay its course, are variations on the theme, sweet-sorrowful predictions of imminent separation.

Parting, as everyone knows, intensifies desire: absence makes the heart grow fonder.

> since want provokes desire
> When we lose what wee before
> Have enjoy'd, as we want more,
> So is Love more set on fire.
>
> (Carew 1949: 61)

Moreover, the narcissistic element in desire thrives on absence, imagining and idealizing its lost object, creating out of its own yearning a fiction of presence which underwrites the omnipotence of the lover. A lyric from Davison's *Poetical Rhapsody*, printed in 1602, makes witty capital out of this ambiguity:

> By Absence, this good meanes I gaine,
>   That I can catch her,
>   Where none can watch her,
> In some close corner of my braine,
>   There I embrace and kisse her,
> And so I both enjoy and misse her.
>
> (Rollins 1931: 225)

Fulke Greville renders a similar account with characteristic brevity: 'Absence records the Stories/Wherein Desire glories/Although she burne.'[8] Edward, it is clear, has also had his fantasies:

> Thy absence made me droope, and pine away,
> For as the lovers of fair *Danae*,
> When she was lockt up in a brasen tower,
> Desirde her more, and waxt outragious,
> So did it sure with me.
>
> (2.2.52–6)

The most notable among the beautiful Danaë's lovers was of course Jupiter, king of the gods, who visited her in a shower of gold, just as Edward showers Gaveston with titles, entitlements, wealth.[9]

We do not need to turn to social history for an explanation of the textual recurrence of absence in the Renaissance. It is not geographical mobility but the problem of writing about desire that generates the preoccupation with separation. Absence constitutes an emblem of desire, its material analogue, its figure. Isn't desire, after all, as Roland Barthes suggests, 'the same, whether the object is present or absent? Isn't the object *always* absent?' – always, that is to say, elusive, unintrojected, unmastered, unpossessed (Barthes 1979: 15)?

Not that absence is figur*ative* in the Renaissance texts. On the contrary, it is understood to be a literal condition, and *its* figures, its metaphors, are winter, a desert, darkness, death. Absence as a signifier of desire does not make desire present, does not produce or reproduce the thing itself, but only generates a succession of further signifiers, further analogies. The metaphor, the emblem or the analogue, however, is inevitably a stand-in for the thing itself, always only a substitute, and in this second process of substitution, something further slips away, just when it seems that meaning is being affirmed.[10] In consequence, these texts of absence, like desire itself, seek an impossible, a metaphysical presence, which is the inscription of love. In each case the figure deflects what it set out to define, paradoxically re-enacting the precise process of deferment which constitutes desire sustained.

If absence is thus the type of desire, it is also the type of signification itself. Separation is the beginning, for Freud, of meaning, the formulation of difference in the *fort-da* game, which *names* and distinguishes the comings and goings of the cotton reel. 'Language is born of absence', Barthes says, invoking Freud. 'The child has made himself a doll out of a spool, throws it away and picks it up again, miming the mother's departure and return: a paradigm is created' (Barthes 1979: 16). But if language is born of absence, so is desire, and at the same moment. This must be so because meaning is always borrowed from the place of the Other, the locus of speech, not invented by the child, not at the disposal of the subject, and never, therefore, introjected, mastered, possessed. In consequence, the subject, which is no more than an effect of language, is finally absent from its own utterances, just as desire, the unutterable residue, is absent from its own formulation, even when it takes the form, Jacques Lacan would say, of the demand for love (Lacan 1977: 263–4, 286–7). Desire resides with the missing subject and the missed meaning in the (absent) place of the Other. The poetic or dramatic representation of absence is thus a critical instance of an impossible project, which is the signification of desire.

ii

Desire is what exceeds the signifier. And since desire's imperatives are absolute, it also exceeds the Law, which is orthodoxy, propriety and, above all, the order of meaning. The Law of the Father links kings indissolubly with kingdoms, monarchs with monarchy. But for Edward II in love, kingdoms are clay, he repeatedly declares. His realm is nothing in comparison with his love, which is all-absorbing:

I have my wish, in that I joy thy sight,
And sooner shall the sea orewhelme my land,
Then beare the ship that shall transport thee hence.

(1.1.151–3)

And again,

> Ere my sweete *Gaveston* shall part from me,
> This Ile shall fleete upon the Ocean,
> And wander to the unfrequented *Inde*.

(1.4.48–50)

> Make severall kingdomes of this monarchie,
> And share it equally amongst you all,
> So I may have some nooke or corner lefte,
> To frolike with my deerest *Gaveston*.

(1.4.70–73)

Has the King of France invaded Normandy? A 'trifle' (2.2.10). He has occupied it?

>   tush *Sib*, if this be all,
> *Valoys* and I will soone be friends againe.
> But to my *Gaveston*: shall I never see,
> Never behold thee now?

(3.1.66–9)

Edward's desire is extravagant: he distributes power and dispenses titles to his favourites, and to the peers when they seem reconciled to his favourites, in a form of conspicuous, unproductive expenditure which far exceeds utility. These displays of patronage do not buy respectability for Gaveston or loyalty to Edward: the barons do not in consequence come into line. On the contrary, they re-enter the circle of power, and the expenditure that corresponds to it, by risking their lands, their armies, and finally their lives in rebellion.

Desire thus lays waste a kingdom, and with it a king, since the relationship between the two is symbiotic. Edward makes Gaveston his 'self', he repeatedly affirms (1.1.143; 1.4.118), and this identification with the object of desire is more than a compliment: the lover finds an imagined wholeness of the self, an illusory unity, in the presence of the other. But the self of a subject identified (named) as a monarch is properly invested in monarchy, not in desire. When Edward appears with Gaveston enthroned at his side, in the place of the Queen, Mortimer Senior knowingly invokes Ovid's pronouncement that majesty and love do not go well together, or long remain in the same seat (1.4.13).[11] In trying to combine majesty and love, in identifying his 'self' with Gaveston, the king throws away his own title to his kingdom.

> what are kings, when regiment is gone,
> But perfect shadowes in a sun-shine day?
> My nobles rule, I beare the name of king . . .

(5.1.25–7)

Finally, he resigns the crown, signifier of monarchy, and with it the name of king, the only (shadowy) identity that now remains to him: 'Come death, and with thy fingers close my eyes,/Or if I live, let me forget my selfe' (5.1.110–11). Desire, which is an absence, takes possession of the subject, tantalizes with an imagined omnipotence, and ultimately delivers nothing more nor less than annihilation.

iii

The desire which so destabilizes the subject is also shown in the play to be in excess of its object. Much would depend on performance, of course, but the text does not explicitly invest Gaveston with beauty or wit, though in his short Italian cloak, and his Tuscan cap with one huge jewel, he has, we are evidently to understand, style (1.4.413–15). In general terms the play presents the object of Edward's obsession with a degree of scepticism: Gaveston, whose interests are at least as mercenary as they are passionate, is arguably not worth what it costs to keep him. The comparison with Danaë, for instance, is two-edged: there was a tradition of representing the beautiful captive as a courtesan showered by golden coins,[12] and the play itself (with some ambiguity) invokes this convention at its second allusion to her. In this instance the French are to be bribed to resist the Queen's appeals for support, and Edward's treasure will leave them 'all enchaunted like the guarde,/That suffered *Jove* to passe in showers of gold/To *Danae* (3.1.266–8).

Even Edward has little to say in praise of Gaveston, and much of the barons' criticism seems to be justified by events. All in all, Edward's expense of far more than spirit seems oddly unmotivated. When he is asked why he loves a man the whole world hates, Edward can only reply, 'Because he loves me more than all the world' (1.4.77). As soon as Gaveston is dead, he adopts Spencer in his place – and showers him with titles. But the play, probably first performed in 1592, belongs to a moment before love was fully moralized and domesticated, when desire was commonly brought into being by forces much more arbitrary than virtue.

Gaveston's mode of seduction is not moral but theatrical:

I must have wanton Poets, pleasant wits,
Musitians, that with touching of a string
May draw the pliant king which way I please:
Musicke and poetrie is his delight,
Therefore ile have Italian maskes by night,
Sweete speeches, comedies, and pleasing showes.

(1.1.51–6)

The emphasis is on pleasure: wanton poets, pleasant wits, sweet speeches. Gaveston's entertainments are offered in return for the king's patronage, and in this way they constitute an alternative kind of conspicuous expenditure. By staging these seductive shows, Gaveston proposes to enter the circle of power, drawing the pliant king to his own will. It is worth noting, in the context of current debates, that though Gaveston's final object is political, there is no suggestion here that the *content* of the shows should be devoted to either containment or subversion.[13] He is not planning to produce court propaganda on the one hand, or revolutionary agitprop on the other. On the contrary, the spectacles Gaveston will direct are to be a staging of desire itself. They are to solicit desire in response to the object of the gaze; a record of desire and its consequences will constitute the plot:

Sometime a lovelie boye in *Dians* shape,
With haire that gilds the water as it glides,
Crownets of pearle about his naked armes,
And in his sportfull hands an Olive tree,
To hide those parts which men delight to see,
Shall bathe him in a spring, and there hard by,
One like *Actaeon* peeping through the grove,
Shall by the angrie goddesse be transformde,
And running in the likeness of an Hart,
By yelping hounds puld downe, and seeme to die.

(1.1.61–70)

A beautiful boy-girl, an Ovidian narrative,[14] voyeurism and violence: Gaveston's princely pastime includes in mythological form many of the staple pleasures of the English Renaissance stage. And indeed Gaveston's intent to entertain the monarch was exactly the presumed official project of the Elizabethan public theatres.[15] But there is also a difference. Gaveston is apparently wholly dependent on the monarch's patronage: it is Edward who pays, directly or indirectly, for Gaveston's 'triumphes, maskes, lascivious showes' (2.2.157). These erotic spectacles themselves constitute a form of courtly excess, a display of indifference to the Law which names the monarch and defines monarchy. The Renaissance theatre, meanwhile, was funded by the audience. It, too, was excessive, unnecessary, non-utilitarian, and its excesses were a constant source of irritation to religious and commercial orthodoxy. The London theatres, as Steven Mullaney has argued, would seem to exceed the boundaries of the city (1988), and the plays they stage commonly exceed the bounds of propriety, taking as their topics those areas that official culture barely acknowledged, but did not exclude. While moralists either denounced or domesticated desire, and lyric poets idealized it, the stage put on display for the purposes of entertainment an account of eroticism which, though presumably widely intelligible at that moment, in some ways differs markedly from our own.

The relationship between the Elizabethan theatre and the court was ambiguous. The Crown retained the right to license plays for performance;

court performances guaranteed that the Privy Council provided a degree of protection against attempts to close the playing houses; patronage by a powerful baron led to court performances (Barroll *et al.* 1975: 26–7); but economically the theatres were independent.[16] Until the mid-sixteenth century most noble households retained troupes of players, who travelled in the liveries of their patrons, returning to base at intervals (Westfall 1990: 124–5). The court was no exception. But during the 1570s the Revels Office supervised a spectacular reduction in court expenditure by substituting plays for masques and progresses. The advantage of plays was that the players were able to provide their own props and costumes (Streitberger 1986: xviii–xix). At exactly this time the theatre was in the process of becoming a commercial venture. In 1574 a patent was granted to the Earl of Leicester's Men authorizing them to perform publicly in or out of London. The London Theatre opened in 1576. From this period until the end of Elizabeth's reign, plays became an increasingly favoured form of court entertainment at the traditional times of Revels,[17] and patronage was increasingly symbolic. The royal and aristocratic theatre of the first half of the century had given way to a commercial theatre which was much more tenuously and uncertainly related to the court.

It follows that we cannot simply read off the meanings of the plays from the power relations in the state.[18] Sometimes love *is* love, not power in disguise, as Mary Beth Rose points out, taking issue with Arthur Marotti (1982) and with a subsequent critical tradition which finds court politics wherever it turns (Rose 1988: 11). The Jacobean and Caroline court masque would show how direct patronage produces works designed to celebrate and instruct. The theatre, meanwhile, was neither a straightforward instrument of court power, nor the consistent location of radical resistance. On the contrary, the plays explore, within certain constraints, the plurality of meanings, including the unacknowledged meanings, in circulation in the culture of which they form a part. They also set out to please, and they do so to a large extent, like Gaveston, by dramatizing desire.

This does not imply, however, that the theatrical representation of desire is necessarily cosy, as Gaveston's projected show indicates. Actaeon, who spies in secret on the naked Diana, dies torn to pieces by his own hounds. Renaissance plays are an instance of what Georges Bataille calls 'symbolic expenditure', depicting and dramatizing loss and degradation. Their extravagance is not accidental. While the court masque represents 'real expenditure', conspicuous excess which puts monarchic and courtly magnificence on display, the theatre, no less excessive, provokes dread and horror, or perhaps laughter, as an effect of its own signifying practices (Bataille 1985). The anti-theatrical writers were not slow to seize on this. Stephen Gosson denounced the stage accordingly:

The argument of Tragedies is wrath, crueltie, incest, iniurie, murther eyther violent by sworde, or voluntary by poyson. The persons, Gods, Goddesses, furies, fiendes, Kinges, Quenes, and mightie men. The grounde worke of Commedies, is loue, cosenedge, flatterie, bawderie, slye conueighance of whoredome; The persons, cookes, queanes, knaues, baudes, parasites, courtezannes, lecherous olde men, amorous yong men.

(Chambers 1923: 215)

In Gosson's view, all this attention to passion and violence can only produce immoderate sorrow: it certainly offers no useful lessons for life. Even if in 1582 Gosson's account reads more like the Church Fathers denouncing Roman drama than an account of the contemporary London stage, there would in due course prove to be something in it. Certainly Phillip Stubbes thought that Gosson's lists were good enough to reprint more or less verbatim in his *Anatomy of Abuses* a year later, though for good measure he added hags among the persons and adultery to the themes (Chambers 1923: 223). As we know with the benefit of hindsight, even in Renaissance romantic comedy, where desire leads finally to a happy ending, traces of a violence which inhabits or accompanies desire are frequently in evidence.[19] In the tragedy of the period, meanwhile, desire commonly causes murder and suicide. It means Virginia's 'execution', Lavinia's rape and mutilation and death, or the extraction of Annabella's heart. And it leads, of course, to the climactic horror of Edward II's appalling death, a murder which is simultaneously torture and emblematic rape.

iv

Much of the information the play offers about Gaveston comes from his enemies, so its reliability is in some doubt. But there is a consistent emphasis on his theatricality and the general staginess of his lover-king's regime. Gaveston himself declares that his followers will sustain his projected dramatic and erotic illusion off the stage and in broad daylight:

Like *Sylvian* Nimphes my pages shall be clad,
My men like Satyrs grazing on the lawnes,
Shall with their Goate feete daunce an antick hay.

(1.1.58–60)

And Mortimer's comments indicate that he has been true to his plans. The base-born Gaveston, he complains,

weares a lords revenewe on his back,
And *Midas* like he jets it in the court,
With base outlandish cullions at his heeles,
Whose proud fantastick liveries make such show,
As if that *Proteus* god of shapes appearde.

(1.4.407–11)

Courtiers up from the country who overspent on clothes in defiance of the sumptuary laws were a common target of satire, but so too were the actors, who obscured the difference between artisans and gentlemen by flaunting their borrowed robes both on the stage and off it. The theatrical wardrobes were often built up from aristocratic cast-offs, and Stephen Gosson denounced the players who 'jet under gentlemens noses in sutes of silke' (Chambers 1923: 204). Mortimer's reference to Proteus, the shape-changer, seems to align Gaveston with the actors here.

Is the object of Edward's tragic desire no more, then, than a poor player who struts and frets his hour upon the stage, a walking shadow, as insubstantial as desire finally renders the king himself? Is the idealizing world of love a mere theatre of illusions? Certainly Spencer, who replaces Gaveston, is adept at instructing Baldock on how to perform, how to 'cast the scholler off,/And learne to court it like a Gentleman' (2.1.31–2). The court of the king who identifies himself as a lover becomes increasingly theatrical, and eventually even Edward's army comes to resemble a pageant: the soldiers march like players, in garish robes, while the king himself rides laughing with them, nodding his 'spangled crest' (2.2.183–6). The image momentarily renders the lover-king hopelessly absurd.

The Earl of Lancaster compares Gaveston to Helen of Troy, the 'Greekish strumpet' who wasted so many lives (2.5.15), and Shakespeare's *Troilus and Cressida*, some ten years later, explicitly presents heroes rendered unheroic by desire. This time the statement is even bleaker, the absurdity more unredeemed. Love's excesses progressively incapacitate Paris, Achilles and Troilus, as they fail to live up to what Linda Charnes calls their 'notorious identities' (Charnes 1989). This is probably the first appearance of Troilus and Cressida on the English stage, but their legend, recounted most notably by Chaucer and Henryson, was familiar enough in the Elizabethan period to ensure the irony of their prophetic exchange of vows: the characters are already proverbial, 'As true as Troilus' and 'As false as Cressid' (3.2.180, 194),[20] in advance of the theatrical representation of their story (Kimbrough 1964: 28–9). Like Linda Charnes, Elizabeth Freund also stresses what she calls the play's 'citationality', its reinscription of a well-known narrative, and the discontinuity between its reiterated familiarity on the one hand, and its mimetic allure on the other (Freund 1985: 24). I want to draw on their analyses in order to suggest that the disjunction they both identify is in part an effect of the differing modes of Greek epic, medieval romance and the Renaissance stage. The Elizabethan theatre characteristically calls idealization into question and foregrounds excess. As an instance of symbolic expenditure, it provokes either horror or laughter, and sometimes both at once. When Shakespeare's play retells the romantic story of enforced absence, of lovers parted by an epic war for a 'placket' (*Troilus and Cressida* 2.3.21), fought on behalf of a cuckold, the dominant mode is exceptionally ironic, and the figure of desire's excess is venereal disease.

'Agamemnon – how if he had boils, full, all over, generally?' ruminates Thersites, 'And those boils did run. . . . Then would come some matter from him' (2.1.2–8). The play is punctuated by images of the human body overflowing with pus or rheum (5.3.104), or extruding skin diseases (2.3.76), surrogates for the syphilitic chancre of the Neapolitan bone-ache (2.3.19–20; 5.3.105; 5.10.35). Love itself is identified as a 'sore' (3.1.115), an 'ulcer' (1.1.53). In Renaissance medical theory desire is an effect of an imbalance in the humours: an excess of blood, which is the origin of semen, leads to obsession with a pleasing form, and if desire is frustrated, the result is lovesickness or erotomania.[21] *Troilus and Cressida* shows a world where desire is everywhere. Here the condition commonly exceeds its outward motive, its object. Helen's worth is a topic for debate (2.2; 4.1.56–75): the 'mortal Venus' (3.1.31) is also a whore (4.1.67). Cressida does not apparently teach the torches to burn bright: the play is more lyrical about Troilus's desire than about Cressida's beauty. As far as Cressida herself is concerned, Diomed will finally do in exchange for Troilus. Achilles is in love with Polyxena, but spends his time with Patroclus. The play stages the extent to which objects of desire, always only a succession of stand-ins, are ultimately interchangeable for the subject.[22] But obsession here is indiscriminate: the characters lose all distinction as desire becomes the element in which they have their being. The body exceeds itself and runs over indifferently with semen[23] and with disease.

But Shakespeare's play is more than parodic gesture, and more too than anti-heroic irony. It also offers to define desire with precision and without sentimentality. Love, the play proposes, exceeds the sexual act; it also exceeds both the desiring consciousness and the subject that utters its own desire.

When Cressida fears to find a monster in Cupid's pageant, Troilus reassures her. There is nothing monstrous in love, he insists, or at least,

> Nothing but our undertakings, when we vow to weep seas, live in fire, eat rocks, tame tigers; thinking it harder for our mistress to devise imposition enough than for us to undergo any difficulty imposed. This is the monstruosity in love, lady: that the will is infinite, and the execution confined; that the desire is boundless, and the act a slave to limit.

> (3.2.75–82)

Love is what can never be made manifest, and this renders it monstrous: dangerous, devouring, out of control. Desire is the unuttered residue which exceeds any act that would display it, including the sexual act. Cressida immediately narrows and fixes Troilus's meaning:

> They say all lovers swear more performance than they are able, and yet reserve an ability that they never perform.

> (3.2.83–5)

But the reserve is not voluntary, not deliberate. On the contrary, it is the absence at the heart of all performance, the lack in being which sets desire itself in motion.

Meanwhile, in Troilus's anticipation the act threatens to annihilate the consciousness that seeks it:

> I am giddy: expectation whirls me round.
> Th'imaginary relish is so sweet
> That it enchants my sense: what will it be
> When that the wat'ry palate tastes indeed
> Love's thrice-reputed nectar? Death, I fear me,
> Sounding destruction, or some joy too fine,
> Too subtle-potent, tun'd too sharp in sweetness
> For the capacity of my ruder powers.
> I fear it much; and I do fear besides
> That I shall lose distinction in my joys,
> As doth a battle, when they charge on heaps
> The enemy flying.   (3.2.16–27)

Here it is the sexual act which is boundless and the experiencing consciousness that is a slave to limit. Troilus fears a sensation so powerful, so excessive, that its consequences must be death, or perhaps the swooning dissolution of consciousness, or at the very least a pleasure too intense to be registered by the subject. The common Elizabethan sexual pun on 'die' indicates that his fears may be by no means eccentric in the period.[24] The expectation is of a loss of consciousness, and with it the loss of 'distinction' in the ruthless impersonality of coition. There is a radical mismatch between desire, which imagines and idealizes a unique object, and this in-different sex which simultaneously exceeds the subject and leaves the object out of account. Cressida is not mentioned: ultimately her place is taken in the imagery by 'The enemy flying'.

In Troilus's presence Cressida herself is in another way beyond control, a victim of contrary imperatives to tell and not to tell. To confess, to be 'unsecret', is to put herself at the disposal of another (3.2.118–32), and indeed to reveal that she is at the mercy of the Other, a speaker unwilling to be the person she speaks of. Troilus reasons with her, inappropriately: 'You cannot shun yourself.' But Cressida recognizes the division in the self that desire prises open:

> Let me go and try.
> I have a kind of self resides with you,
> But an unkind self, that itself will leave
> To be another's fool. I would be gone.
> Where is my wit? I know not what I speak.
>   (3.2.144–9)

In *Edward II* desire creates a division of the self in terms of conflicting obligations, seen as conflicting subject positions: to be a lover is to invest the self in another person and not in kingship. To be a lover and a king is therefore to be a king without regiment, which is in the end to be nothing. But in *Troilus and Cressida* the division is within the desiring subject, uncertain whether to speak or not to speak. The uncertainty invades the signifier itself: the syntactic relationship between the selves that appear in Cressida's utterance is unspecified. Is the 'kind of self' that resides with Troilus synonymous with the 'unkind self' that wants to abandon Cressida's self-determining self, in order to be Troilus's fool? ('I have a kind of self resides with you, But [it is] an unkind self'). Or is the unkind self an alternative to the self that resides with Troilus, already determined to leave Troilus and become another's fool? ('I have a kind of self resides with you, But [also] an unkind self').[25] How many selves are there in this miniature drama of division? For a subject at the mercy of the signifier the unitary, self-determining self was always imaginary. Desire, which invests the self in another, necessarily precipitates a division in the subject. And to the degree that desire speaks, it does so from the place of the Other, and so reveals the self to be precisely an Other's fool. Cressida knows not what she speaks: the I that knows (or doesn't) is not the same as the I that speaks. Cressida is in an oddly literal sense beside herself here, out of her wits, mad, since, as she goes on to explain, 'to be wise and love/Exceeds man's might' (3.2.154–5). For the uncertain subject, which is an effect of the unstable, undecidable signifier, there is no ground, no resting place, no guarantee, and least of all in another subject. Love is folly, as Troilus has known all along: 'I tell thee I am mad/ In Cressid's love' (1.1.51–2).

v

If lovers are mad, they should clearly be locked up. This was the age, as Foucault has reminded us, of the great incarceration of the insane in institutions which contained and confined them. At the same historical moment desire was to be more thoroughly contained and confined within the institution of marriage, and thus brought under the control of the Law (and the law). The project was to ground desire in true love, its moralized, domesticated version, based on partnership, companionship, the fitness of mind and disposition.

The theatre, however, was not quite as optimistic about marriage as the moralists who prescribed it. In the 1590s alone, *Arden of Faversham, A Warning for Fair Women, Page of Plymouth* and *The History of Friar Francis* all showed women murdering their husbands for love of another man. In *A Woman Killed with Kindness* (1603) desire exceeds marriage in a curiously unmotivated way. Anne Frankford is not driven to adultery by her husband's indifference or her lover's charms. On the contrary, she simply does it, as if we could take for granted the improbability of lifelong monogamy. But the strangest case of all must surely be *Othello*, a year later, where the adultery is only imagined, but Othello's desire is so far in excess of the domestic institution designed to contain it that he strangles his wife in their wedding sheets. Like Edward II, like Troilus and Cressida, Othello, who loves not wisely but too well, submits to the absolute imperatives of desire and finds his apparently unitary self annihilated in the process.

Beginning in this period, eroticism was to find its proper and circumscribed place within marriage. Marriage was to be the remedy for absence. 'I did love the Moor, to live with him', Desdemona insists (*Othello* 1.3.248):[26] in this play war does not separate the lovers. Marriage makes desire legitimate,[27] brings it within the bounds of propriety and orthodoxy, on condition, of course, that it is suitably heterosexual, non-incestuous and duly based on consent. The Law of the Father, the order of meaning, backed by the law of the land, comes to differentiate increasingly systematically, increasingly solemnly, between love and lust, propriety and licence, natural and unnatural passion, and in each case the privileged term becomes incorporated into the meaning of marriage.

This newly valorized state now encompasses a private world of reciprocity and affection based on the household. The unmarried Desdemona is torn between desire and domesticity. Othello tells his entrancing adventure stories, and she longs to listen:

> this to hear
> Would Desdemona seriously incline;
> But still the house-affairs would draw her thence,
> And ever as she could with haste dispatch,
> She'ld come again . . .
>
> (*Othello* 1.3.145–9)

But marriage, by contrast, reconciles the two concerns: husband and wife are 'housed' together forever in love:

> But that I love the gentle Desdemona,
> I would not my unhoused free condition
> Put into circumscription and confine
> For the sea's worth.
>
> (*Othello* 1.2.25–8)

When the married Othello is called away from that private world by his public responsibility to the Senate, he must first 'spend a word here in the house' (1.2.48), in parting from his new wife. And when the journey to Cyprus temporarily parts them again, Othello legitimately makes time, however briefly, for his matrimonial obligations:

Come, Desdemona, I have but an hour
Of love, of worldly matters, and direction,
To spend with thee; we must obey the time.

(1.3.298–300)

Othello's list (love, worldly matters, direction) perfectly summarizes the
responsibilities of a husband as they are specified in the contemporary
domestic conduct books.

But since married lovers must obey the time, Othello sets out for Cyprus.
Now that public and private are so firmly distinguished, however, there is
apparently no conflict of commitments, identities, or subject positions. On
the contrary, Othello assures the Senate that he will keep them rigorously
separate:

And heaven defend your good souls that you think
I will your serious and great business scant,
For she is with me, . . . no, when light-wing'd toys,
And feather'd Cupid, foils with wanton dullness
My speculative and active instruments,
That my disports corrupt and taint my business,
Let housewives make a skillet of my helm.

(1.3.266–72)

Though this invocation of Mars unarmed, sporting with Venus (Colie 1974:
153) is commonly taken as an indication of Othello's individual contempt
for sexuality, or even his personal sexual anxiety,[28] the trivialization of
desire seems to me not very surprising in this transitional period, especially
in an address to the Senate. The speech does not repudiate 'disports', but
it aligns them with domesticity and distinguishes them from 'business'.

The syntax of the speech is not very surprising either: 'when I allow
myself to be distracted, let housewives use my helmet to cook in'. But the
rhetorical 'when', which momentarily permits us to glimpse the distraction
as a real possibility, anticipates Othello's later formulation of his passion:
'I do love thee, and when I love thee not,/Chaos is come again' (3.3.92–3).
The Arden editor, since he has seen it misunderstood, hastens to assure us
in a note on this declaration that the verbs are in the future tense. This
seems to me not quite right. ('When I shall not love you, chaos will
come again'?) Although the utterance is, of course, proleptic, it is so only
ironically: Othello is not making a declaration of intent. Here too 'when'
means 'if'. But because the word is 'when', once again the utterance permits
us to glimpse as reality what the speech rejects, and the present tenses allow
the appalling possibility, contained but not dispelled by the commonsense
reading, that the loving, the not loving and the chaos are simultaneous
conditions. Othello's utterance betrays the trace of antipathy which inhabits
desire itself. And at the same time it calls into question the system of

differences which distinguishes private and public, domestic and political, disport and business. Chaos is all-encompassing: it cannot be kept indoors.

In practice, the play deconstructs this system of differences from the beginning. Iago, Othello's colleague, sets out to destroy his marriage; the first wedding night of Othello and Desdemona, and then the second, are interrupted by military affairs; the island of Cyprus, threatened by the Turks, is also sacred to Venus; when Desdemona pleads for the professional reinstatement of Cassio, her action is on a par with entreating her husband to wear his gloves, eat well and keep warm (3.3.77–9). Marriage is not purely private: it is itself public and institutional, and it necessarily interacts, therefore, with the world of work and politics.

But the tragic irony of the play is the return of the trivialized desire to destroy 'the plumed troop, and the big wars' of Othello's formerly privileged 'occupation' (3.3.355–63). Othello becomes other than he is, explicitly the 'aftermath' of a soldier (Fineman 1990: 38), differentiating between the self he was and what he has become: 'That's he that was Othello; here I am' (5.2.285). Desire does not stay confined in its domestic place, does not obey the Law of meaning, nor indeed the law of the land. On the contrary, desire's own Law proves absolute: it turns murder to 'justice' and makes a 'cause' of jealousy (5.2.17). Othello-the-husband exceeds Othello-the-soldier, and if the soldier reasserts himself in Othello's final speech, it is only in order to destroy both these 'perplexed' and imbricated selves that the institution of marriage was to preserve in perfect independence of each other (5.2.340–57).

vi

An earlier generation of critics found Othello's final speech theatrical, self-dramatizing.[29] We are less inclined to believe this now, and more likely to attribute the theatricality in question to the Renaissance stage, the theatre of excess. But a tradition of humanist criticism has continued to find in the characters the causes of these tragedies of desire. Whether the central figures themselves or, more recently, the cultures they inhabit, are to blame, the real problems, we have been led to believe, are that Edward II is homosexual, Troilus naive, Cressida a whore, and Othello black and an outsider. Sexuality, the Enlightenment insists, is 'natural': if people have trouble with it, that is in one way or another a failure of adjustment. Where these differences between the protagonists are textually supported, they are clearly important, but there is a danger that by concentrating exclusively on the characters, we leave desire unproblematically in place. Might it be, in other words, that we have been unduly reluctant to attend to the problems that reside in the (excessive) desire which the Renaissance theatre so remorselessly dramatizes?

Since then, desire has become fully official. Its laws, its taxonomies, its norms and proprieties are now largely consensual. Love has been carefully distinguished from lust, the homoerotic from heterosexuality. We know what is mature and immature, or we imagine we do. True love still leads to marriage, which is now highly rated as a source of satisfaction: British cabinet ministers resign in order to spend more time with their families. And there are approved ways of holding marriages together: the Marriage Guidance Council would have sorted Othello out in no time. Meanwhile, however, the Law-lessness of desire returns to destabilize the institutions set up to bring it under control, and love unpredictably exceeds the norms designed to contain it. The divorce rate is high, and rising. Heterosexual monogamy is not to everyone's taste.

The theatre, too, has become official, along with cinema and television, and family values are conspicuously promoted by all three institutions. But this is so only in consequence of constant vigilance. Modern western culture fiercely polices propriety: it draws the line at what it calls (at any particular moment) pornography. Might it be that pornography is the price we pay precisely for drawing the line? Is it possible that the inculcation of norms is itself the force which drives desire's now unacknowledged excess to re-enter the circle of power as a direct challenge to both the Law of the Father and the law of the land?

Notes

1 Gaveston's death in 3.1 divides the play into two halves. It creates a new political order by altering what seemed an unalterable impasse (McCloskey 1985).
2 References to *Edward II* are to Bowers (1973).
3 Shakespeare, *Sonnets* 97, 98.
4 Ben Jonson, 'An Elegie. Since you must goe' (Jonson 1947: 199).
5 'Absens absenting causithe me to complain' (Wyatt 1969: 231–2)
6 'A Farewell' (Sidney 1962: 148); 'Sweetest love, I do not goe' (Donne 1965: 31).
7 'A Valediction Forbidding Mourning' (Donne 1965: 63).
8 'Absence, the noble truce', *Caelica* 45 (Greville 1938: 100).
9 For a similar fantasy of omnipotence see 'Would I were chaung'd into that golden showre' (Raleigh 1951: 81–2).
10 Cf 'Throes of love: The field of the metaphor' (Kristeva 1987: 267–79).
11 'Non bene conveniunt nec in una sede morantur/maiestas et amor', *Metamorphoses* II.846–7.
12 Two of Titian's paintings of Danaë seems to invoke this tradition. In the version in the Prado, Madrid the fabrics are rich and embroidered, the bedclothes rumpled, and an aged servant holds out her apron to catch the falling coins. The Vienna painting of the same subject shows some of the coins lying on Danaë's sheets, and this time the servant holds up a dish to catch them.
13 For the framework of the debate see Dollimore (1989: xx–xxii).
14 Ovid, *Metamorphoses* III.155–252.
15 In 1600, for example, the Privy Council declared that if the Queen was to be supplied with entertainment, there must be provision for the supply of good actors, '& consequentlie of the houses that must serve for publique playenge to keepe them in exercise' (Wickham 1972: 22).

16 I am indebted to John Astington and Leeds Barroll for information about court patronage and the Elizabethan theatre.
17 Progresses were revived in the 1590s, but Elizabeth no longer expected to have to pay for them (Streitberger 1986: xix).
18 For the case against easy assumptions about the relationship between the court and the stage see Barroll (1988).
19 See, for example, Lyly's *Love's Metamorphosis* and Shakespeare's *A Midsummer Night's Dream* or *Much Ado About Nothing*.
20 References to *Troilus and Cressida* are to Palmer (1982).
21 See Ferrand (1990: 42, 75–81); Ferrand (1640: 64); Wack (1990: 39).
22 In a challenging Lacanian analysis of the play's account of (masculine) desire as always idealizing, always independent of the object, Carol Cook goes on to suggest that Cressida has to be false, as Desdemona has to be killed, in order to preserve intact desire's illusory ('unbodied') ideal object (Cook 1986).
23 This is not as sexually differential as it sounds: women were widely held to ejaculate 'seed' (Laqueur 1990: 35–52).
24 Modern French retains the parallel between orgasm and death in 'la petite mort'.
25 Most commentators settle for the first of these meanings, but Linda Charnes sees the unkind self as proleptic and 'will leave' as a future tense rather than a wish (Charnes 1989: 421).
26 References to *Othello* are to Ridley (1962).
27 Greenblatt takes the opposite position, and finds instances of a continuity between the Church Fathers' celebration of (monastic) celibacy and the Reformers' fear of sexual immoderation in marriage. In my view these are not quite the same, and there is, as Greenblatt acknowledges, among the Puritan writings a new legitimation of married sexual pleasure (Greenblatt 1980: 242–52). For a discussion of the shift of emphasis see Rose (1988).
28 See for example Colie (1974: 153); Greenblatt (1980: 250); Barthelemy (1987: 152–3); Rose (1988: 133–4); Calderwood (1989: 71 ff.). The attribution of anxiety here is surely anachronistic, an effect of the post-Victorian preoccupation with sexual health, which has only recently begun to seem coercive.
29 See for example Leavis (1952: 152); Rossiter (1961: 200–1).

References

Barroll, J. Leeds (1988) 'A new history for Shakespeare and his time', *Shakespeare Quarterly* 39: 441–64.

——, Leggatt, A., Hosley, R. and Kernan, A. (eds) (1975) *The Revels History of Drama in English, Volume III, 1576–1613*, London: Methuen.

Barthelemy, Anthony Gerard (1987) *Black Face Maligned Race: The Representation of Blacks in English Drama from Shakespeare to Southerne*, Baton Rouge: Louisiana State University Press.

Barthes, Roland (1979) *A Lover's Discourse: Fragments*, trans. Richard Howard, London: Cape.

Bataille, Georges (1985) 'The notion of expenditure', *Visions of Excess: Selected Writings, 1927–39*, trans. Allan Stoekl, Minneapolis: University of Minnesota Press, 116–29.

Bowers, Fredson (ed.) (1973) *The Complete Works of Christopher Marlowe*, 2 vols, Cambridge: Cambridge University Press, vol. 2.

Calderwood, James L. (1989) *The Properties of 'Othello'*, Amherst: University of Massachusetts Press.

Carew, Thomas (1949) *Poems*, ed. Rhodes Dunlap, Oxford: Clarendon Press.

Chambers, E. K. (1923) *The Elizabethan Stage*, 4 vols, Oxford: Clarendon Press, vol. 4.

Charnes, Linda (1989) ' "So unsecret to ourselves": Notorious identity and the material subject in Shakespeare's *Troilus and Cressida*', *Shakespeare Quarterly* 40: 413–40.

Colie, Rosalie L. (1974) *Shakespeare's Living Art*, Princeton, NJ: Princeton University Press.

Cook, Carol (1986) 'Unbodied figures of desire', *Theatre Journal* 38: 34–52.

Dollimore, Jonathan (1989) *Radical Tragedy: Religion, Ideology and Power in the Drama of Shakespeare and his Contemporaries*, Hemel Hempstead: Harvester-Wheatsheaf.

Donne, John (1965) *The Elegies* and *The Songs and Sonnets*, ed. Helen Gardner, Oxford: Clarendon Press.

Ferrand, Jacques (1640) *Erotomania*, trans. Edmund Chilmead, Oxford.

—— (1990) *A Treatise on Lovesickness* (Paris, 1623), ed. and trans. Donald Beecher and Massimo Ciavolella, Syracuse, NY: Syracuse University Press.

Fineman, Joel (1990) 'The sound of O in *Othello*: The real tragedy of desire', in Richard Feldstein and Henry Sussman (eds) *Psychoanalysis and . . .* , New York: Routledge, 33–46.

Freund, Elizabeth (1985) ' "Ariachne's broken woof": The rhetoric of citation in *Troilus and Cressida*', in Patricia Parker and Geoffrey Hartman (eds) *Shakespeare and the Question of Theory*, New York: Methuen, 19–36.

Greenblatt, Stephen (1980) *Renaissance Self-Fashioning from More to Shakespeare*, Chicago: University of Chicago Press.

Greville, Fulke (1938) *Poems and Dramas*, ed. Geoffrey Bullough, 2 vols, Edinburgh: Oliver & Boyd, vol. 1.

Jonson, Ben (1947) *Ben Jonson: The Poems, The Prose Works*, ed. C. H. Herford, Percy and Evelyn Simpson, Oxford: Clarendon Press.

Kimbrough, Robert (1964) *Shakespeare's 'Troilus and Cressida' and its Setting*, Cambridge, Mass.: Harvard University Press.

Kristeva, Julia (1987) *Tales of Love*, trans. Leon S. Roudiez, New York: Columbia University Press.

Lacan, Jacques (1977) *Ecrits*, trans. Alan Sheridan, London: Tavistock.

Laqueur, Thomas (1990) *Making Sex: Body and Gender from the Greeks to Freud*, Cambridge, Mass.: Harvard University Press.

Leavis, F. R. (1952) *The Common Pursuit*, London: Chatto & Windus.

McCloskey, Susan (1985) 'The worlds of *Edward II*', *Renaissance Drama* n.s. 16: 35–48.

Marotti, Arthur (1982) ' "Love is not love": Elizabethan sonnet sequences and the social order', *ELH* 49: 396–428.

Mullaney, Steven (1988) *The Place of the Stage*, Chicago: University of Chicago Press.

Palmer, Kenneth (ed.) (1982) *Troilus and Cressida* (The Arden Shakespeare) London: Methuen.

Raleigh, Walter (1951) *The Poems*, ed. Agnes Latham, London: Routledge & Kegan Paul.

Ridley, M. R. (ed.) (1962) *Othello* (The Arden Shakespeare) London: Methuen.

Rollins, Hyder E. (ed.) (1931) *A Poetical Rhapsody 1602–21*, 2 vols, Cambridge, Mass.: Harvard University Press, vol 1.

Rose, Mary Beth (1988) *The Expense of Spirit: Love and Sexuality in English Renaissance Drama*, Ithaca: Cornell University Press.

Rossiter, A. P. (1961) *Angel With Horns*, London: Longman.

Sidney, Philip (1962) *The Poems*, ed. William A. Ringler, Oxford: Clarendon Press.

Streitberger, W. R. (1986) *Jacobean and Caroline Revels Accounts, 1603–42*, Oxford: Malone Society Collections.

Wack, Mary Frances (1990) *Lovesickness in the Middle Ages: The 'Viaticum' and its Commentaries*, Philadelphia: University of Pennsylvania Press.

Westfall, Suzanne R. (1990) *Patrons and Performance: Early Tudor Household Revels*, Oxford: Clarendon Press.

Wickham, Glynne (1972) *Early English Stages, 1300–1660*, London: Routledge & Kegan Paul, vol. 2 (ii).

Wyatt, Thomas (1969) *Collected Poems*, ed. Kenneth Muir and Patricia Thomson, Liverpool: Liverpool University Press.

Chapter 7

'Lawless desires well tempered'

Kathleen McLuskie

i

Teaching a course on Renaissance Poetry in 1976, I encountered for the first time the contradictions of feminist politics in Renaissance criticism. The class was discussing Marvell's 'To his Coy Mistress' and a young woman protested 'that's a really heavy trip he's laying on her'. I was nonplussed, completely unable to track through the connections between the politics of sexual harassment and the aesthetic pleasures of the *carpe diem* convention in Renaissance love poetry. Fifteen years and a whole critical movement later, I am still concerned with the question of how to relate the witty play with sexuality, the locus of pleasure and desire, which informs the literary treatment of sexuality, to what we know of the sexual politics of early modern England.

The contrast between these two realms of knowledge, loosely defined as 'literature' and 'history', is not just a matter of conflicting data. Rather it is a matter of different ways of conceptualizing sexuality so as to deal with contrasting sources of evidence and to locate them in the social experience of early modern culture (Dollimore and Sinfield 1990: 91–100).[1] However, in contrasting the discourses of pleasure and social regulation we ourselves accept a discursive distinction defined by Foucault (1976) as the contrast between an *ars erotica* and a *scientia sexualis*. The literary critic deals with the *ars erotica* of the pleasures of the text while the social historian investigates the *scientia sexualis* of sexual relations in the social world, themselves seen as epiphenomena of larger social and economic movements.

The unsatisfactory character of those distinctions has been emphasized by Rosalind Coward who enquired, 'Why is the study of sexuality when it appears in the social sciences frequently subsumed under studies of institutionalised social forms of regulation, like marriage?' (1983: 4). In the case of early modern church court material widely used by historians of sexual behaviour, this institutionalization seems inevitable. One of the functions of the church courts was the regulation of sexuality in marriage, and their terms of reference imposed the terms of reference on the depositions they heard. Martin Ingram has therefore concluded:

> the single most important reason why unmarried women were prepared to commit fornication was with marriage in mind. Both in the 1580s and in the late 1610s between 30 and 40% in the better recorded cases before the bishop's court at Salisbury claimed some kind of promise of expectation of marriage; and the proportion rises even higher if cases involving married men are excluded. . . . But the willingness of some of them to appear in court and submit to penance suggests that they were not total nonconformists. . . . The overall figures, considered in relation to the total population of these parishes are consistent with the assumption that sexual immorality was by no means rampant in this period.
>
> (1987: 269)

These complex and fascinating constructions of the terms in which sexual behaviour was described present early modern sexual activity firmly embedded in the structures of rural social existence. They have been modified by feminist historians who have drawn attention to the differential treatment afforded to women and men,[2] but for the most part we are offered an image of early modern sexual experience in which the behaviour of both women and men was dominated by financial considerations and was part of a complex economy of honour and shame which regulated early modern social existence.

However the very evidence which is used for this analysis could be seen in terms of what Foucault has called The Incitement to Discourse: the sense that sex is spoken about and the terms of that speaking have an important influence on the social construction of sexual identity. The high proportion of poor women and servants presented for bearing a bastard, together with the frequent instances of rape or attempted rape, suggest a model of sexuality in which men were opportunist and predatory, while women were constantly concerned to regulate sexuality within sociability. Moreover, the imagery of the church court depositions, their references to 'carnal knowledge' or 'making use of a woman's body' institutionalize sexual identities based on male exploitation of women, an organization of desire which is predominantly heterosexual, with a firm gender division between active men and passive women whose bodies are to be known or possessed by them, shaping narratives of desire in which men impose sexual actions on women.

In different contexts, similar narratives of desire were used to contest the social norms enforced by institutions of control. Ingram (1985) cites fascinating evidence of popular modes of erotic production in satiric rhymes and mockery both of sexual behaviour and attempts to control it.[3] Ingram reads this mockery as part of the shaming rituals which enforced community norms but he extends his analysis to a consideration of what they reveal about the sexuality of those who produced and consumed them: 'mocking rhymes and the like involved a prurient or even pornographic element which suggests that they sometimes served as a proxy form of sexual indulgence rather than a clear-cut condemnation of it' (1985: 165). Moreover he suggests that the activities of the church courts themselves may have been a manifestation of unexamined and unarticulated sexual characteristics, presenting the 'endemic gossip about sexual reputation, which served both as an informal means of social control and an outlet for the prurience and spite of the bored and sexually repressed' (1987: 305). The church courts as social institutions could not have functioned without the willingness of members of the rural community to spy and investigate and follow those thought to be involved in illicit sex. Again and again, the depositions quoted present people in the act of seeing, creating and repeating the formulae by which sex was sought out and represented to the judging community, listing the signs of sexual activities, sexualizing certain parts of the body and cataloguing the sounds and images of sex.[4]

All of this evidence about early modern sexual behaviour can be read in a variety of ways. On the one hand it can be used to ask historical questions about the processes of social change, the patterns of bastardy, the connections between economic factors and attempts at social control, the changing social relations between men and women and the connections between the ideological and material determinants of sexual behaviour. However, our understanding of the Incitement to Discourse and the importance of speaking about sex can complicate those questions. With his characteristic ability to entangle the terms of his enquiry, Foucault has asked 'whether, since the nineteenth century, the *scientia sexualis* . . . has not functioned, at least to a certain extent as an *ars erotica*' (1976: 70–1). Evidence about the discourses of sex suggests that in the early modern period, too, the *scientia sexualis* of social control embodied an *ars erotica* of proxy sexual experience.

This entangling of the terms, the suggested connection between the processes of social control and sexual pleasure provides an important link between literary and historical evidence. It allows the possibility of connecting actual sexual behaviour and the pleasure of both sex and text, acknowledging the continuity of the social world shared by the producers of literary *ars erotica* and the fragments of evidence which inform the *scientia sexualis* of historical accounts of early modern sexual behaviour.

ii

The narratives of desire which shape accounts of sexual behaviour in popular culture were formed by the questioning assumptions of the church courts or, like the mocking rhymes Ingram discusses, were casual, amateur productions. Similar accounts of sexual behaviour found a commercial outlet in the many exemplary narratives about sexual transgressions which became part of early modern pamphlet literature. The antics of women who in real life might have been presented before the church courts were the subject of jest books and merry tales[5] with which literate people were entertained. The commercial conditions of their production place these texts at one remove from the social interaction of popular culture, making it difficult to read them simply as endorsing or contesting social norms. Rather these texts created the forms in which sex could be experienced and discussed away from direct engagement with its immediate social consequences.

Narratives of misdemeanour and repentance, for example, provided a way of writing sex and negotiating the complex relations between sex as social behaviour and as the locus of pleasure and desire. Robert Greene's *The Conversion of an English Courtesan* consists of a series of set pieces which draw on a repertory of stories both exemplary and bawdy. It shapes its narrative so as to endorse the official disapproval of women's free sexual activity, charting her decline from a wanton uncontrolled youth, followed by loose behaviour in freely consorting with men, to her ultimate fall into prostitution and rescue by a virtuous country gentleman. This narrative leaves open the question of her motives, of how she is able to resist the moral pressures of her rural community, and the process by which she comes into contact with her virtuous rescuer: the pleasures of the text offer the more entertaining possibility of a creative tension between the explicitly stated moral position and the pleasure of exposition.

Early in the story, the young woman's uncle addresses her with a 'watch-word to wanton maidens', a set piece statement of conventional morality. He then offers to rescue her from sin through marriage to a substantial farmer of forty. This solution, often indeed involved in bastard bearers' defences, is completely unsuitable as a narrative resolution: it would abort the story and close off both the possibility of variety and the pleasures of closure which the courtesan's conversion would bring about.

This tension between moral and artistic requirements permits a much more wide-ranging account of the young woman's sexuality, focusing less on a single illegal act of fornication and more on the varying social signs of sin.[6] Her potential for sin, for example, lies in her indulgence not of lust but of luxury consumption:

> pride creeping on, I began to prank myself with the proudest, and to hold it in disdain that any in the parish should exceed me in bravery. As my apparell was costly, so I grew to be licentious, and to delight to be looked on, so that I haunted and frequented all feasts and weddings, and other places of merry meetings, where, as I was gazed on of many, so I spared no glances to surview all with a curious eye favour.
>
> (Greene 1913: 229)

The freedom to look and to wear costly clothes inexorably becomes the freedom to dispose of her body. She betrays the first young man for a

sequence of friends and is once again instructed by a set piece which establishes the connection between promiscuity and prostitution (ibid.: 233).

The story of her decline into common whoredom follows after she has
been abandoned by the system of exchange among friends and forced to
shift for herself in a whore house. The evil of her sexuality is associated with
commodification. She is no longer fulfilling her own desires, 'clamorous for
my lust', but

> I gave myself to entertain all companions, sitting or standing in the door
> like a stale, to allure or draw in wanton passengers, refusing none that
> would with his purse purchase me to be his ... now I began not to
> respect good personage, good qualities, to the gracious favour of man,
> when eye had no respect of person, for the oldest lecher was as welcome
> as the youngest lover, so he brought meat in his mouth.
>
> (ibid.: 242)

The complicated interaction of pleasure, social exchange and commerce
is only resolved in this text by invoking the higher authority of God as the
ultimate judge of sin and salvation. However the text also reveals the
competing forms in which the questions of pleasure and sex and their
regulation could be narrated in the contrasting styles of the 'watchword to
wanton maidens', the joky story of the man who paid his wife for sex, the
authenticating detail of the brothel scenes and the enacted allegory of the
virtuous young man looking in vain for a dark place in which his sin would
not be seen.

The tension between moral, aesthetic and commercial considerations evident in this narrative was also evident in the social relationships generated
by the production and consumption of these texts. Their authors objectified
the social pressures of sexual behaviour and turned them into narrative. In
doing so they addressed their audience as free individuals whose status as
consumers rendered them judges, free from the regulating bodies' concern.
The audience was invited to distance themselves both from the world of
rural poor women, the perpetrators and victims of sexual immorality, and
from the values of the middling sort (the dreary author of the 'watchword
for wanton maidens') who were responsible for their regulation. By equat-
ing sex and prostitution they separated the male consumers of sex and text
from the women who were both their subject and their object.

This distance is most clearly established in the opening lines of Nashe's
'Choice of Valentines' (1972),[7] which invokes a past, idealized world of free
sexuality in which

> young men in their jolly roguery
> Rose early in the morn 'fore break of day
> To seek them valentines so trim and gay.
>
> (1972: 458)

The narrator, however, cannot find his mistress, for

> Good Justice Dudgeon-haft and Crabtree-Face
> With bills and staves had scar'd her from the place;
> And now she was compell'd for sanctuary
> To fly unto an house of venery.

(ibid.: 459)

For the sophisticated urban writer, the world of the countryside is both the idealized, simple arena of true love and the locus of control effected by the puritanical justices of the church courts.

Once the narrator finds his true love in the brothel, the poem shifts to a graphic account of his sexual encounter with her. The details of its description of sex and its self-conscious literary wit represent sexuality, uncontrolled by social concerns, as a matter of mutual and sophisticated indulgence. This style does not, of course, posit an alternative *social* reality. Its frame of reference is emphatically literary. The opening stanzas evoke the world of medieval romance, the idealized country pleasures of former times. When the action moves to the brothel, the personifications of the body parts, the invocations to Cupid, Danaë and Priapus place the action in the traditions of classical erotica, the style of 'Ovid's wanton Muse' (ibid.: 468). It offers the fantasized illusion of a free space of erotic pleasure, an escape from the repressive social relations of official ideology.

However, this escape is only achieved by moving to a different social arena, that of the commercial relations of whore and client. The poem acknowledges this shift if only to make it the subject of literary play. The lover urges his whore to

> Hold wide thy lap, my lovely Danae
> And entertain the golden shower so free

and the familiar metaphor works both to glamorize the physical activity and to echo the commercial. The same effect is achieved when he laments his failure to satisfy her:

> I want those herbs and roots of Indian soil,
> That strengthen weary members in their toil.
>   . . .
> Drugs and electuaries of new device
> Do shun my purse that trembles at their price.

(ibid.: 467)

This rejection of commercially available support for an ailing sexual performance suggests a contradiction between notions of natural and spontaneous sexual power and the evidently commercial context in which it must find fulfilment. The whore's private and autonomous sexual satisfaction, though wittily enough treated, is seen as robbing the man of his sexual power. She in fact prefers to fulfil her desire by mechanical means since it

> will refresh me wel
> And never make my tender belly swell. (ibid.: 466)

For her the social considerations of avoiding bastardy still exist but for the young man sex is equated with pleasure, which masks the commercial relations through which it finds fulfilment.

This fantasy of a free space of erotic pleasure was a mark of much of the sophisticated writing on sexuality at the turn of the seventeenth century. Raymond Waddington (1990: 40–69) has written about the way that even the tropes of platonic love theory were turned into bawdy jokes,[8] and quotes Donne's letter to Sir Henry Wotton in which he celebrates both the high cultural philosophy of love and the physical pleasures which it allows: 'You (I think) and I am much of one sect in the philosophy of love; which though it be directed upon the mind, doth inhere in the body, and find pretty entertainment there' (65).

The writers who could fantasize a sexuality free from social constraints were part of a special group in early modern London, constructed as much by the discourses of their writing as by their actual social existence. In his study of the wits of the Inns of Court, Finklepearl (1969) characterizes their poetry as displaying 'a sense of belonging to an elite of wits in a world of gulls; a tradition of free and candid speech; upper class condescension to the taste of the professional writers' (73). Love, or at least sexual passion, seems to have been an essential element of Inns of Court culture. As George Turberville (1587: 70) explains:

> being there although my minde were free:
> yet must I seeme love wounded eke to be.

But this practice of love when it was turned into poetry produced for a commercial market involved a finely tuned negotiation among the discourses of pleasure and of commerce. Marston, for example, presents the philosophy behind the witty play of his satires as part of a private exchange between connoisseurs. However even this private world is intruded on by commercial considerations when, through publication, the poems are misinterpreted by the general populace. In *The Scourge of Villainie*, he demands:

> Is not he frantique, foolish, bedlam mad,
> That wastes his spright, that melts his very braine,
> In deepe designes, in wits darke gloomie straine?
> . . .
> To be perus'd by all the dung-scum rable
> Of thin-braind Ideots, dull, uncapable?

For mimicke apish schollars, pedants, gulls,
Perfum'd Inamoratoes, brothel trulls?[9]

(Marston 1961: Satire X: 10–18)

In Marston's satirized world, the sexual behaviour that is disapproved of is the commodified activity which wastes inheritance (see Satire III) and which is debased by being indulged in by anyone who has the money. It becomes the image of all commodity and the only commodity worth the transaction:

But now I see, he findes by his accounts
That sole Priapus by plaine dealing mounts.
How now? what droupes the new Pegasian Inne?
I feare mine host is honest. Tut, beginne
To set up whore-house. Nere too late to thriue.

(ibid.: Satire V: 88–92)

This attack on sexual indulgence and libertinage as commodified and commercialized offers a critique of sexual behaviour which is quite distinct from the representation of sexuality in the discourses of the church courts or the popular culture of jest books and merry tales. In Marston's satires sex stands in for and acts as the emblem of other social ills. He is less concerned with its immediate social and economic consequences in bastardy and the crisis of order than with the way in which it can represent all the newfangled luxuries 'that soile our soules and dampe our reasons light' (ibid., Satire VII, 183).

However the philosophical concerns which Marston makes explicit cannot fully account for the pleasure of these texts and the ways they embody social and sexual ideology for the young men who produced and consumed them. Nashe distinguished his witty, free indulgence of sexuality as appropriate for his audience who were free from the rural courts, and in Marston's denunciation of commercialized sex we see the process of constructing a different sense of an elite audience defined in terms of literary and sexual connoisseurship which can be entered through shared taste as much as through class and education. This elite identity is constructed negatively, rejecting the indulgence in and consumption of sex which turns heterosexuality into whoredom and erotica into pornography. Any attempt to define the particular characteristics of the sexuality which lies behind this construction, to understand the pleasures and anxiety through which this identity is positively constructed, requires a different and, as it were, more penetrating method.

For this construction of literary pleasure focuses almost entirely on the men who are constructed as its readers. An interesting angle on that pleasure is provided by Laura Mulvey in the introduction to *Visual and Other Pleasures* (1989). She suggests that Freud's theory of fetishism provides the vital clue to understanding the representation of sex: 'The fetishist becomes fixated on an object in order to avoid knowledge, he has to abandon the desire to know the true nature of sexual difference in order to avoid castration anxiety' (ix). In Marston's 'Metamorphosis of Pygmalion's Image' there is a striking moment which seems to endorse this Freudian reading. When Pigmalion looks over his creation, he works his way down her body, stopping at

Loues pauillion
Where Cupid doth enjoy his onely crowne
Where Venus hath her chiefest mantion:
There would he winke, & winking looke againe,
Both eies and thoughts would gladly there remaine.

(Marston 1961: stanza 9)

But the poem goes no further with the description of the woman's sex. It moves instead into a satiric simile of the Citty-dame

In sacred church, when her pure thoughts shold pray
Pierce through her fingers, so to hide her shame,
When that her eye, her minde would faine bewray.

(stanza 10)

This mockery of a city woman's debauchery is offered as a generalized displacement of the knowledge of women's sexuality. The effect partly increases the suspense and thwarts the expectation of detailed description but it also offers misogynistic and class-specific generalization as an alternative to the troubling vision of a woman's genitals.

When Pygmalion proceeds to make love to his statue, the language offers an image of matching perfection between Pygmalion's and his lover's body which glosses over the defining sexual difference:

His eyes, her eyes, kindly encountered,
His breast, her breast, oft ioyned close unto
His arms embracements oft she suffered,
Hands, armes, eyes, tongue, lips, and all parts did woe.
His thigh, with hers, his knee played with her knee,
A happy consort when all parts agree.

(stanza 17)

When the statue finally comes to life, the poet refuses to offer 'The amorous discription of that action', acknowledging that the power of erotic poetry lies in its fulfilment of fantasy:

Let him conceit but what himself would doe
When that he had obtayned such a favour.

(stanza 34)

Elsewhere, in the Satires, the displacement of sexual knowledge is less obvious but their representation of women, whether the idealized mistress or the 'brothel trull' is overdetermined. Women act as the signs of sexual activity, objects of sexual fantasy but more often than not they are accompanied, like the whore of 'The Choice of Valentines', by an explicit penis substitute: 'her instrument/Smooth fram'd at Vitrio' (Satire III) or 'in ioulting Coach with glassie instrument'. Saturio in Satire VIII who 'wish'd himself his Mistress buske', the other who 'Her silver-handled fanne would gladly be', or Publius who wished to get his mistress's 'itch-allaying pin' only serve to make the point.

It is less the case that Marston is satirizing fetishism than that the whole activity of misogynist satire and erotic poetry are themselves fetishistic. Marston is sarcastic about the dolt who after one kiss might 'three-score sonnets write / Upon a pictures kisse' (Satire VIII), but his own obsession with anatomizing sex, only in order to displace it in satire embodies the fetishism at the centre of his representation of sexuality. As Mulvey explains: 'Women may seem to be the subjects of an endless parade of pornographic fantasies, jokes, day dreams and so on, but fundamentally most male fantasy is a closed-loop dialogue with itself' (1989: 11).

Understanding this psychoanalytic dimension of the representation of sexuality helps to locate the discourses of sex. It explains how representation of sexuality readily slides into a concern over commodification or satire of immoral behaviour which serves to allay anxiety about knowledge of sex itself. These anxieties seem to inform the erotic politics of early modern culture and go some way to explaining the pleasures of these sexual discourses. The psychoanalytic reading offers an analysis of these texts which goes beyond the extent to which they reinforce dominant moral ideology and makes possible a treatment of their poetic dimension, their choice of imagery and their recurring motifs.[10]

iii

In the preceding pages I have attempted a sketch of the overlapping discourses which mediate between sexual behaviour and sexual representation and inform the ideology of sexuality in early modern culture. I have suggested that within the moral constraints of the dominant ideology of sex, texts dealing with sexual activity also point to a construction of male sexual identity which places itself within metropolitan culture by negotiating the relationship between commoditized sexual relations and the literary fantasy of a free space of erotic pleasure. The principal relationship of this male sexuality to women is misogynistic but the terms and imagery in which this misogyny is represented reveal a fetishism which allays the threat presented by the absence at the centre of women's sexual being.

In the remainder of the paper, I want to suggest that these discourses of pleasure and commerce are similarly negotiated in early modern drama and understanding their interaction might serve to complicate our readings of its erotic politics. The contrasts I have suggested between the low culture of the church courts and the traditions of bawdy jesting, and the high culture of intellectualized and fetishistic eroticism were also acted out in plays which centred on sexual narratives in the changing theatrical environment of the turn of the century. For the theatre acted as a vital link between high and low culture. It was connected to low culture in that it took place in public and was subject to official scrutiny, but the dramatists who wrote for it worked within the literary traditions of high culture. Indeed, at the turn of the century, the cultural situation of the theatre was argued over in terms of a contest between commercial culture and the culture of patronage (McLuskie 1991).

Part of that contest over the proper location of theatre involved a search for dramatic materials which would appeal to a new and extended audience and was conceptualized in terms of a contest between elite and popular culture. The domestic tragedies of the 1590s, for example, made an explicit bid for a popular audience in the production of a domesticated drama which rejected the high cultural traditions of Senecan revenge. *A Warning for Fair Women*, produced in 1599 by the Chamberlain's Men, addressed itself to the problems of clichéd theatrical conventions by offering truthful reportage as an explicit alternative to the tragedy of revenge. In the Induction, the figure of Comedy dismissed the conventions of revenge tragedy, set at court:

> How some damn'd tyrant to obtain a crown
> Stabs, hangs, impoisons, smothers, cutteth throats:
> And then a Chorus, too, comes howling in
> And tells us of the worrying of a cat:
> Then, too, a filthy whining ghost,
> Lapt in some foul sheet, or a leather pilch,
> Comes screaming like a pig half stick'd.
> And cries, Vindicta! – Revenge, Revenge!
>
> (Cannon 1975: 43–50)

This was no abstract discussion of artistic theory but a contest over theatrical styles. Tragedy defended the appeal of his art for audiences, insisting on an alternative to the conventions of revenge in the tears which the true events of the story brought forth. The play replaced the conventions of revenge with a true story of sexual misdemeanour in which George Browne murdered George Saunders in order to gain the love of his wife Anne. Sexual relations between ordinary people were presented as a spectacle, but both the play and the pamphlet source of the story addressed the problem of how this spectacle was to be viewed. The pamphlet fell back on the familiar image of the *theatrum mundi*, comparing the scaffold on which the lovers were executed to a theatre in which God is the director of productions:

> when God bringeth such matters upon the stage, unto ye open face of the world, it is not to the intent that men should gaze and wonder at the persons, as byrdes do at an Owle. . . . His purpose is that the execution of his judgements, should by the terrour of the outward sight of the example, drive us to the inward consideration of ourselves . . . that we myght both detest wickednesse with perfect hatred and rue the persons with christen modestie.
>
> (Golding 1878: 233–4)

God's intentions, however, were less easily effected by a dramatist who had to acknowledge that part of his audience's pleasure involved 'that they should delight themselves & others with the fond and peradventure sinister reporting' of the story. The balance between the spectacle of pleasure and its moral meaning was difficult to achieve in the theatre, and the writer fudged the issue completely, interspersing the narrative with a series of allegorical dumb-shows of Lust and Chastity. This old-fashioned and static mode of representation was an attempt to solve the problem of dramatizing Anne's sexuality in purely moral terms. Even outside the dumb-shows, the representation of sexuality was locked into existing poetic and moral conventions, constructed literally from a male point of view as Browne views Anne, sitting in the doorway of her husband's house or playing with her child, her significance for the action subsumed in the poetic imagery of Browne's speeches.[11]

This physical organization of the stage, which presented women as the visual emblem of sexual action, elaborated in the 'word' of a male onlooker's speech, is repeated in numerous other plays. In Heywood's treatment of *Edward IV*, 'his loue to faire Mistresse Shore', the setting of the seduction scene presents Mistress Shore '*with her worke in her hand*' and while she '*sits sowing in her shop. Enter the King disguised*'. His soliloquy both explains his disguise and expresses his wonder at Jane's beauty:

> Oh rare perfection of rich Nature's work!
> Bright twinkling spark of precious diamond,
> Of greater value than all India . . .
> Her radiant eyes, dejected to the ground,
> Would turn each pebble to a diamond.
>
> (1964: 64)[12]

The commonplace images of women's beauty as a jewel[13] can here be extended into the dialogue with the familiar but none the less powerful irony of bargaining over a jewel in a shop when the true jewel of chastity is part of the market. The intersection of moral and commercial considerations is evident when Jane Shore, troubled by the loss of her honour,

discusses her plight with Mistress Blague who presents a clear account of
the profit and loss involved, weighing the loss of her honour with the
protection of being 'folded in a prince's arms'. The argument does not
touch on the feelings, nor, far less, the potential pleasures involved.

The distinct discourses of sexuality for people of different ranks is evident
and is played upon in the following scene where Edward comes to woo
Jane once again. She reminds him of his responsibilities as a king:

> The sunne that should all other vapours dry,
> And guide the world with his most glorious light
> Is muffled up himself in wilful night.
>
> (75)

Edward responds with the language of love poetry:

> The want of thee, Fair Cinthia, is the cause.
> Spread thou thy silver brightness in the aire
> And straight the gladsome morning will appeare.
>
> (76)

The high cultural language of love poetry is presented both as a seduction
technique and as a mask for his true sexual intentions which are soon made
explicit:

> But leaving this our enigmatick talke,
> Thou must sweete Jane, repaire unto the Court.
>
> (76)

Jane's final seduction is indicated unequivocally in the unmistakeable sign
of sexual wrongdoing when her husband's boy reports:

> Master, my mistresse, by a nobleman,
> Is sent for to the King, in a close coach.
>
> (78)

This use of familiar signifiers of sexuality makes the action perfectly clear,
but by displacing the explicit discussion of sexual pleasure and desire, it
allows the tension between the moral and the emotional response to the
action to be left unresolved.

Like the young woman cited in the church court cases, Jane is repentant
and constantly chides herself for her immoral conduct. As such she can act
as the emotional centre of the action, producing scenes in which the morality
of adultery is transformed into the dramatic materials of pathos and suspense. Once again, the point of view is male: in the scenes where she
compensates for her adultery by dispensing charity and patronage, her
husband looks on and his soliloquy contrasts her new role as influential
courtesan with her former life as a chaste city wife. The woman character

can thus become a theatrical symbol seen by both man and audience, the object of his desire and of their narrative attention.

In the play's finale, Jane's sexuality is subsumed within her emotional appeal as she becomes the central dramatic focus for King Richard's tyranny. In Heywood's characteristically economical combination of physical and verbal effects, the final stage picture sums up the story of Jane's adultery. She is wearing a penitent's white sheet and the presence on stage of the dead body of 'yong Aire', one of her former clients, reminds the audience of her repentant good works and charity. Her final suffering is evoked in her affecting farewell to her forgiving husband:

> O dying marriage! oh, sweet married death
> Thou grave which only shouldst part faithful friends
> Bringst us togither, and dost joine our hands.
> O living death! even in this dying life,
> Yet ere I go, once Matthew kiss thy wife.
> *He kisseth her, and she dies.*

(183)

This play, like *A Warning for Fair Women*, illustrates the dramatic raw materials which the narrative of sexual misdemeanour centred on a woman character provided for the popular drama. A woman character extended the action into the arena of men's sexual honour but also provided the drama with a direct emotional dimension with which to engage the audience, a sense that the drama could engage with their day-to-day existence. It transformed tragedy into melodrama and displaced the politics of tyranny into a sexual action involving the lives of people like themselves. The narrative of sexuality effaces the distinction between royal honour and the honour of citizens since both can be located in domestic relations.

In their representation of sexuality, these domestic melodramas occupy a similar discursive arena to the depositions of the church courts in which the sexual act is never seen but is displaced into a series of signs. On the stage these signs were both the verbal and physical signifiers of jewels and clothes, displacing the knowledge of sex into the signs of honour and status. The figures of women (played on stage by boys) were both the signs of sexuality, observed and constructed as such by men, and exemplars of the consequences of deviant behaviour. In the church courts these signs had social consequences in shame and punishment, but on the stage the sexual narratives existed only in order to elicit emotional responses which subsumed morality within pathos and suspense.

There remained, however, a theatrical tension between women's exemplary function in a moral schema and their roles as dynamic characters in a mimetic narrative, the focus of sympathetic identification. In Dekker and Middleton's two-part play, *The Honest Whore*, written for the Prince's Men and performed at the popular Red Bull Theatre, the central character is a repentant whore, and the action turns uneasily round the possibilities of sympathy for such a figure. She is variously represented with a sophisticated acceptance of the alternative values of commodified sex (see 1955, part 1: 2.1) and denounced with the misogynist rhetoric of the *memento mori* (see 2.1.290–423). These oppositions cannot be resolved in action and the play is concluded by bringing all the characters together at Bridewell where the dramatists attempt to displace the sophistry of literary representations of sexuality by dramatic truth. However they can only do so by returning to the simplest form of dramaturgy in which the physical action on stage is glossed by an authoritative figure who is not implicated in the complexities of dramatic action. The stage becomes the simple scaffold invoked in Golding's account of the theatre as the emblem of God's judgement.

Each whore enters, flanked by the Masters of Bridewell carrying the emblems of their oppression: 'th'one with a wheele, the other with a blue Gowne . . . one with a blue Gowne, another with Chalke and a Mallet . . . &c' (5.2.265, 313, SDs). However, even in this simple dramatic form, representation complicates the very process of judgement. The women are presented as objects of revulsion but they also arouse intense interest for their dress is not simply emblematic and their speeches complicate simple judgment. Penelope Whore-hound, for example, is a whore dressed as a citizen and she complains,

> if I goe amongst Cittizens wiues they ieere at me: if I goe among the Loose bodied Gownes, they cry a pox on me, because I goe ciuilly attyred, and sweare their trade was a good trade, till such as I am tooke it out of their hands.
>
> (5.2.330–4)

The whores' vivid and violent account of how they were 'burnt at fourteene, seuen times whipt, six times carted, nine times duck'd, search'd by some hundred and fifty Constables' (5.2.373–5) has a social authenticity which makes it rhetorically powerful and suggests a chaos of sexual vice and exploitation. But it is held in place by the Master of Bridewell's complacent account of the effectiveness of the institution in his charge offered as a combination of civic pride and reassurance that the social legislation of Elizabethan London has fulfilled its purpose (5.2.37–40). The Master's homily is less theatrically powerful than the whores' abusive resistance and the juxtaposition of the two highlights the difficulty of the play as a whole. Conventional moral values are constantly asserted but the play cannot find a theatrical form which will give them dramatic life.

These dramatic representations of sexual behaviour may have played some role in forging the social identity of the popular audience and the significance of women within it.[14] In his *Ghost of Richard III* (1614) Christopher Brooke addressed the question of how far the exemplary function

of displaying women's sexual misdemeanours was outweighed by the pathos
with which it was dramatized. His Richard remarks,

And what a piece of Iustice did I shew
On Mistress Shore? when (with a fained hate
To unchast Life) I forced her to goe
Bare-foote, on penance, with deiected state?
But now her Fame by a vild Play doth grow:
Whose Fate, the Women so commiserate,
That who (to see my Iustice on that Sinner)
Drinks not her Teares; and makes her Fast, their dinner?

(1844: 16)

In the new theatrical styles of the turn of the century, this melodramatic
sympathy for the adulterous woman, associated with ignorant women's
taste, was contested by a vogue for satiric misogyny. The new writers
sought to construct a different, more self-consciously elite audience for
their plays and did so by denouncing as popular the melodrama of domestic
tragedy. Jane Shore was particularly mocked both in the description of a
popular audience of 'Civill Throats stretchd out so lowd' who 'Came to
see Shore or Pericles',[15] and when Beaumont sneered at citizen women's
taste for exemplary narratives in *The Knight of the Burning Pestle*. His
Citizen's wife, the antithesis of his desired new audience, had never been
to the theatre before, 'but I should have seen Jane Shore once and my
husband hath promised me anytime this twelvemonth to carry me to *The
Bold Beauchamps*' (Beaumont 1966: Induction 11).

Where the domestic tragedies for the popular theatre had assimilated
comic material of low-life sexual action to tragic form, the new satiric style
presented the threat to marriage as comic: not a matter of pathos and regret
but a matter of trickery and wit. The theatrical pleasures it offers are not
those of moral certainty but of witty games and the power to see through
role-playing and affectation, distinguishing gallant from gull rather than
good from evil. Wit in these plays is less a matter of verbal dexterity than
a set of social attitudes which endorses the style and behaviour of the 'witty
young masters of the inns of court' who were its targeted audience. Its
theatrical values are those of comedy which attempts to appropriate female
sexuality from a moral to a comic world.

In their treatment of sexuality, these boys' plays dramatize the world of
verse satire. The new 'realism' of this style of boy-player comedy is a
result of taking old devices and exploiting their sexual potential to the full,
presenting its audience with an eroticized view of its world. Sex and women
are presented as part of the infinitely available variety of consumption and
the audience is invited to identify with the male characters as the consumers.
Dekker and Webster's *Westward Ho* written for Paul's Boys, for example,
presents a scene set in a brothel where, as it turns out, all the husbands are

frequent clients. Moral judgements of their behaviour are swamped in laughter as the scene plays out the classic farce of each arrival forcing the previous one to hide until all four husbands are secreted about the stage. Shakespeare had used a similar device in *Love's Labour's Lost* (4.3) but where in that play the courtiers are involved in an intrigue of courtly love, the men in *Westward Ho* are consumers of commoditized sex.

In its representation of women's sexuality, the play offers the delicious illusion of a private view of women's vice in which the humour comes from simply displaying the wives' arch raillery as they offer mocking summaries of their husbands' and lovers' failings. This familiar fantasy of women's insubordination is given a particular edge by being placed in an explicitly modern setting. Mistress Honysuckle, for example, talks of 'going to puritan Lectures' and to a banquet and warns Mistress Wafer against breastfeeding her child:

> if a Woman of any markeable face in the World giue her Child sucke, looke how many wrinckles be in the Nipple of her breast, so many will bee in her foreheade by that time twelue moneth.
>
> (1955: 1.2.117–20)

They talk of a world where fashion and style are everything even to the extent of women learning to write.

The novel realism of this comic mimesis is held firmly in place by older comic form. The women's eagerness to learn writing is sexualized in a scene where Iustiano, one of the husbands, comes to see them, disguised as a writing master. The resulting sequence draws on the comic schoolmaster routine familiar from *Love's Labour's Lost* (4.2) or *The Merry Wives of Windsor* (4.1) In the new satiric style the dreary puns in bawdy dog latin are transformed into sexual play with the idea of a woman's skill in holding a pen, a *double entendre* which comically escapes the foolish, indulgent husband but is offered up for the audience's enjoyment.

In these comic sequences, women's sexuality is presented as completely available for men, both as the subject of bawdy talk and as desire that can be used or dismissed at will. When Birdlime, the bawd, tells the gallant Master Monopoly that Mistress Tenterhook is in love with him, the comedy, once more, is all at her expense:

MONOPOLY: Fewh? pray thee stretch me no more uppon your *Tenterhook*: pox on her? Are there no Pottecaries ith Town to send her Phisick-bils to, but me: Shees not troubled with the greene sicknesse still, Is she?

BIRDLIME: The yellow Iaundis as the Doctor tels me: troth shees as good a peat: she is falne away so, that shees nothing but bare skin and bone: for the Turtle so mournes for you.

MONOPOLY: In blacke?

BIRDLIME: In blacke? you shall find both black and blew if you look
under her eyes.
MONOPOLY: Well: sing over her ditty when I'me in tune.

                                                            (1955: 2.2.209–19)

Monopoly's arrogance is typical of the gallants' attitude to women's
sexuality which assumes women are available to be consumed or not at
will. They are presented as the sum of the commodities which make them
attractive as in Master Monopoly's description of how he is

In an excellent humour to go to a valting house, I wold break downe all
their Glass-windowes, hew in peeces all their ioyne stooles, tear silke
petticotes, ruffle their periwigges, and spoyle their Painting.[16]

                                                            (3.2.15–18)

This eroticized humour is to some extent at odds with the play's narrative.
The city wives accept the gallants' invitation to go 'Westward Ho' with
them and their plotting to do so generates a lot of entertaining action.
However the wit with which they deceive their husbands is also used to
thwart their lovers and the adultery is never consummated. The resulting
tension between witty eroticism and conventional morality is, however,
treated much more censoriously in the Earl's plan to seduce Mrs Iustiano.
Having accepted the bawd's invitation to visit the Earl, Mrs Iustiano nevertheless denounces him with all the fervour of outraged chastity. She excuses
her visit to the Earl as womanly healing 'in pitty of your sick hart',[17] but
she claims that pity has caused her to forsake her true self: 'see I cloth'd/
My limbes (thus Player-like) in Rich Attyres,/Not fitting mine estate, and
am come forth' (2.2.108–10), and then she laments her fate in the language
of moral abstractions, 'Pouerty, thou bane of Chastity . . . /Oh tis rare/To
find a woman chast, thats poore and faire' (2.2.146–7). The Earl is eventually
punished by an elaborate trick: he is courted at a banquet by her husband
in disguise and when, appalled, he realizes his mistake, is forced to confront
both the horror of his action and the corpse of 'Mistress Iustiano as though
dead' (4.2.110 SD). He is then denounced before the citizens and acknowledges his guilt.

Moralizing critics have suggested that the difference in tone between the
scenes with the Earl and the rest of the play may be the result of a difference
in taste and style between Dekker and his young collaborator (see Hoy
1980 II: 160). However, a simple opposition between conventional morality
and sexual libertarianism cannot account for the complex interaction of
styles in the play's representation of sexuality. It is interesting that the Earl
alone among the would-be adulterers is punished. He is quite explicitly
contrasted with the witty gallants by Birdlime, who urges Mrs Iustiano to
prefer him to 'A Templer or one of those cogging Cattern pear-coloured-
beards, that by their good wils would have no pretty woman scape them'

or 'some yong perfum'd beardles Gallant... that spits al his braines out ats tongues end' (2.2.149–51; 170–1). However he violates both the moral and the comic codes by being both lascivious and old. When he meets Mistress Iustiano he is presented not as a witty young rake but as an example of the 'lustful duke' paradigm of contemporary tragedy (Potter 1981 IV: 188–96). His passion for Mistress Iustiano is not the wild oats of youth but a consuming desire which he glamorizes with the rhetoric of love:

> You giue my loue ill names, It is not lust
> Lawless desires well tempered may seem Iust
>
> (2.2.83–4)

The 'tempering' of his lawless desires takes the form of an eroticized worship expressed in poetic imagery. He is not playing with lust but is totally committed to his passion, so that 'my Hart/My Happiness, and State lie at your feet' (2.2.72–3). In the world of boy-player comedy, such language smacks of an old-fashioned style and the self-deluding, foolish worship of women is treated as comically as uppity citizens or overdemanding whores.

The potentially terrifying theatrical *memento mori* in which the audience as well as the Earl is confronted by the contrasting images of the banquet of lust and the dead object of that lust, has accordingly to be neutralized into another joke. Mistress Iustiano is alive and the affair is simply another story, available to be sold in the popular book trade:

> the book of the siedge of *Ostend*, writ by one that dropt in the action, will neuer sell so well, as thy report of the siedge between this *Graue*, this wicked elder and thy selfe, an impression of you two, wold away in a May morning:
>
> (4.2.186–9)

Like the boy-players' work itself, moral (or immoral) stories are grist to the commercial mill, part of the market in which sexuality itself is another commodity.

When Mrs Iustiano rejects the Earl's advances, Birdlime contemptuously reminds her of the market in which her beauty must function: 'you must thinke that the commodity of beauty was not made/to lye dead upon any young woman's hands' (2.2.186–7). Moreover she explicitly connects the market for sex with the market for drama:

> A woman when there be roses in her cheekes, Cherries on her lippes, Ciuet on her breath, Iuory in her teeth, Lyllyes in her hand and Lickorish in her heart, why she's like a play. If new, very good company, very good company, but if stale, like old Ieronimo, goe by, go by.
>
> (2.2.181–5)

This connection between plays and sex was commonplace and suggested the way in which the representation of sexuality becomes a form of pleasure which in the market place is associated with fashion and style. The domestic drama offered the pleasure of sympathetic engagement and pathos, but the elite boy-player comedies offered a kind of sexual pleasure in which actions involving women are removed from the arena of moral judgement and offer extensions of sexual fantasy. The audience can indulge in representations of sexuality denied them in the social world but held in place by a narrative which regulates consumption by norms of taste. The old-fashioned moralizing is as unacceptable as the rhetoric of love, and both are replaced by eroticized narratives of wit and trickery in a free space of theatrical pleasure. Moreover the social and sexual identity of fashionable young men is offered a pleasing reflection of itself.

Conclusions

In our excitement at the discovery that Shakespearean drama was implicated in the real social relations of early modern England, we have perhaps neglected the formal and material circumstances of its operation; the way in which sexuality as dramatic material is differently inflected according to the rhetorical and dramatic requirements of different stages and audiences. Mary Beth Rose has described the significance for comic form of John Lyly's 'aesthetic realisation that the theme of erotic love could be used to organise the disparate materials of early romantic comedy into a coherent design' (1988: 13). What she calls the 'erotic teleology' of marriage, 'this celebratory sexual and social configuration', provided a structure for sexual narratives which was both artistically satisfactory and endorsed by contemporary moral norms. Rose's findings apply in particular to the development of Shakespearean comedy and I have been suggesting that a similar relationship between ideology and form exists for the treatment of sexuality in other theatrical conditions.

The analysis of sexual relations provided by recent social history has indicated the extent to which they were built into the demographic and economic circumstances of the rural communities of early modern England. In their formulaic repetition of the details of sexual encounters and their public display of narratives of sexuality, the church court depositions suggest interesting connections with the representation of sexuality on the contemporary stage. In dealing with the drama, however, we need to recognize the extent to which it is not purely mimetic but is also negotiating with a variety of literary discourses which represent sexual relations outside the parameters of immediate social existence.

For when we turn to the literary representations of sexuality in Renaissance poetry and drama, we find ourselves, almost literally, in another world. Marvell's coy mistress could almost be imagined thinking about her marriage prospects or the dangers of bastardy but the result would be bathos, and though some of the mistresses of metaphysical poetry and satire fear for their honour, most of those sexual encounters represented take place in a fantasized free world of erotic pleasure. Even when the controlling eye of the poet condemns, we can glimpse the possibility of court women controlling their sexual pleasure and fertility, indulging a taste for pre-pubescent boys, or even extending their passions beyond heterosexuality. Women poets such as Katherine Phillips and Amelia Lanyer open up the possibility of an affective realm centred entirely on women in which relations of patronage or platonic love are expressed in terms of pleasure and desire (Andreadis 1989: 34–50; Montefiore 1990).

The world of sexual behaviour suggested by this literary evidence offers tantalizing suggestions of an alternative to the sexuality discussed by social historians which is constructed out of a heterosexual libido, moulded by the official instruments of ecclesiastical control and the unofficial sanctions of neighbourly authority into an acceptable expression in courtship and marriage. However such a positivist reading of literary material would ignore the importance of fantasy in both literature and sexuality, the way in which literary representation transforms sexuality into aesthetic pleasure, an *ars erotica* of pathos, suspense and witty comic play. These competing knowledges of poetry and social history have somehow to be combined if we are to arrive at an adequate understanding of the place and politics of the erotic in the cultural history of early modern England.

The connections between the two can perhaps be found in the contemporary commercialization of culture which included the commercialization of sex. This process of commercialization divided the audience in terms of its old-style taste for 'huge bombasted plaies, quilted with mighty words to leane purpose' or its modish preference for 'the nicenes of our Garments, single plots, quaint conceits, letcherous iests, drest up in hanging sleeves'. (Middleton 1958: Preface).[18] It offered the possibility that like the commercial consumption of drama, sex could also be consumed in the free space of commerce:

> for Plaies in this Citie are like wenches new falne to the trade, onlie desired of your neatest gallants while they are fresh; when they grow stale they must be vented by Termers and Cuntrie Chapmen.
>
> (Middleton 1608: A2)

However, as with wider market relations, such unregulated access to sex remained a distant fantasy, pleasing to the imagination (and perhaps the libido) while the play took place but whose social consequences were held in place by the regulation of dramatic form in the theatre and social regulation in the life world of early modern society.

Notes

1 This essay examines the relationship between texts and contexts in cultural materialist criticism.
2 See Amussen (1988), Chaytor (1980) and Sharpe (1981).
3 The view that jokes express conservative anxiety is offered in Thomas (1977: 7). Compare McLuskie (1989: 41).
4 A number of these depositions are quoted *in extenso* by Quaife (1979). His conclusions about early modern sexuality have been contested by Ingram (1985 and 1987).
5 See Heywood (1624) and Dekker (1963) especially jests 8, 43, 50, 55, 56, 58.
6 The slide from social to sexual pleasure exemplified in this narrative echoes Moll Frith's insistence that her deviant behaviour though similar to that of a roaring *boy* does not imply sexual licence:

> being pressed to declare whether she had not byn dishonest of her body & hath not also drawne other women to lewdnes by her perswasions & by carrying her selfe lyke a bawde, she absolutely denied y^t she was chargeable wth eyther of these imputacions.
>
> *Consistory of London Correction Book* (quoted in Hoy 1980 III)

Compare Amussen's observations about the prevalence of sexual misdemeanours in slander against women (1988: 102–3).
7 Steane's edition, used here, has no lineation. References are to page numbers.
8 This attempt to validate erotic verse by invoking classical precedent was more sceptically viewed by John Taylor, the water poet who, in *A Common Whore*, deplored the tendency 'To turne good humane studies and divine/Into most beastly lines like Aretine' (1622 sig. B3v). Taylor's work itself offers an interesting example of the overlap of sexual discourses with concerns about the commodification of literature in his prefatory comparison of a book with a whore. The classical and the moral discourses of sexuality are also explicitly contrasted in Dekker's *2 The Honest Whore* 4.1, in the dialogue in which Hippolito takes pleasure in the image of the whore as a free spirit, endorsed and justified by classical learning, while Bellafront invokes the low cultural tradition of the bible and the argument from origins while insisting on the social reality of the whore's life.
9 Compare the opening lines of his address to the reader of *The Scourge of Villainie* in which he is indignant that 'each mechanick slaue,/Each dunghill pesant, free perusal have/Of thy well labor'd lines.'
10 This Freudian reading is not a reflection on Marston's personal psychopathology but an attempt to understand the pleasures of the text. It is reinforced by similar fetishistic displacement found in the phallic symbolism of other texts, for example the lance, beard and feathers of Rich (1959); the amputated finger of *The Changeling* 3.4, or Ferdinand's dagger in *The Duchess of Malfi* 1.2.
11 Compare Dekker, *The Shoemakers' Holiday*, scene XII SD, in which Hammon soliloquizes while watching 'Jane *in a sempster's shop, working*'.
12 Pearson's edition, used here, has no lineation. References are to the page numbers.
13 Compare *Romeo and Juliet*, 1.5.45, and for a more sexualized version John Webster, *The White Devil*, 1.2.227–8. This trope is discussed in full in McLuskie (1989: 126–8).
14 For discussion of women in the theatre audience see Levin (1989) and compare McLuskie (1989: 87–99).
15 *Pimlico or Run Redcap*, 1609 sig. C; quoted in Clark (1931: 16).

16 Compare the sexualization of commodities in the jokes about ruffs and pokers in the catalogue of a whore's accoutrements in Dekker and Middleton, *1 The Honest Whore* 2.1.
17 Compare Julia, the Cardinal's mistress in Webster's *The Duchess of Malfi*, 2.4.37.
18 In this Preface to the Reader of *The Roaring Girl* Middleton offers another example of the assimilation of boy-player theatrical styles to a popular theatre audience.

References

Amussen, S. (1988) *An Ordered Society: Gender and Class in Early Modern England*, Oxford: Blackwell.
Andreadis, H. (1989) 'The Sapphic Platonics of Katherine Philips 1632–1664', *Signs* 15: 34–60.
Beaumont, F. (1966) *The Knight of the Burning Pestle*, in Fredson Bowers (ed.), *The Dramatic Works in the Beaumont and Fletcher Canon*, vol. 1, Cambridge: Cambridge University Press.
Brooke, C. (1844) *The Ghost of Richard III*, ed. J. Payne Collier, London: Shakespeare Society.
Cannon, C. D. (1975) (ed.) *A Warning for Fair Women* (anon.), The Hague: Mouton.
Chaytor, M. (1980) 'Household and Kinship: Ryton in the late sixteenth and early seventeenth centuries', *History Workshop Journal*, 10: 25–60.
Clark, A. M. (1931) *Thomas Heywood Playwright and Miscellanist*, New York: Russell & Russell.
Coward, R. (1983) *Patriarchal Precedents: Sexuality and Social Relations*, London: Routledge & Kegan Paul.
Dekker, T. (1963) 'Jests to Make you Merry', in A. Grosart (ed.) *The Non-Dramatic Works of Thomas Dekker*, New York: Russell & Russell.
—— (1979) *The Shoemakers' Holiday*, R. L. Smallwood and S. Wells (eds), Manchester: Manchester University Press.
—— and Middleton, T. (1955) *1 and 2 The Honest Whore*, in Fredson Bowers (ed.), vol. III, *The Dramatic Works of Thomas Dekker*, Cambridge: Cambridge University Press.
—— and Webster, J. (1955) *Westward Ho*, in Bowers, vol. II.
Dollimore, J. and Sinfield, A. (1990) 'Culture and textuality: debating cultural materialism', *Textual Practice* 4, 1: 91–101.
Finklepearl, P. J. (1969) *John Marston of the Middle Temple*, Cambridge, Mass.: Harvard University Press.
Foucault, M. (1976) *The History of Sexuality*, vol. 1, trans. Robert Hurley, Harmondsworth: Penguin.
Golding, A. (1878) *A briefe discourse of the late murther of master George Saunders a worshipfull Citizen of London: and of the apprehension, arreignement, and execution of the principall and accessaries of the same* in R. Simpson (ed.), *The School of Shakespeare*, vol. II, New York: J. V. Bouton.
Greene, R. (1913) *The Conversion of an English Courtesan*, in F. Aydelotte (ed.) *Elizabethan Rogues and Vagabondes*, Oxford: Clarendon.
Heywood, T. (1624) *Guneikeon: Or Nine Books of Various History Concerninge Women*, London: Aslip.
—— (1964) *The First and Second parts of King Edward the fourth* in J. Pearson (ed.) vol. I, *The Dramatic Works of Thomas Heywood*, New York: Russell & Russell.

Hoy, C. (1980) *Introductions, notes and commentaries to texts* in *The Dramatic Works of Thomas Dekker*, 4 vols, Cambridge: Cambridge University Press.

Ingram, M. (1985) 'Ridings, rough music and mocking rhymes in early modern England', in Barry Reay (ed.) *Popular Culture in Early Modern England*, London: Croom Helm.

—— (1987) *Church Courts, Sex and Marriage in England 1570–1640*, Cambridge: Cambridge University Press.

Levin, R. (1989) 'Women in the Renaissance theatre audience', *Shakespeare Quarterly* 40: 165–73.

McLuskie, K. (1989) *Renaissance Dramatists*, Hemel Hempstead: Harvester.

—— (1991) 'The Poets' Royal Exchange: Patronage and commerce in early modern drama', *The Yearbook of English Studies* 21: 53–62.

Marston, J. (1961) *The Poems of John Marston*, ed. A. Davenport, Liverpool: Liverpool University Press.

Middleton, T. (1608) *The Family of Love*, London: John Holmes.

—— (1958) *The Roaring Girl*, in F. Bowers (ed.) vol. III, *The Dramatic Works of Thomas Dekker*, Cambridge: Cambridge University Press.

Montefiore, J. (1990) 'Women and the poetic tradition', in M. Coyle (ed.) *Encyclopedia of Literature and Criticism*, London: Routledge.

Mulvey, L. (1989) *Visual and Other Pleasures*, London: Macmillan.

Nashe, T. (1972) 'Choice of Valentines', in J. B. Steane (ed.) *The Unfortunate Traveller and Other Works*, Harmondsworth: Penguin.

Potter, L., Bentley, G., Edwards, P., and McLuskie, K. (eds) (1981) *The Revels History of Drama in English*, vol. IV, London: Methuen.

Quaife, G. R. (1979) *Wanton Wenches and Wayward Wives*, London: Croom Helm.

Rich, B. (1959) *Farewell to Military Profession*, ed. T. N. Cranfill, Austin: University of Texas Press.

Rose, M. B. (1988) *The Expense of Spirit: Love and Sexuality in English Renaissance Drama*, Ithaca: Cornell University Press.

Sharpe, J. (1981) *Defamation and Sexual Slander in Early Modern England: The Church Courts at York*, Borthwick Papers 58, York: St Antony's Press.

Taylor, J. (1622) *A Common Whore*, London: Henry Gosson.

Thomas, K. (1977) 'The place of laughter in Tudor and Stuart England', *Times Literary Supplement*, 21 January 1977: 78.

Turberville, G. (1587) *Tragical Tales Translated by Turberville*, London: Abel Ieffs.

Waddington, R. (1990) ' "All in All": Shakespeare, Milton, Donne and the soul in body topos', *English Literary Renaissance* 20: 40–6.

Chapter 8

Making a difference

Male/male 'desire' in tragedy, comedy, and tragi-comedy

Bruce R. Smith

First we should get a few things straight. Let us begin with difference.

   Me   /   not me

The biggest difference of them all embodies two truths about the dynamics of difference in desire. First, two things marked out as being different are never equal. One of them inevitably defines the other. We may draw the line down the middle, but what lies to the left of that line is more important than what lies to the right. What comes first predicts what comes second. What lies to the left of the line is, we might say, the *radical* of difference. It defines the standard against which whatever comes next is different.[1]

   The second dynamic is this: desire is all about 'Me' wanting to incorporate the 'not me'. On this point, Plato, Aristotle, and Freud are in agreement. Plato's purchase on desire is characteristically idealistic. To see the beautiful is to love it. And to love it is to want to possess it.[2] For Aristotle, one person's use of another person to satisfy a need or lack in himself is the criterion that distinguishes attachments based on usefulness or on pleasure from the mutual self-sufficiency of true friendship. Secondary 'friendships', Aristotle argues in the *Nicomachean Ethics*, are always self-referential; they cease to exist when the need or the lack ceases to exist. Falling in love, desiring another person sexually, is a perfect example of such transient attachments.[3] For Freud, sexual contact with another body simultaneously satisfies two kinds of libido: 'object-libido', psychic energy attached to an external object, and 'narcissistic-libido', psychic energy attached to parts of one's own body. In puberty, so Freud observes in one of his early *Contributions to the Theory of Sex*, narcissistic-libido becomes focused on the genitals, while object-libido (in healthy males) rediscovers the satisfactions of the female body, particularly the satisfactions of the female breast.[4] In the act of sexual union self and object become one. Beauty, the useful or pleasurable person, the female breast: with each of these objects, desire is fulfilled when difference is obliterated. The satisfaction of desire is in making the 'not me' mine.

   Before Me, there was already radical difference. 'So God created man in his own image, in the image of God created he him; male and female created he them' (Genesis 1:1–27).

Male / female

To unthink 'male' as a radical is perhaps the greatest challenge today in feminist theory and in that newest colony of the English enterprise, men's studies. To speak of 'male/male "desire" ' is, then, something of a tautology. To conjoin two radicals – or, rather, to set down one radical and then set it down again – would seem to be making an equation, not drawing a distinction. When it comes to desire, how *is* difference to be marked between 'male' on the right and 'male' on the left?

But let us go back to 'make'. To early modern theorists such as Sidney, a poet is not only a seer but a 'maker', a man who makes things out of words.[5] In one of those nice coincidences that convince postmodern critics that the world (almost) makes sense after all, 'make' in early modern English could be both a substantive and a verb, both a conjoining and a disruption. With only a slight movement of the tongue from the palatal position to the dental, and with no difference at all in meaning, Phillip Stubbes *might* have said that on their way from theatre to sodomitical conclave 'every *make* sorts to his *make*', since 'mate' and 'make' operated as synonyms in early modern English if not as variant pronunciations of the same word (*OED* s.v. *Make sb.*[1]).[6] In early modern English, as in English today, 'make' was more commonly a transitive verb. Besides sense, merry, and sport, we might also 'make' love (*Hamlet* 3.4.83), the beast with two backs (*Othello* 1.1.118–19), and Edmund under the Dragon's tail (*Lear* 1.1.22, 1.2.126–30).[7] If we were verging on obsolescence, we might during Shakespeare's adulthood 'make' two things or two people by mating them, pairing them, or matching them (*OED* s.v. *Make v.* [2]*Obs.*). 'To make' a sexually desired person, with all that *that* invites in the way of scholarly discourse, we have to wait until the twentieth century. In the meantime, we can still 'make' a difference with quite enough to think about.

When it comes to desire, we ought, strictly speaking, to differentiate among three different kinds: 'desire' enacted by characters in the fiction for one other, 'desire' prompted in a spectator for characters in the fiction, and desire aroused in a spectator for actors onstage. Only the last of these three kinds of desire can be spoken of without quotation marks. The characters in the fiction do not, after all, exist. Consummation of the 'desire' these characters articulate toward each other can be no more than an imagined thing, a simulation. In the drama of early modern England such consummation is not even simulated directly: it happens offstage, out of hearing, out of sight. Whatever Phillip Stubbes and other Puritan detractors may have said, a spectator's 'desire' for characters onstage is likewise an act of imagination, not an act of the body. (Playing the sodomite, as Stubbes realized, was something that came later, in private.) Only the desire of spectators for the actors onstage, or for people outside the theatre who might resemble characters inside the theatre, involves actual people with actual bodies capable of satisfying actual desire.

About spectators' desire for people outside the theatre we are in a position to say nothing. About spectators' desire for actors onstage the evidence is radically contradictory. Puritan divines and academic snobs may have chafed in print to the very pitch of passion, yet all the unpolemical witnesses we have from the seventeenth century – John Manningham, Henry Jackson, Simon Forman, Abraham Wright – register no erotic interest whatsoever in the characters they saw onstage, much less a specifically homoerotic interest in the boy actors they watched in *Twelfth Night*, *Othello*, *Macbeth*, *Cymbeline*, *The Winter's Tale*, and *Philaster*. Every one of these informants writes about the fictional female characters he saw as if those female characters were female persons, persons who engaged delight or pity but not *eros* (Salgado 1975: 23, 31–3, 47; Gurr 1980: 209; Gras 1991). Even for a single performance of a single play on a single afternoon how could we ever hope to generalize about spectators whose numbers might run into the thousands? Middleton's prologue to *No Wit, No Help Like a Woman's* (Lady Elizabeth's Men?, 1613) sounds a cautious note that we, too, should heed when we survey the pit and the galleries of London's public theatres – not from fifty feet away, but across an expanse of 400 years:

> How is't possible to suffice
> So many ears, so many eyes?
> Some in wit, some in shows
> Take delight, and some in clothes;
> Some for mirth they chiefly come,
> Some for passion – for both some;
> Some for lascivious meetings, that's their arrant;
> Some to detract, and ignorance their warrant.
> How is't possible to please
> Opinion toss'd in such wild seas?
>
> (Pro. 1–10)

We can speak with confidence, not about what spectators might have felt, must have felt, or ought to have felt about characters in the fiction or about actors on the stage, but about what the characters in the fiction are scripted to say they 'feel' toward one another. And the kind of 'desire' they articulate depends very much on the kind of play they happen to inhabit.

Gendering genre

When seventeenth-century eye-witnesses do talk about sexual desire on-stage, it is not boys who set them to talking. Among the differences that distinguish drama in early modern England from drama on the continent, the most conspicuous has come to seem, to our own moment in political history, the all-male composition of English professional acting companies. To Marlowe, Shakespeare, and their contemporaries the really telling difference was just the opposite. It was the sight of *women* playing women's parts that had power to startle, intrigue, disturb, and call into question assumptions that otherwise might never be made explicit. If we can credit Thomas Nashe, differences of gender in this regard were qualified by differences of genre and differences of geography. The peroration of *Pierce Penilesse His Supplication to the Divell* (1592) contains this virile defence of English playhouses, English players, English playing, and English plays:

> Our Players are not as the players beyond sea, a sort of squirting baudie Comedians, that have whores and common Curtizens to playe womens partes, and forbeare no immodest speech or unchast action that may procure laughter; but our Sceane is more statelye furnisht than ever it was in the time of *Roscius*, our representations honourable, and full of gallant resolution, not consisting like theirs, of a Pantaloun, a Whore, and a Zanie, but of Emperours, Kings, and Princes; whose Tragedies (*Sophocleo cothurno*) they do vaunt. Not *Roscius* nor *Aesope*, those admyred tragedians that have lived ever since before Christ was borne, could ever performe more in action than famous *Ned Allen*. I must accuse our Poets of sloth and partialitie, that they will not boast in large impressions what worthy men (above all Nations) *England* affoords.
>
> (1910 1:215)

Tongue in cheek or not, Nashe sets up in this little expostulation an interlocked series of differences in gender and genre that are keyed to a difference in geography: English/male/tragedy is situated at a scornful distance from Italian/female/comedy. To the 'whores and common Curtizens' of *commedia dell'arte* Nashe consigns sexual desire; to the 'Emperours, Kings, and Princes' of tragedy he concedes 'honourable' representations and 'gallant resolution'.

Nashe is presumably describing *commedia dell'arte* performances by travelling Italian troupes that he had seen or heard about in England. The same differences in gender, genre, and geography are implicit in several first-hand accounts by Englishmen who found themselves 'beyond sea' and ventured while there to the theatre. Thomas Coryate's story of his visit to one of the playhouses in Venice displays the same conflation of setting, sex, and scenario that we witness in Nashe. At first taste, this particular tidbit among *Coryate's crudities. Hastily gobled up in five moneths travells* seems to be about a difference in dramatic conventions. Coryate is frankly astonished that Italian women could be as *artful* as English boys in playing fictitious women:

I was at one of their Play-houses where I saw a Comedie acted. The house is very beggarly and base in comparison of our stately Play-houses in England: neyther can their Actors compare with us for apparrell, shewes and musicke. Here I observed certaine things that I never saw before. For I saw women acte, a thing that I never saw before, though I have heard that it hath beene sometimes used in London, and they performed it with as good a grace, action, gesture, and whatsoever convenient for a Player, as ever I saw any masculine Actor.

What Coryate notices here seems to be simply a matter of theatrical artifice. But when he turns his back on the disguised characters onstage and trains his attention on certain disguised members of the audience, we realize that 'Italy', 'courtesans', and 'comedy' constitute, for Coryate, a distinct category of experience:

Also their noble & famous Cortezans came to this Comedy, but so disguised, that a man cannot perceive them. For they wore double masks upon their faces, to the end they might not be seene: one reaching from the toppe of their forehead to their chinne, and under their necke; another with twiskes of downy or woolly stuff covering their noses. And as for their neckes round about, they were so covered and wrapped with cobweb lawne and other things, that no part of their skin could be discerned.

(1611: 247–8)

The same implicit linkages can be discerned in George Sandys' account of his stop-over at Messina on a voyage back from the Middle East in 1610. 'Here live they in all abundance and delicacy', Sandys begins. Delicate food, wine chilled in summer by snow, sumptuous silks, piles of money, and women publicly displaying their beauty in carriages lead Sandys' memory to the playhouse door – and to the spectacle of women playing women's parts:

Every evening they solace themselves along the Marine (a place left throughout betweene the Citie wall and the haven) the men on horse-backe, and the women in large Carosses, being drawne with the slowest procession. There is to be seen the pride and beauties of the Citie. There have they their play-houses, where the parts of women are acted by women, and too naturally passionated; which they forebeare not to frequent upon Sundayes.

(1615: 246–7)

By 'too *naturally* passionated' Sandys may sound as if he is talking only about theatrical conventions, about the want of art in women playing women. But the context in which he makes that observation describes a debauchery of taste, touch, and sight. The moral disapproval Sandys registers about performances on Sunday qualifies whatever delight he has taken in describing all the rest. The Italian theatre, Sandys suggests no less insistently than Nashe and Coryate, is an arena of erotic action.

When the women onstage are really women, Nashe, Coryate, and Sandys seem as eager to talk about sexual titillation as Manningham, Jackson, Forman, and Wright are reticent when the women onstage are boys. If we attend carefully to the context in which actual witnesses to plays in performance (as opposed to moral polemicists) talk about sexual desire in the theatre, it seems inappropriate if not impossible to disentangle differences in gender from differences in genre and differences in geography. What Nashe, Coryate, and Sandys do in effect is to give genre both gender and national identity. In allying 'us' and 'male', Nashe, Coryate, and Sandys are asserting two of the most powerful radicals in all forms of discourse in early modern England. In conjoining 'tragedy' with 'us' and 'male', they may be isolating a radical that is no less powerful when the mode of discourse is drama and the subject is sexual desire. We do no more than respect categories of experience constructed by early modern witnesses themselves if we attempt to decipher the dramatic signs of homoerotic desire according to these differences between male/English/tragedy and female/Italian/comedy. And in doing so, the witnesses suggest, we should assume a specifically male point of view.

Differentiating likenesses in tragedy

Nashe notwithstanding, tragedies and history plays on the English public stage do contain verbal cues to sexual desire. But, true to Nashe's claim, many of those cues have nothing to do with women. It is difficult to hear a woman's voice – or even a boy actor's – in one of the most blatant declarations of homoerotic desire in all of early modern drama:

> *Enter* Gaveston *reading on a letter that was*
> *brought him from the king.*
> *My father is deceast, come* Gaveston,
> *And share the kingdom with thy dearest friend.*
> Ah words that make me surfet with delight:
> What greater blisse can hap to *Gaveston*,
> Then live and be the favorit of a king?
> Sweete prince I come, these these thy amorous lines,
> Might have enforst me to have swum from *France*,
> And like *Leander* gaspt upon the sande,
> So thou wouldst smile and take me in thy armes.
> The sight of *London* to my exiled eyes,
> Is as *Elizium* to a new come soule.
> Not that I love the citie or the men,

But that it harbors him I hold so deare,
The king, upon whose bosome let me die,
And with the world be still at enmitie:
What neede the artick people love star-light,
To whom the sunne shines both day and night.

(Marlowe, Edward II: 1.1.1–17)

In raising the rhetorical force that spends itself in the pun on 'die' – just at the moment that blank verse reaches a climax in rhyme – Gaveston may appropriate metaphors from Petrarchan sonnets (the poet's beloved as a sun outshining the stars beloved by other men, the poet's beloved as a city waiting to be entered), but the only 'she' who figures in his declaration of desire is Hero. The implied object of Leander's race through the waves, Hero remains without a name, offstage, out of mind. Instead, the actor's attention in these opening lines to Marlowe's *Edward II* is focused, just as it is in Marlowe's narrative poem 'Hero and Leander', on the pursuing male – on the body of Leander gasping upon the sand. In person, in his own eyes at least, Edward turns out to be not 'Hero' but *the hero*. 'Not *Hilas* was more mourned by *Hercules*,/ Then thou has beene of me since thy exile', the king exclaims when he and Gaveston are reunited face to face (1.1.144–5).

Hercules, the role Edward sees himself as playing to Gaveston's Hylas, is corroborated later in the play by the elder Mortimer. 'The mightiest kings have had their minions', Mortimer consoles his disgruntled nephew and goes on to catalogue them: Alexander and Hephaestion, Hercules and Hylas, Achilles and Patroclus, Cicero and Octavius, Socrates and Alcibiades (1.4.391–401). Each of these classical male lovers is, in Mortimer's terms, a 'king' or a 'wise man' and his 'minion' – in Greek terms, an *erastēs* and an *erōmenos* (Dover 1978: 16). The differences between the two are spelled out in Mortimer's qualifiers: 'great', 'conquering', 'stern', 'grave' find their erotic opposites in 'wild', 'vain', 'light-headed'. Difference in each case is measured by age, by social station, by political power, but not by gender. Likewise in Gaveston's opening speech the eroticized differences are by and large *political* differences: king/commoner, this man/all other men, we two/the world.

In such a context, the sexual desire of male for female becomes a metaphor, a way of drawing likenesses. But ultimately it becomes a way of marking differences. Male/male desire stands as the reality; male/female desire is invoked to describe it. In *Troilus and Cressida*, for example, the relationship of Patroclus to Achilles – in Thersites' satiric view, at least – is that of *erōmenos* to *erastēs*, of 'masculine whore' (5.1.17) to an 'idol of idiot-worshippers' (5.1.7). But the Greek warriors bring to their battle with the Trojans a vocabulary of sexual passion that springs from romance, not satire. That passion finds its release, not in sexual union, but in man-to-man combat. When Ajax accepts Hector's challenge to a Greek 'That loves his mistress more than in confession' (1.3.266). the Greeks come to the fight, in Aeneas' words, 'with a bridegroom's fresh alacrity' (4.5.145). The combat between Ajax and Hector turns out to be the 'maiden battle' Achilles predicted it would be: 'Let me embrace thee, Ajax', declares Hector as he abruptly leaves off fighting. 'By him that thunders, thou hast lusty arms./ Hector would have them fall upon him thus' (4.7.19–21). And with that 'thus' he embraces the man he hoped to kill. Achilles himself confesses to have 'a woman's longing,/ An appetite that I am sick withal,/ To see great Hector in his weeds of peace' (3.3.230–2).

'Appetite' is the image Achilles keeps to the fore when later in the play he meets Hector face to face and proceeds to 'feed his eyes' on his enemy's body in what sounds like a lover's blazon (4.7.114–22). A similarly startling conjunction of lovers' affection and enemies' hostility marks *Coriolanus*. Marriage is the controlling likeness in Aufidius' welcome when Coriolanus deserts the Romans and arrives in the camp of his sometime enemy:

> O, let me clip ye
> In arms as sound as when I wooed, in heart
> As merry as when our nuptial day was done,
> And tapers burnt to bedward!
>
> (4.5.110–13)

As important as these likenesses are in suggesting the intensity of feeling that connects Achilles with Patroclus, Ajax with Hector, Achilles with Hector, and Aufidius with Coriolanus, desire in each case is articulated through difference. In each case it is combat – a graphically *physical* difference – that occasions the rhetoric of homoerotic desire. The most important difference of all is the very fact that the desiring speaker and the object of his desire are both male. Aufidius goes on to make the point explicit:

> Know thou first,
> I loved the maid I married; never man
> Sighed truer breath. But that I see thee here,
> Thou noble thing, more dances my rapt heart
> Than when I first my wedded mistress saw
> Bestride my threshold.
>
> (4.5.113–18)

Man and wife, arch enemy and arch enemy: likeness is less important than difference in setting Aufidius' raptured heart to dance. For the desire to which Aufidius gives voice in this speech, the bond between man and wife may be a particularly powerful metaphor, but it remains just that: a metaphor. Desire of man for man becomes the radical according to which desire of man for wife is measured.

That Jonson in *Sejanus* should read the politics of imperial Rome in homosexual terms is not simply an accident of Tiberius' notorious debauches. As with Thersites in *Troilus and Cressida*, it is a satirist-figure, Arruntius, who points a finger at the fleshy realities of sodomy. Tiberius, 'an emperor only in his lusts' (Jonson [1981] 4.4.376), has rusticated himself on Capri, whither

> He hath his boys, and beauteous girls ta'en up,
> Out of our noblest houses, the best formed,
> Best nurtured, and most modest: what's their good
> Serves to provoke his bad. Some are allured,
> Some threatened; others, by their friends detained,
> Are ravished hence, like captives, and, in sight
> Of their most grieved parents, dealt away
> Unto his spintries, sellaries, and slaves,
> Masters of strange, and new-commented lusts,
> For which wise nature hath not left a name.

Though it happens offstage, on 'an obscure island' far from Rome (4.378), sodomy becomes, in Arruntius' view, a way of reading politics at the centre – specifically, the politics practised by Sejanus. Tiberius' 'strange, and new-commented lusts' are not the worst of Rome's political plight.

> To this (what most strikes us, and bleeding Rome)
> He is, with his craft, become the ward
> To his own vassal, a stale catamite:
> Whom he, upon our low and suffering necks,
> Hath raised from excrement to side the gods,
> And have his proper sacrifice in Rome . . .

(4.392–407)

On the stage of his island, Tiberius is, in Arruntius' telling phrase, 'acting his *tragedies* with a comic face' (4.4.381, emphasis added)

'English', 'male', and 'tragedy': these three radicals define the imagined space within which plays such as *Edward II*, *Troilus and Cressida*, *Coriolanus*, and *Sejanus* were written, rehearsed, acted, and remembered. In that ethos, homoerotic desire assumes a shape and a voice that may admit the 'not English' in the guise of ancient Rome, but it radically excludes the female. In the violent politicized male worlds of these plays, desire is constructed out of differences that are violent, political, and male. The desiring subject defines the object of his desire in terms of power; desire finds its end in violence. The playing out of desire may take the form of struggle between dominant and dominated (Gaveston exploits the difference between 'king' and 'favourite', Edward defies the nobles and denies difference by treating Gaveston as 'friend', Tiberius raises Sejanus to power only to hurl him from power in the end); struggle between equals for supremacy (Achilles and Hector, Aufidius and Coriolanus); or a mutuality that achieves its distinction by being different from the animosity that surrounds it (Achilles and Patroclus). Senate house, council chamber, military encampment, battlefield: as the imagined universe of tragedy on the London public stage, this virile ethos supplies the images in which homosexual desire is seen in tragedy; it dictates the terms in which homosexual desire is heard. No less remarkable than the sexual energy that charges male power-struggles in these plays is the violence in which that energy spends itself. None of the protagonists dies the death prescribed for sodomites by 5 Elizabeth, Chapter 17, the law that finally fixed sodomy as a felony: death by hanging. Penetration and dismemberment are, in Southwark if not at Tyburn, more compelling forms of death. The red-hot spit that Lightborne thrusts up Edward's fundament is only the most blatant among the images of cutting and/or entering that mark the deaths of Gaveston at the hands of Mortimer and his lackeys, of Patroclus at the hands of Hector, of Hector at the hands of Achilles and his Myrmidons, of Coriolanus at the hands of Aufidius and his conspirators, of Sejanus at the hands of the Roman mob. Having stabbed the man who killed his lover, Achilles gives the imagery of sexual appetite a final twist in the lines with which he exits from *Troilus and Cressida*: 'My half-supped sword, that frankly would have fed,/ Pleased with this dainty bait, now goes to bed' (5.9.19–20). 'Thou *boy* of tears': stung by the epithet with which Aufidius has cancelled his earlier speeches of adversarial wooing, Coriolanus positively begs the fate that befalls him at the end of the play: 'Cut me to pieces, Volsces. Men and lads,/ Stain all your edges on me' (5.6.103, 112–13). Sejanus' death is anatomized by Terrentius digit by digit, limb by limb, and organ by organ, ending with the liver and the heart (5.818–26).[8] It is remarkable how many of these acts of punitive violence are carried out, not by individuals, but by men in groups.

The violence that consummates homoerotic desire in tragedy may have its origins in the desiring subject himself (Achilles, Aufidius) or in the hostile world that constructs and contains his desire (the nobles who destroy Gaveston and Edward, the Trojans who slay Patroclus and so inspire Achilles' bloody assignation with Hector, the Roman mob that tears apart Sejanus) or, with greater verisimilitude, in a complicated combination of the two. Whatever the circumstances, one law of tragedy remains sacrosanct: the ending of homoerotic desire is death. That eventuality probably tells us less about the moral and legal proscriptions of sodomy in early modern England than it does about Hegel's contention, elaborated by structuralist critics in this century, that tragedy enacts the irreconcilable conflict, not of right against wrong, but of two rights with each other (Hegel 1975: 2,1196; Vernant 1972, 1983). In Achilles and in Aufidius we witness an urge to enact homoerotic desire countered by the political necessity of containing that desire within orthodox moral and legal ideas. In that conflict of desire and necessity resides the pathos of tragedy. Achilles' Greece and Coriolanus' Rome may not be the England of Edward II, but

as settings for tragedy Greece and Rome set in place all-male power structures that replicate the all-male power structure of early modern England,
with its legal proscription of sodomy, its economic investment in marriage
– and its privileging of male/male friendship above all other bonds. In the
structuralist view, it is just such a conflict between hero and context that
generates tragedy. In early modern England the erotic politics of tragedy
seems to have been, in certain plays at least, a specifically homoerotic
politics.

Likening differences in comedy

Whatever erotic delight certain spectators may have taken in the very sight
of a boy actor in women's clothes, it is specifically the case of a boy actor
dressed up as a girl dressed up as a boy, *in a comedy*, that prompts from
Shakespeare and other playwrights the sort of verbal cues that suggest a
jokey but interested awareness of the boy's body beneath the woman's
weeds – an awareness that some critics, among them several contributors
to this volume of essays, have taken as a universal fact about boy actors
playing female roles in all plays, in all circumstances (Jardine 1989; Howard
1988; Orgel 1989; Garber 1991). The quips exchanged by Julia and Lucetta,
Portia and Nerissa, and Rosalind and Celia as they put on men's clothes
and go off to turn catastrophe into comedy have become the *loci classici*
for such generalizations. Provocative as their speeches may be, Shakespeare's Julia, Portia, Rosalind, and Viola can hardly speak for the more
than seventy-five female pages, in scripts by nearly forty different playwrights, who appeared on the Elizabethan, Jacobean, and Caroline stage
(Freeburg 1915; Shapiro, forthcoming). Those English-speaking exemplars
of the maid in male disguise represent a character-type with its own Stith
Thompson motif-number (K–1837, to be exact) that recurs in narratives
throughout history, in cultures all over the world. Such plenitude, even if
we limit our attention to the seventy-five surviving English scripts, demands
a respect for differences – in date, in venue, in authorship, in genre.

In the mid–1590s at least two plays with transvestite heroines were to be
seen on London's stages, each of them belonging to a different dramatic
tradition, each of them working out its own distinctive differences with
respect to homoerotic desire.[9] Having given the device a trial run in *Two
Gentlemen of Verona* (1590), Shakespeare was handing the female page an
even more prominent part in *The Merchant of Venice* at the Theatre,
Shoreditch. At the Rose, meanwhile, the Admiral's Men, perhaps responding to the success of *Two Gentlemen*, were mounting their own version of
the male-turned-female-turned-male in Heywood's *The Four Prentices of
London with the Conquest of Jerusalem*. (Shakespeare in his turn may have
appropriated the device from Robert Greene's romance play *The Scottish
History of James IV*, probably acted by the Queen's Men in 1590. The fact

that *Two Gentlemen of Verona* was acted by the Chamberlain's Men, perhaps during the very season Greene's *James IV* was acted by the Queen's Men, makes one wonder whether the maid-in-male disguise was not one of the feathers stolen by the upstart crow.)

Whatever commercial rivalry may have inspired his play, Heywood's way with the female page is decidedly not Shakespeare's. *Two Gentlemen of Verona*, *The Merchant of Venice*, *As You Like It*, *Twelfth Night*: all but one of Shakespeare's transvestite comedies, let it be noted, are set in Italy. 'Illyria' may not be findable on a map, but the characters who inhabit it proclaim their Italian origin with their names. If Nashe, Coryate, and Sandys can be believed, it may have been that specific fictional setting that prompted Shakespeare to invest the speeches of Julia/'Sebastian', Portia/'Balthazar'. and Viola/'Cesario' with the sexual flirting and gender teasing that have attracted the attentions of Jardine, Howard, Orgel, Garber, and other modern scholars. Heywood's *Four Prentices* is set closer to home. Despite the romance adventure announced in the play's subtitle, despite the fact that the four apprentices are really the sons of the dispossessed Earl of Boulogne, the mode of *The Four Prentices of London*, if not exactly 'city comedy', is something like 'domestic romance' – with an emphasis on the 'domestic'. In the merchant-class world of *The Four Prentices* – and in the city comedies by Jonson, Chapman, and Middleton that held the stage for nearly thirty years – the maid-in-male-disguise becomes an object, not of romantic fascination as he/she/he is in Shakespeare's scripts, but of satiric derision. When Guy discovers that the page who has been sharing his bed is really the French king's daughter, he and his brothers share a laugh that comes from the belly, not from the heart. As in *James IV*, the lady's change of identities from page to lady has occurred offstage. When the French king's daughter walks onstage, she occasions a series of jokes that start with the breeches – but end with the gown:

> GUY: Leape heart, dance spirit, be merry jocund soule,
>   Tis she undoubtedly.
> LADY: You know me then!
> GUY: I do, 'twas that disguise,
>   That all this while has blinded my cleere eyes.
> EUSTACE: Fye, are you not asham'd to kisse a boy,
>   And in your armes to graspe him with such joy?
> GUY: She is no boy, you do mistake her quite.
> EUSTACE: A boy, a Page, a wagtaile by this light:
>   What say you sister?
> BELLAFRANCA: Sure he told me so,
>   For if he be a maide, I made him one.
> EUSTACE: Do not mistake the sex, man, for he's none.

>It is a rogue, a wag, his name is *Jacke*,
>A notable dissembling lad, a Cracke.
>GUY: Brother, 'tis you that are deceiv'd in her.
>Beshrew her, she hath beene my bedfellow
>   A yeare and more, yet I had not the grace—
>
>*(Four Prentices, 2.252–3)*

All those missed opportunities are soon made right when Guy marries his sometime lady, sometime page, sometime bedfellow. In these lines there may be jokes about gender (one wonders about 'crack' as a synonym for 'lad', despite the *OED*'s innocent citations), but those jokes ultimately serve to *differentiate* genders, not to confuse them.

In the theatrical history of the maid-in-male disguise the plays acted in 1593–4 chart out two trends that can be traced all the way down to 1642. *The Merchant of Venice* and *The Four Prentices of London* define two viable but very different directions in genre and in venue. In the tradition of *The Merchant of Venice* follow not only Shakespeare's own romantic comedies *As You Like It* (1599) and *Twelfth Night* (1601) but tragi-comedies such as *Cymbeline* (1609–10), Beaumont and Fletcher's *Philaster* (King's Men, 1609), and Fletcher's *The Night Walker* (Lady Elizabeth's?, 1611) and *The Honest Man's Fortune* (Lady Elizabeth's, 1613). In the city comedy tradition of *The Four Prentices* follow Haughton's *Englishmen for My Money* (Admiral's, 1598), Chapman's *May Day* (Chapel boys, 1602?), Heywood's *The Wise Woman of Hogsdon* (Queen Anne's, 1604), Barry's *Ram Alley* (King's Revels, 1608), Field's *Amends for Ladies* (Queen's Revels, 1611), and Middleton's *No Wit, No Help like a Woman's* (Lady Elizabeth's?, 1613) and *More Dissemblers Besides Women* (King's Men, 1615). The fact that the romances and tragi-comedies were, by and large, productions by the King's Men, and that the satiric comedies were, by and large, productions by other companies may not be altogether happenstance. Nor may the fact that satiric comedies far outnumber romantic comedies and tragi-comedies.

Satiric comedy's parodic ways with the female page's part are particularly high-spirited in Middleton's *More Dissemblers Besides Women*. 'Antonio' is constantly in comic danger of having her cover blown – by being asked to sing ('a pretty, womanish, faint, sprawling voice', one of the characters comments [4.2.78]), to share a bed, to go swimming in the nude, to dance ('did you ever see a boy begin a dance and make curtsy like a wench before?' [5.1.183–4]). Dancing proves especially awkward, since 'Antonio' is pregnant and is on the verge of giving birth! Not only his Italo-Shakespearean name but the fact that the Antonio of *Dissemblers* is supposed to have lost all his friends and money in a shipwreck (1.2.156–7), suggest that the object of parody in Middleton's play might specifically be *Twelfth Night*. The erotic interest this androgynous figure arouses is assigned by the speeches to the fools of the play. Most egregious among them is

Dondolo (cf. Italian *dondolone*, 'idler', 'loafer', from *dondolare*, 'to swing', 'to rock', 'to dally',), who presents himself as an experienced wencher but complains that 'Antonio' will not play the usual page's part and 'suffer me to come to bed to him' (3.1.84) nor ever go in swimming:

> There's no good fellowship in this dandiprat,
> This dive-dapper, as in other pages:
> They'd go a-swimming with me familiarly
> I' th' heat of summer, and clap what-you-call-'ems;
> But I could never get that little monkey yet
> To put off his breeches:

(3.1.91–6)

The Italy of *More Dissemblers* is no Illyria. Dondolo is no Orsino. The desires *he* entertains are not yours or mine – or so go the politics of satire. '*Enter* Page *in a female dress*' (5.2.214.SD): when reality triumphs over Dondolo's illusions in the play's last scene, the spectators are invited to laugh at the sport, not give themselves up to seduction. *This*, the script says, is reality; *that* is illusion.

From an inventory of scripts that feature female pages we come away with an impression of differences – differences not only with respect to gender and genre but differences with respect to who wrote the plays in question, just when those plays were acted, and which company it was that bought the script, mounted a production, and took a chance on its success. Stolen or not from the plumage of Robert Greene, boy-heroines disguised as pages seem to have been something of a speciality of the King's Men. In the romantic comedies of Shakespeare's earlier career and in the romantic tragi-comedies of his later career, as well as in the tragi-comedies that Beaumont and Fletcher supplied after Shakespeare's retirement, the King's Men seem, for a time, to have capitalized on this particular plot device. Not to be outdone, other companies – in particular, the Admiral's company at the Red Bull Theatre in Clerkenwell – seem to have seized on the *satiric* potential of their rivals' device. In this exchange of satire for romance we find just the pattern of appropriation and parody that Roslyn Knutson and Andrew Gurr have traced in the capitalist rivalry that governed London's public theatre companies from at least the 1590s through 1642 (Knutson 1991, Gurr, forthcoming). Even among plays acted by the King's Men, Shakespeare's scripts stand out by their difference: where scripts by other playwrights play up differences in gender among boy actor, female role, and male disguise, Shakespeare's scripts play up their ambiguity. Only in a script by Shakespeare does a boy actor, in the very last lines of the play, offer to kiss the audience.

Verifying differences in tragi-comedy

The homoerotic difference in comedy is gender; in tragedy it is power status. One might say that romantic comedy turns on gender difference that ends in likeness; tragedy, on gender likeness that ends in difference. Holding these differences in mind, we can see what a genuinely subversive figure Gaveston is. From his opening soliloquy straight through to the offstage fall of the executioner's axe in 3.2, Gaveston constantly threatens to turn the high-mimetic seriousness of the history play in which he happens to be a character into the low-mimetic liminality of a comedy. Music and poetry, he tells us, are Edward's delight. 'Therefore ile have Italian maskes by night,/ Sweete speeches, comedies, and pleasing showes.' Gaveston's idea of the theatre sounds very much like the Italian entertainments that Nashe, Coryate, and Sandys saw and scorned. When the actor playing Gaveston turns to specify the contents of these 'pleasing shows', he has in mind, not the actresses of Italy, but the transvestite boys of England: 'Like *Sylvian* Nimphes my pages shall be clad.' One particularly 'lovelie boye' will be dressed as Diana and hide with an olive branch 'those parts which men delight to see' (1.1.50–73). What Gaveston does, in effect, is to take Nashe's triad of serious drama and turn it on its head: English/male/tragedy would, if Gaveston had his way, become Italian/female/comedy. The masks, comedies, and shows that Gaveston proposes as royal entertainments admit a rampant eroticism for which the high seriousness of a history play has no room. Gaveston's threat of turning virile history into effeminate comedy is recognized from the start – and vigorously resisted – by Edward's peers. They see themselves as principals in an altogether different kind of play. After Gaveston's removal midway in Act 3, it is their vision of the play that holds sway. The consummation of homoerotic desire in *Edward II* is death.

Something of the same clash between comedy and tragedy, with happier results for the hero, can be witnessed in Marlowe's earlier play *Dido, Queen of Carthage*. As an induction to the Virgilian tragedy of Dido and Aeneas, Marlowe stages a comic scene out of Ovid and Lucian. When Ganymede asks a small favour, Jupiter promises the world: 'What ist sweet wagge I should deny thy youth?/. . . . / Sit on my knee, and call for thy content,/ Controule proud Fate, and cut the thred of time' (1.1.19, 24–5). What Ganymede wants has nothing to do with Fate, however: 'I would have a jewell for mine eare,/ And a fine brouch to put in my hand,/ And then Ile hugge with you an hundred times' (1.1.46–8). The most visible symbol of male homosexuality in Renaissance art, 'Ganymede' was likewise the commonest slang term for the *erōmenos*, the minion, in male/male couplings (Bray 1982: 13–32; Saslow 1985: 1–5; Brown 1990; Barkan 1991). 'Wild', 'vain', 'light-headed': the Ganymede of Marlowe's *Dido* shows himself to be just such a minion as Mortimer sees in Gaveston. As such, Ganymede provides a comic foil to Aeneas – 'great', 'conquering', 'stern', and 'grave' – who earns his tragic greatness by renouncing sexual desire.

To elide the generic differences between tragedy and comedy is to bring together two very different modes of simulating homoerotic desire onstage: a mode that defines erotic difference in all-male terms, with a mode that defines that difference in male/female terms; a mode that enacts desire through violence, with a mode that affirms concord; a mode that ends in difference, with a mode that celebrates likenesses; a mode that frustrates desire, with a mode that gives desire satisfaction. By displacing the radical 'tragedy', tragi-comedy calls into question those other radicals 'English' and 'male'.

The indeterminacy of tragi-comedy with respect to these radicals can be witnessed in four intertextually connected scripts acted in the first burst of tragi-comedy's popularity, between 1609 and 1613. *Philaster* and *Cymbeline*, two plays that the King's Men mounted on the same stage with the same cast in 1609–10, may both have last-minute happy endings brought about by maids in male disguise – maids played, perhaps, by the same boy actor – but Beaumont and Fletcher's characteristic way of deploying that device differs from Shakespeare's in one crucial detail. In his disguise as 'Fidele', the boy actor playing Imogen works the same erotic magic on the exiles in Wales as Rosalind does on Orlando in Arden or as Viola does on Orsino in Illyria. When 'Fidele' first shows up in Wales, the old royal retainer Belarius is thunderstruck by 'his' beauty. 'By Jupiter, an angel', he first exclaims, and then decides to grant the figure gender:

> or, if not,
> An earthly paragon. Behold divineness
> No elder than a boy.

(3.6.42–4)

The king's estranged sons, having never seen a woman before, don't know what to make of 'Fidele'. Guiderius almost believes him to be a maid ('Were you a woman, youth,/ I should woo hard but be your groom in honesty,/ Ay, bid for you as I'd buy'); Arviragus is willing to accept him as a boy ('He is a man, I'll love him as my brother' [3.6.66–91]). For all that, the two princes and their foster-father treat 'Fidele' as if he were a girl. 'Pray be not sick', Belarius pleads, 'For you must be our housewife' (4.2.43–4).

No such teasing is possible in *Philaster*, for one simple reason: the audience is no less deceived by the disguised heroine's gender than the characters in the play are. 'Bellario', the page who has taken service with Philaster before the play begins, seems, as far as the audience is concerned, to *be* Bellario. Only when the page has maliciously been accused of seducing Philaster's true lover – and Philaster himself believes it – does 'Bellario' step forward and reveal her true identity as Euphrasia, a nobleman's daughter who is herself enamoured of Philaster and has taken on a boy's disguise in order to be with him. 'Bellario'/Euphrasia pointedly denies having acted out of sexual passion. 'After you were gone', she confesses to Philaster in the play's last scene,

I grew acquainted with my heart, and search't
What stir'd it so, alas I found it Love,
Yet farre from Lust, for could I but have lived
In presence of you, I had had my end.   (5.5.167–71)

Her sentiments are convenient, since Philaster is presently betrothed to his true love Arathusa, who graciously takes Euphrasia into her service. Even if some members of the audience have suspected a ruse all along – and have taken erotic pleasure in the secret – Euphrasia's disavowal of passion in the end gives such spectators an excuse to disown their pleasure, just as they would at the end of a city comedy. In *Philaster*, as in Jonson's *Epicoene*, also acted in 1609, the final effect of confidence tricks on the audience is to play up *differences* in gender, not their ambiguity (Rackin 1987). Having been tricked, however delightfully, the audience gets a first-hand lesson in the difference between appearance and reality.

If one suspects Beaumont and Fletcher of making sport with a shop-worn theatrical prop in *Philaster*, those suspicions are confirmed in Fletcher's *The Honest Man's Fortune*, acted four years later, when the page Veramour – who, it turns out, really *is* the boy he appears to be – arouses suspicion that he is a lady in disguise. The character who thinks so is Laverdine, a clothes-horse courtier familiar from the verse satires of Jonson, Donne, and Marston. 'A woman! how happy am I! now we may lawfully come together, without fear of hanging', Laverdine exclaims when Veramour first confirms his suspicions in 4.1 (Fletcher 1843:419). To encourage the fool further in his delusion Veramour shows up for the play's last scene in woman's clothes. When Laverdine seizes the occasion to beg the 'lady's' hand, 'her' master Montague assures Laverdine that 'she' is really a he:

MONT.   This! 'tis my page, sir.
VER.   No, sir; I am a poor disguiséd lady,
         That like a page have follow'd you full long,
         for love, God wot.
ALL.   A lady!
LAV.   Yes, yes; 'tis a lady.
MONT.   It may be so; and yet we have lain together,
         But, by my troth, I never found her lady.
DUCH.   Why wore you boy's clothes?
VER.   I'll tell you, madam;
         I took example by two or three plays, that methought
         Concerned me.
                                                    (5.3, p. 450)

Among those two or three plays, surely, were *Cymbeline*, *Philaster* and *Epicoene*. The happy ending of *The Honest Man's Fortune* may turn on totally unexpected changes of heart on the part of the political protagonists, but, in moments like this one, the comedy in Fletcher's tragi-comedy is not romance but satire. The Orlando-figure, the character who falls in love with Ganymede, is ostracized as a fool.

The mercurial place of homoerotic desire in tragi-comedy is illustrated most strikingly, perhaps, by an episode in another tragi-comedy inspired by *Cymbeline*, Heywood's *The Golden Age*. Mounted at the Red Bull Theatre in Clerkenwell in 1610 as the first in a series of *Ages* plays that extended to 1612, Heywood's epic trivialization of every pagan myth in the book is full of divine epiphanies and spectacular effects that capitalize on the commercial success that Jupiter's descent in *Cymbeline*, Hermione's metamorphosis in *The Winter's Tale*, and Prospero's feats of magic in *The Tempest* were commanding in the Blackfriars and across the river. When it comes time for Ganymede's brief quarter-hour on the stage, Heywood turns to tragedy, not comedy, as the mode for his appearance. Unlike the cheeky boy who opens Marlowe's *Dido* or inspires Rosalind's disguise, Heywood's Ganymede strides onstage with the swagger of an Achilles or an Aufidius. He squares off against Jupiter as a combatant in the war of Saturn's offspring against their father. The taunting speeches, the physical fight, the swift passage from steel weapons to a muscular embrace distinctly recall the confrontations of Ajax and Hector and of Aufidius and Coriolanus:

Alarme. Enter Ganimed *compast in with soliders, to them* Jupiter, Neptune, Pluto, Archas, Melliseus.

JUP.   Yeeld noble Troian, ther's not in the field
    One of thy Nation lifts a hand save thee.

GAN.   Why that's my honour, when alone I stand
    Gainst thee and all the forces of thy land.

JUP.   I love thy valour, and would woo thy friendship,
    Go freely where thou wilt, and ransomlesse.

GAN.   Why that's no gift: I am no prisoner,
    And therefore owe no ransome, having breath,
    Know I have vow'd to yeeld to none save death.

JUP.   I wish thee nobly Troian, and since favour
    Cannot attaine thy love, I'le try conclusions,
    And see if I can purchase it with blowes.

GAN.   Now speak'st thou like the noblest of my foes.

JUP.   Stand all a-part, and Princes girt us round.

GAN.   I love him best, whose strokes can lowdest sound.

Alarme, they fight, and loosing their weapons embrace.

JUP.   I have thee, and will keep thee.

GAN. Not as prisoner.
JUP. A prisoner to my love, else thou art free,
    My bosome friend, for so I honour thee.
GAN. I am conquer'd both by Armes and Courtesie.

(8:75–6)

However ambiguous 'love' and 'friend' may be, it is hard to imagine that Heywood, his actors, or his audience could forget what Ganymede meant in art – or in slang. Certainly, in his *Pleasant Dialogues and Dramma's* (1637) Heywood seems altogether savvy about Jupiter's interest in the sometime shepherd boy: 'Although this Fable to the gods extends,/ Base sordid lust in man it reprehends', Heywood warns in his prefatory remarks to the jealous dialogue between Jupiter and Juno on the subject of Ganymede (1903: ll.3680–1). Jupiter and Ganymede, characters who figure in Marlowe's *Dido* as the conquering *erastēs* and light-headed *erōmenos* of satiric comedy, are thrust by Heywood into the ethos of an Elizabethan history play. In that ethos, Jupiter and Ganymede enact homoerotic desire in the same high-mimetic guise as Achilles and Patroclus, Ajax and Hector, and Aufidius and Coriolanus – but with this tragi-comic difference: the embrace that closes their combat is never ruptured by swords. Tragedy/comedy, male/female, England/not England: in the tragi-comedy of *The Golden Age* Heywood has dramatized two of these radicals but not the third. Heywood's *Ages* plays, like the repertory of the Red Bull Theatre in general, exhibit a groundedness in the English here-and-now that seems far removed from the liminal horizons of Shakespeare's tragi-comedies, or even of Beaumont and Fletcher's. Likely sharing the boards with the *Ages* plays at the Red Bull in 1610–12 were Heywood's *The Fair Maid of the West*, John Cooke's *The City Gallant*, and Dekker's *Match Me in London*. It is the indeterminacy of tragi-comedy, its fusion of high mimetic modes and low, that allows Heywood to make room for homoerotic desire in his Olympus-on-the-Fleet where most city comedies close it out. The variable and volatile place of homoerotic desire in Jacobean tragi-comedy has much to do with the variable and volatile place of homosexual behaviour in Jacobean society (Bray 1982: 76; Goldberg 1983: 141–7; Bray 1990; Smith 1991: 73–6; Bergeron 1991: 29–31).

Genres with different conventions for portraying sexual 'desire', plays with different plots, playwrights with different temperaments and abilities, acting companies with different clienteles and different specialities, individual actors with different talents and different habits, spectators with different preoccupations and different sensibilities: all of these things make a difference. If homosexual 'desire' is so difficult to fix in fiction – and in only one medium of fiction-making, at that – we should be wary indeed of saying anything about the desires of historical subjects who have been dead for 400 years. It is suggestive, none the less, that tragedy and satiric comedy both seem calculated to engage homosexual desire, only to deny it in the end. In Freud's terms, both genres look like strategies of displacement; in Foucault's terms, like mechanisms of social control; in Derrida's terms, like a means of reifying 'male' as a radical and ridding it of contradictions. Dead men and fools: these are the characters who speak about homosexual desire in tragedy and in satire. They are 'not me', with a vengeance. Only in romantic comedy, and in tragi-comedies played out within that comic mode, does homosexual 'desire' assume a face, a body, and a voice that desire can congenially inhabit beyond the two hours' traffic of the stage.

Notes

1 The attention I give in this essay to difference is informed, of course, by Jacques Derrida, *Of Grammatology*, trans. Gayatri Chakravorty Spivak (Baltimore: Johns Hopkins University Press, 1976). Semiological concerns are, however, qualified here by respect for the dictates of genre, for the exigencies of script-writing as a commercial enterprise, and for categories of experience constructed by early modern witnesses themselves. On genre see Frye (1957), particularly pp. 186–206, 223–39, on romance and satire as two quite distinct modes of comedy. On the commercial conditions of writing plays and acting them in early modern London see Gurr (1980 and forthcoming). On the new awareness that many contemporary cultural anthropologists bring to differences between their own analytical categories and the subjective experience of their informants see Clifford (1986), Tyler (1986), and Shweder (1991).

2. 'When a man loves the beautiful, what does he desire?' Diotima asks Socrates in one of the great set-pieces of the *Symposium*. Socrates replies, 'That the beautiful may be his' (329).

3. 'Those who love for the sake of utility love for the sake of what is good for *themselves*, and those who love for the sake of pleasure for the sake of what is pleasant to *themselves*, and not in so far as the other is the person loved but in so far as he is useful or pleasant.' Falling in love, and out of love, is particularly characteristic of young people, 'for the greater part of the friendship of love depends on emotion and aims at pleasure; this is why they fall in love and quickly fall out of love, often changing within a single day' (*Nicomachean Ethics* 1156a).

4. In infancy, Freud postulates:

   when the very incipient sexual gratifications were still connected with the taking of nourishment, the sexual instinct had a sexual object outside one's own body, in the mother's breast. This object is later lost, perhaps at the very time when it becomes possible for the child to form a general picture of the person to whom the organ granting him satisfaction belongs. The sexual instinct later regularly becomes autoerotic, and only after overcoming the latency period is the original relation re-established. It is not without good reason that the suckling of the child at the mother's breast has become a model for every love relation. Object-finding is really a re-finding.

   (614)

5. 'The Greeks called him a "poet", which name hath, as the most excellent, gone through other languages. It cometh of this word *poiein*, which is, to make:

wherein, I know not whether by luck or wisdom, we Englishmen have met with the Greeks in calling him a maker . . .' (Sidney 1966: 22).

6. 'Than, these goodly pageants being done, every mate sorts to his mate, every one brings another homeward of their way verye freendly, and in their secret conclaves (covertly) they play *the Sodomits*, or worse. And these be the fruits of Playes and Enterluds for the most part' (Stubbes, 1877–9: 144–5).

7. 'Nay, but to live / In the rank sweat of an inseamèd bed,/ Stewed in corruption, honeying and making love / Over the nasty sty—' (*Hamlet* 3.4.81–4); 'your daughter and the Moor are now making the beast with two backs' (*Othello* 1.1.117–19); 'Though this knave came something saucily into the world before he was sent for, yet was his mother fair, there was good sport at his making, and the whoreson must be acknowledged' (*The Tragedy of King Lear* 1.1.20–3); 'My father compounded with my mother under the Dragon's tail and my nativity was under Ursa Major, so that it follows I am rough and lecherous. Fut! I should have been that I am had the maidenliest star in the firmament twinkled on my bastardizing' (*The Tragedy of King Lear* 1.2.126–30).

8. By order of the Senate, Terrentius tells Lepidus, Sejanus was condemned to lose his head, 'which was no sooner off,/ But that, and the unfortunate trunk were seized/ By the rude multitude; who not content/ With what the forward justice of the state/ Officiously hath done, with violent rage/ Have rent it limb from limb./ . . . / These mounting at his head, these at his face,/ These digging out his eyes, those with his brain,/ Sprinkling themselves, their houses, and their friends;/ Others are met, have ravished thence an arm,/ And deal small pieces of the flesh for favours;/ These with a thigh; this hath cut off his hands;/ And this his feet; These fingers, and these toes; That hath his liver; he his heart: there wants/ Nothing but room for wrath, and place for hatred!' (5.796–801, 808–16).

9. The dates and auspices that I have adopted are those specified or suggested in the chronological table appended to *The Cambridge Companion to English Renaissance Drama* (Braunmuller and Hattaway 1990: 419–46). Michael Shapiro's forthcoming book *Shakespeare and the Tradition of Boy Heroines in Male Disguise* will include two appendices, one cataloguing sources, analogues, and models, another providing a complete chronological listing of plays with heroines in male disguise.

References

Anon. (1913) *Look About You*, ed. W. W. Greg, Malone Society Reprints, vol. 37, Oxford: Oxford University Press.

Aristotle (1925) *Ethica Nicomachea*, in *Works*, trans. W. D. Ross, vol. 9, Oxford: Clarendon Press.

Barkan, Leonard (1991) *Transuming Passion: Ganymede and the Erotics of Humanism*, Stanford: Stanford University Press.

Beaumont, Francis, and John Fletcher (1966), *Philaster*, in Fredson Bowers (gen. ed.) *The Dramatic Works in the Beaumont and Fletcher Canon*, vol. 1, Cambridge: Cambridge University Press.

Bergeron, David M. (1991) *Royal Family, Royal Lovers: King James of England and Scotland*, Columbia: University of Missouri Press.

Braunmuller, A. R., and Michael Hattaway (eds) (1990) *The Cambridge Companion to English Renaissance Drama*, Cambridge: Cambridge University Press.

Bray, Alan (1982) *Homosexuality in Renaissance England*, London: Gay Men's Press.

————(1990) 'Homosexuality and the signs of male friendship in Elizabethan England', *History Workshop Journal* 29: 1–19.

Brown, Steve (1990) 'The boyhood of Shakespeare's heroines: Notes on gender ambiguity in the sixteenth century', *Studies in English Literature* 30: 243–64.

Clifford, James (1986) 'On ethnographical allegory', in James Clifford and George E. Marcus (eds) *Writing Culture*, Berkeley: University of California Press.

Coryate, Thomas (1611) *Coryate's crudities. Hastily gobled up in five moneths travells in France, Savoy, Italy, Rhetia . . . Switzerland, some parts of high Germany, and the Netherlands . . .* , London: William Stansby.

Derrida, Jacques (1976) *Of Grammatology*, trans. Gayatri Chakravorty Spivak, Baltimore: Johns Hopkins University Press.

Dover, K. J. (1978) *Greek Homosexuality*, New York: Random House.

Fletcher, John (1843) *The Honest Man's Fortune*, in Alexander Dyce (ed.) *Works* (of Beaumont and Fletcher), vol. 3, London: Edward Moxon.

Foucault, Michel (1978) *The History of Sexuality: An Introduction*, trans. Robert Hurley, New York: Pantheon.

Freeburg, Victor Oscar (1915) *Disguise Plots in Elizabethan Drama*, New York: Columbia University Press.

Freud, Sigmund (1938) *Three Contributions to the Theory of Sex*, in A. A. Brill (ed.) *Basic Writings*, New York: Modern Library.

Frye, Northrop (1957) *The Anatomy of Criticism*, Princeton: Princeton University Press.

Garber, Marjorie (1991) *Vested Interests: Cross-Dressing and Cultural Anxiety*, New York: Routledge.

Goldberg, Jonathan (1983) *James I and the Politics of Literature*, Baltimore: Johns Hopkins University Press.

Gras, Henk (1991) ' "As I am a man": Aspects of the presentation and audience perception of the Elizabethan female page', paper presented at the World Congress of the International Shakespeare Association, Tokyo.

Greene, Robert (1970) *The Scottish History of James the Fourth*, ed. Norman Sanders, London: Methuen.

Gurr, Andrew (1980) *The Shakespearean Stage, 1574–1642*, Cambridge: Cambridge University Press.

————(forthcoming) *A History of the London Playing Companies to 1642*, Cambridge: Cambridge University Press.

Hegel, Friedrich (1975) *Aesthetics: Lectures on Fine Art*, trans. T. M. Knox, Oxford: Clarendon Press.

Heywood, Thomas (1874a) *The Four Prentices of London*, in *Dramatic Works*, vol. 2, London: J. Pearson.

————(1874b) *The Golden Age*, in *Dramatic Works*, vol. 8, London: J. Pearson.

————(1903) *Pleasant Dialogues and Dramma's*, ed. W. W. Bang, Louvain: Uystpruyst.

Howard, Jean E. (1988) 'Crossdressing, the theatre, and gender struggle in early modern England', *Shakespeare Quarterly* 39, 4: 418–40.

Jardine, Lisa (1989) *Still Harping on Daughters*, rev. edn, New York: Columbia University Press.

Jonson, Ben (1981) *Sejanus*, in G. A. Wilkes (ed.) *The Complete Plays*, Oxford: Clarendon Press.

Knutson, Roslyn (1991) *The Repertory of Shakespeare's Company 1594–1613*, Fayetteville: University of Arkansas Press.

Marlowe, Christopher (1973) *The Complete Works*, ed. Fredson Bowers, 2 vols, Cambridge: Cambridge University Press.

Middleton, Thomas (1885) *More Dissemblers Besides Women* in A. H. Bullen (ed.) *Dramatic Works*, vol. 6, London: John D. Nimmo.
——(1976) *No Wit, No Help Like a Woman's*, ed. Lowell E. Johnson, Lincoln: University of Nebraska Press.
Nashe, Thomas (1910) *Pierce Penilesse His Supplication to the Divell*, in Ronald B. McKerrow (ed.) *Works*, vol. 1, London: Sidgwick & Jackson.
Orgel, Stephen (1989) 'Nobody's perfect: or why did the English stage take boys for women?', *South Atlantic Quarterly* 88, 1: 7–29.
Plato (1937) *Symposium*, in *The Dialogues*, trans. B. Jowett, vol. 2, New York: Random House.
Rackin, Phyllis (1987) 'Androgyny, mimesis, and the marriage of the boy heroine on the English Renaissance stage', *PMLA*, 102: 29–41.
Salgado, Gamini (1975) *Eyewitnesses of Shakespeare: First-hand Accounts of Performances 1590–1890*, New York: Barnes & Noble.
Sandys, George (1615) *A Relation of a Journey begun Anno Domini 1610 . . . Containing a description of the Turkish Empire, of Aegypt, of the Holy Land, of the Remote parts of Italy, and Ilands adjoyning*, 2nd edn, London: W. Barrett.
Saslow, James M. (1985) *Ganymede in the Renaissance: Homosexuality in Art and Society*, New Haven: Yale University Press.
Shakespeare, William (1986) *The Complete Works*, gen. eds Stanley Wells and Gary Taylor, Oxford: Clarendon Press.
Shapiro, Michael *Shakespeare and the Tradition of Boy Heroines in Male Disguise*, forthcoming.
Shweder, Richard A. (1991) *Thinking Through Cultures: Expeditions in Cultural Psychology*, Cambridge, Mass.: Harvard University Press.
Sidney, Philip (1966) *A Defence of Poetry*, ed. J. A. Van Dorsten, Oxford: Oxford University Press.
Smith, Bruce R. (1991) *Homosexual Desire in Shakespeare's England: A Cultural Poetics*, Chicago: University of Chicago Press.
Stubbes, Phillip (1877–9) *The Anatomie of Abuses*, ed. F. J. Furnivall, London: New Shakespeare Society.
Thompson, Sith (1955–8) *Motif-Index of Folk-Literature*, 6 vols, Bloomington: Indiana University Press.
Tyler, Stephen A. (1986) 'Post-modern ethnography: From document of the occult to occult document', in James Clifford and George E. Marcus (eds) *Writing Culture*, Berkeley: University of California Press.
Vernant, Jean-Pierre (1972) 'Greek tragedy: Problems of interpretation', in Richard Macksey and Eugenio Donato (eds) *The Structuralist Controversy*, Baltimore: Johns Hopkins University Press.
Vernant, Jean-Pierre (1983) 'Ambiguity and reversal: On the enigmatic structure of *Oedipus Rex*', rpt in Erich Segal (ed.), *Greek Tragedy: Modern Essays in Criticism*, New York: Harper & Row.

Chapter 9

The (in)significance of 'lesbian' desire in early modern England

Valerie Traub

The 'lesbian desire' of my title is a deliberate come-on. If this is the last you hear of it, it is because, enticing as it may sound, it doesn't exist. Not, at least, as such. For the conceptual framework within which was articulated an early modern discourse of female desire is radically different from that which governs our own modes of perception and experience. If, as David Halperin reminds us, we have witnessed only one hundred years of homosexuality (Halperin 1990), then how is the even more recent discursive invention, the lesbian, to be related to sexual systems of four hundred years ago? The following discussion attempts to begin to answer that question by examining the asymmetrical representations of three early modern discursive figures: the French female sodomite, the English tribade, and the theatrical 'femme'. My intent is to keep alive our historical difference from early modern women and at the same time to show how historically distant representations of female desire *can* be correlated, though not in any simple fashion, to modern systems of intelligibility and political efficacy. This essay is at once an act of historical recovery and a meditation on the difficulties inhering in such an act.

In *A View of Ancient Laws Against Immorality and Profaneness*, published in 1729, John Disney reviews ancient vice laws from the perspective of a Protestant Englishman. Beginning his compendium of sexual sins with a chapter entitled 'Of the Incentives to Vice, ill company, obscene Talk, and lewd Books or Pictures' and proceeding to such matters as 'Of Polygamy', 'Of Incestuous Lewdnesse' and 'Of Rape', the ten chapters of Section One exhaustively order people and behaviours according to their alleged deviations from 'nature'. What immediately strikes anyone who has read Michel Foucault's *The History of Sexuality* is the implicit shift as the volume progresses from categories of being – 'Common Whores, and such that frequent them', 'Bawds, Procurers, Pimps, &c' – to categories of acts – concubinage, adultery, sodomy and bestiality. But something more peculiar than this division animates Disney's categories. In the final chapter, 'Of Sodomy and Bestiality', not only are these two deviations linked, as they commonly were, in a rather strained narrative of causality,[1] but no mention is made of women. Defining sodomy as 'the unnatural Conjunction of Men with Men or Boys' (Disney 1729: 180–1), Disney thwarts our modern expectation that all those engaged in same-gender erotic acts belong together. Used as we are to linking the identities and political fates of gay men and lesbians under the medico-scientific label of 'homosexuality' or the political banner of 'gay rights', Disney's silence about sexual 'conjunction' among women seems odd, especially when we note that the only chapters focusing on women are 'Of Common Whores' and 'Of What the Roman laws called Stuprum; the Lewdnesse of (or with) unmarried Women, who are *not* Common Whores' (emphasis mine). This exacting division between those women who are lewd with men for money and those who are lewd with men for free provides a negative contrast against which must be measured any attempt to articulate a discourse of lewdness (pecuniary or not) between women.

A second curiosity arises when we note that in his discussion of prostitution, Disney conventionally cites Deuteronomy 23:17: 'There shall be no Whore of the Daughters of Israel; nor a sodomite of the sons of Israel', parenthetically glossing 'sodomite' as 'whoremaster', and registering his incredulity that 'How our [biblical] Translators came to think of a *Sodomite* here, is hard to say . . .' (Disney 1729). For Disney, the biblical 'sodomite', linked in Deuteronomy to female prostitution, must refer to a pimp, not to a male prostitute. Disney's dependence upon discrete, mutually exclusive categories of sexual sin gives his treatise an acute definitional clarity: not only can women not be sodomites; men cannot be whores.

We know, however, that men *could* be whores, not only because early modern plays employ the word and its variants to describe male characters, but because anti-theatrical tracts obsessively articulate the anxiety that men will use their 'feminized' bodies as loose women do (Kinney 1974; Stubbes 1583; Prynne 1632–3). Indeed, in the anti-theatricalists' conflation of the male sodomite and the male whore we find precisely the interpenetration of categories that Disney's treatise, one hundred years later, so assiduously denies.[2]

If we recognize in Disney's tract not the idiosyncrasies of an individual but the discourse of a culture, we gain a point of access into the historical obscurity of early modern women's erotic desires for one another. For if the gender of the whore was not delimited in early modern culture, other categories of sexual sin may not have been as rigidly fixed as Disney would have us believe. In so far as *A View of Ancient Laws Against Immorality and Profaneness* demonstrates an Enlightenment attempt to stabilize, codify and delimit those desires and practices which previously may have been unstable, resistant to codification, and defiant of limits, it suggests that what is at stake is the instability of gender within categories of sexuality.

Such anxiety about gender instability usefully illuminates and contextualizes the historical vacuum into which early modern women's erotic desires for one another seem to fall.[3] We know that prior to the codifications and normalizations initiated by eighteenth- and nineteenth-century criminology, sexology, and psychology, same-gender desire *in England* was, despite the apocalyptic talk about sodomy, hardly regulated at all (Bray 1982). We also know that theology and the law are only *two* social discourses, and not necessarily the most revealing of popular ideologies or practices. And yet, within our contemporary critical discussions, the theological and, more importantly, legal category of sodomy has functioned implicitly as a regulatory mechanism, pre-empting all possibility of analysis precisely because the discourse of law has stood as arbiter of social fact: if no Englishwoman was brought to trial under the sodomy statute, *ipso facto* no women practised such behaviours.

If we look for the inscription of Englishwomen within the confines of the category of sodomy, we will find only absence, hear only silence. But if we shift our gaze slightly, away from exclusive attention on theological treatises, legal statutes, and court cases, and toward other discourses concerned with the representation and regulation of female sexuality – gynaecology and stage-plays, for instance – we discover a discourse of desires and acts that not only can be articulated but correlated with our modern understanding of diverse erotic practices among women. That discourse, of course, is not authored by women; it is highly mediated by the protocols of patriarchal control. At the same time, in its particular representations of female desire, and in its expression of anxiety (or, perhaps more significantly, *lack* of anxiety) about desire among women, it dramatizes the particular conventions according to which such desire was culturally 'staged'. As critics and historians, the difficulty we face is not necessarily the lack of erotically desiring women, but our inability to crack the code organizing the conceptual categories of an earlier culture. Once that code is recognized, our task becomes not only the detection of a discourse of such desire, but delineating that discourse's proper parameters and evaluating its various ideological effects.

Before moving to gynaecological and theatrical discourses, however, it is necessary to point out that the conceptual categories and codes of different nations varied. Contrary to the experience of Englishwomen, Frenchwomen *were* prosecuted under sodomy statutes (Daston and Park 1985). Consider the following anecdote with which Stephen Greenblatt begins his essay 'Fiction and friction':

In September 1580, as he passed through a small French town . . . Montaigne was told an unusual story that he duly recorded in his travel journal. It seems that seven or eight girls . . . plotted together 'to dress up as males and thus continue their life in the world.' One of them set up as a weaver . . . fell in love with a woman, courted her, and married. The couple lived together for four or five months, to the wife's satisfaction, '*so they say.*' But then, Montaigne reports, the transvestite was

recognized . . . 'the matter was brought to justice, and she was condemned to be hanged, which she said she would rather undergo than
return to a girl's status; and she was hanged for using *illicit devices* to
supply her *defect* in sex'.[4]

(Greenblatt 1988: 66, emphasis mine)

I recall Greenblatt's use of Montaigne's anecdote in order to suggest that
desire among women is revealed less in the discourse of the authorities – the
trial and execution that took place just days before Montaigne's visit to the
French town where the story was narrated to him – than in the discourse of
the community, whose members were sifting the controversy through their
own understandings of appropriate gender roles and their curiosity about
the variety of erotic practices. That popular discourse is apparent in those
ambivalently coded, anonymously referring words 'so they say', which
follow the widespread community affirmation of 'the wife's satisfaction'.
People in that small French town were talking, and talking publicly enough
for a stranger to overhear the details of the couple's conjugal relations,
including their four or five months of apparently mutual erotic pleasure.

As this and other cases suggest, in the French context, sodomy for women
is defined as the use of illicit sexual devices, devices which, as Greenblatt
later remarks, 'enable a woman to take the part of a man' (Greenblatt 1988:
67).[5] Indeed, we possess a historical record of such cases not primarily
because the women desired or seduced other women, but because of their
prosthetic use of implements of penetration.[6] French sodomy, by definition,
entails penetration; legal discourse demanded rigorous definitions of *proof*,
and penetration seemed to meet that test. By means of this definition, an
implicit distinction is set up between, on the one hand, sinful *desires* and
criminal *acts* and, on the other hand, those sexual practices that do not
involve penetration and those that do.[7] Neither a Frenchwoman's *desire* for
another woman, nor any nonpenetrative acts she might commit were crimes,
but the prosthetic supplementation of her body was grounds for execution.

This concern about the supplementation of women's bodies crosses the
Channel in those French and English gynaecological texts which repeatedly
refer to female sexual organs growing beyond 'normal' bounds.[8] An
enlarged clitoris was believed to cause 'unnatural' desires in a body already
defined as sexually excessive. Writes Helkiah Crooke in the 1631 edition
of *A Description of the Body of Man*:

[S]ometimes [the clitoris] groweth to such a length that it hangeth without
the cleft like a mans member, especially when it is fretted with the touch
of the cloaths, and so strutteth and groweth to a rigiditie as doth the
yarde [penis] of a man. And this part it is which those wicked women
do abuse called Tribades (often mentioned by many authors, and in some
states worthily punished) to their mutual and unnatural lusts.[9]

(Crooke 1631: 238)

The reference to tribadism in the discourse of gynaecology complicates the operation of sodomy as a legal if not moral category. Indeed, the asymmetrical prosecution of French and English 'tribades' under sodomy statutes brings to light an irregular fracturing of the early modern conceptual terrain. Yet, when we shift our focus from legal categories, we find a previously undetected structural coherence unifying the French and English divide: both gynaecological tribadism and statutory sodomy depend upon a logic of supplementarity for their condition of possibility, with tribadism functioning through anatomical rather than artificial supplementation. The discursive shift from a legal concern with prosthesis to a medical focus on clitoral hypertrophy enacts only a slight distinction within an overall economy of the supplement. Both discourses fail to distinguish between specific sexual acts: penetration, rubbing of clitoris on thigh or pudendum, and auto-erotic or partnered masturbation. Instead, they employ vague analogies to male sexual practices, as in Jane Sharp's *The Midwives Book* (1671), which reports that sometimes the clitoris 'grows so long that it hangs forth at the slit like a Yard, and will swell and stand stiff if it be provoked, and some lewd women have endeavoured to use it as men do theirs' (Sharp 1671: 45).[10] Whether employing a dildo or her enlarged clitoris, a sodomite's or tribade's 'natural', 'feminine' body becomes, in the gendered discourse of both nations, 'masculine'.

And yet . . . the terms by which such supplementation have been defined heretofore not only describe but *reproduce* gender ideology. In particular, in the passages cited above, Greenblatt's rhetorical style collapses any distance that might obtain between early modern ideology and a postmodern feminist understanding of female-centred erotic acts. His rigorous adherence to the replication of not only Renaissance discourses, but dominant discourses within the Renaissance, leads to a failure to articulate the multiple, sometimes contradictory, meanings that erotic acts can express, and, in particular, obscures whatever meanings the use of 'illicit devices' signified for the women involved. Within Greenblatt's rhetoric, as within the rhetoric of early modern authorities, the commingling of two female bodies is subsumed by a heterosexual, male-oriented narrative: female penetration signifies an *imitation* of male (body and role-defined) '*parts*'. Whatever independent agency obtains in the performance of such erotic acts is rendered invisible at the same time as it is resecured into a patriarchal economy. Gaining no metacritical distance on the problems of representation and power posed by the 'conjunction' of female bodies, Greenblatt implicitly, if unintentionally, preserves gender as an essence – it can be imitated, but not, ultimately, subverted.

The fact that the model of imitation was favoured by early modern legal and medical authorities prompts my search for a more dynamic and heteronomous understanding of the ways erotic pleasure was achieved. Here, it seems necessary to employ a postmodern feminist analytic to create a conceptual space wherein erotic acts might be conceived differently than in the terms inscribed by the dominant ideology. Although we possess no first-person accounts written by 'tribades' or female 'sodomites', their actions were neither wholly imitative nor wholly autonomous. Taking place within a system of signification that precedes them, their erotic practice is moulded by a set of conventions and contingencies for possible action – which does not, however, exhaust the meanings such practices signified to and for the women themselves.

If, as Judith Butler argues, gender is not only a representation, but a performance staged within the enclosure of cultural coordinates; and if masculinity is not an essential trait but a cultural production (Butler 1991), then what these women perform is, in the words of Jonathan Dollimore, a 'transgressive reinscription' of gender and erotic codes (Dollimore 1991). At once repetition *and* transgression, such reinscription displaces conventional understandings from *within* dominant systems of intelligibility. Indeed, by using the term 'supplement', I have been importing deliberately a Derridean instrument to break open the gender codes that have heretofore delimited the terms by which tribadism and sodomy are conceived. Derrida employs the notion of supplementarity as that which both adds to *and* replaces the original term; an instance of 'différance', the supplement deconstructs the putative unity, integrity, and singularity of the subject, of its gender and its sexual desires, and registers them as always internally *different* from themselves (Derrida 1974). Early modern women's prosthetic supplementation of their bodies is, I would argue, both additive and substitutive: as a material addition to the woman's body and as a replacement of the man's body *by* the woman's, it not only displaces male prerogatives, but exposes 'man' as a simulacrum, and gender as a construction built on the faulty ground of exclusive, binary difference. Indeed, in the authorities' discourse, the enlarged clitoris and the dildo become objects of cultural *fantasy*. Which is not to imply that there did not exist real confusion about the status of and differentiation between male and female 'yards'; but it is to suggest that the meanings attached to women's appendages exceed the biological. It is not scientifically established anatomical norms, but gender expectations that manifest themselves in descriptions of 'tribades'. I would go so far as to argue that the enlarged clitoris and the dildo take on the quality of a fetish, a stand-in for a lost object of desire. The question is, whose desire is being represented in these accounts? What the authoritative discourse reveals is less the desire of the women than the authorities' desire for the (always already missing) phallus precisely at the moment of its literal displacement; and Greenblatt's account tacitly repeats this gesture by focusing on the replacement rather than the pleasures afforded by the performance of erotic supplementarity.

Primarily at issue, it seems to me, is not sexuality but gender. In England and in France, in gynaecology and the law, it is not woman's desire for other women, but her usurpation of male prerogatives that incites writers to record and thus reveal the anxieties of their (and our) culture. What, then, of a female erotic practice that did not involve the use of a supplement? Although I have only a tentative response to this question, it seems worth noting that whereas such practices are *not* recorded by gynaecology and the law, they *are* the subject of many early modern stage-plays. From Shakespeare's *A Midsummer Night's Dream* (1594–5) to his collaboration with Fletcher on *The Two Noble Kinsmen* (1613), from Heywood's *The Golden Age* (1611) to Shirley's *The Bird in a Cage* (1632–3), what we might call not a little anachronistically 'femme-femme' love is registered as a viable if ultimately untenable state.[11] By turning to early modern theatrical representations, I want to stress that although they do not function mimetically to reveal erotic practices, they indicate discursively a broader range of desires than those inscribed by gynaecology and the law. Early modern drama does not express women's self-perceptions and experiences, but it does provide an index to how the male-authored culture imagined, impersonated, and regulated their desires.

In the absence of a historically accurate term for such desires, I will provisionally call them 'homoerotic', in order to differentiate between, on the one hand, the early modern legal and medical discourses of sodomy and tribadism and, on the other hand, the modern identificatory classifications of 'lesbian', 'gay', and 'homosexual'. Neither a category of self nor normatively male, the term 'homoerotic' retains both the necessary strangeness and historical contiguity between early modern and postmodern forms of desire.

Before discussing female homoeroticism, it is important to note that when placed within the context of gynaecological and legal discourses, the prominence of female cross-dressing on the English Renaissance stage takes on a very specific meaning. It is not just that transvestism accorded female characters the linguistic and social powers of men, nor that the phenomenon itself registered cultural anxieties about the instability of gender identity, but that male clothes worked as external projections, theatrical equivalents, of the cultural fantasy of the enlarged clitoris. Theatrical transvestism, in short, was also prosthetic; the donning of masculine dress enacts the logic of the supplement through the displacement of the body to the clothes. Signifying the independent use of a woman's always possibly inordinately endowed clitoris, cross-dressing not only masculinizes but eroticizes the female body. Such a displaced equivalence gives a more situated, more *embodied* meaning to many critics' current understanding of female transvestism as a strategic appropriation of the phallus.[12]

The prosthetic logic of cross-dressing also enables us to achieve some metacritical distance from our dependence on the transvestite heroine as the privileged stage representative of early modern female desire. The mutability of desire that infuses so many early modern plays tempts us to depend on the changeability of dress as the originating instance of homo-eroticism. But, I wonder whether we have not inadvertently brought the 'epistemology of the closet', to invoke Eve Sedgwick's phrase, to bear on a world prior to closets (Sedgwick 1990). Did homoeroticism have to be physically disguised to be articulated? Or were there other ways of register-ing the expression of female homoeroticism while psychologically dispelling any anxieties such expression might elicit? The problem is not only that female transvestism has seemed the only means of access into homoerotic-ism, but that the result has been a privileging of Viola's self-indictment in Shakespeare's *Twelfth Night* (1603):

> Disguise, I see, thou art a wickedness
> Wherein the pregnant enemy does much. . . .
> How will this fadge? My master loves her dearly,
> And I, poor monster, fond as much on him.
>
> (2.2.27–34)

Not only is cross-dressing presented as wicked, but a homoerotic position to desire is implicitly monstrous. In contemporary critical practice, Viola's articu-lation of anxiety has implicitly served as the summation of sixteenth- and seventeenth-century attitudes toward female homoeroticism, whereas it is more appropriately viewed as the expression of the *dominant* discourse on *tri-badism* and *sodomy*. In addition, however much a fantasy of monstrosity underlies the discourse of tribadism, it hardly sums up the self-perception and experience of women who were erotically compelled by other women.

Shakespeare's *A Midsummer Night's Dream* and *As You Like It* both present two pairs of female characters whose initial erotic investment is in one another. The dialogues between Helena and Hermia, and Celia's speeches to Rosalind, are as erotically compelling as anything spoken in the heterosexual moments in these comedies. This eroticism, however, does not depend upon a cross-dressed figure like Rosalind who is not, in fact, the enunciator of homoerotic desire, but instead depends upon the 'feminine' Celia, who urges Rosalind to 'love no man in good earnest' (1.2.26), and later asserts, 'We still have slept together,/Rose at an instant, learn'd, play'd, eat together,/And wheresoe'er we went, like Juno's swans,/Still we went coupled and inseparable' (1.3.71–4). Their love is presented as both excep-tional in quantity, and unexceptionable in type: 'never two ladies lov'd as they do' (1.1.107), says Charles, and Le Beau describes their love as 'dearer than the natural bond of sisters' (1.2.265). Similarly, when Hermia compares the 'primrose beds where' she and Helena 'were wont to lie' (1.2.215) to the meeting place, and later the bedding place, of Hermia and Lysander, we are encouraged to notice a repetition and displacement of one bedmate for another. Indeed, *A Midsummer Night's Dream*, a play thoroughly concerned with the tension between unity and duality, merger and separ-ation, oneness and twoness, presents Lysander's seductive come-on, 'One

heart, one bed, two bosoms, and one troth' (2.2.42) as no different –
qualitatively, emotionally, physically – from Helena's pained admonition:

> We, Hermia, like two artificial gods,
> Have with our needles created both one flower,
> Both on one sampler, sitting on one cushion,
> Both warbling of one song, both in one key,
> As if our hands, our sides, voices, and minds
> Had been incorporate. So we grew together,
> Like to a double cherry, seeming parted,
> But yet an union in partition;
> Two lovely berries molded on one stem;
> So, with two seeming bodies, but one heart.
>
> (3.2.203–12)

Helena concludes this passionate appeal with the question, 'And will you
rent our ancient love asunder . . . ?' (3.2.215), a motif repeated by Celia,
who complains, 'Rosalind lacks then the love/Which teacheth thee that thou
and I am one./Shall we be sund'red?' (1.3.94–6). That these texts formulate
the divorce of female unity in such similar terms substantiates James Holstun's contention that female homoerotic desire was figured in seventeenth-
century poetry primarily in an elegiac mode (Holstun 1987). Likewise, in
Fletcher and Shakespeare's *The Two Noble Kinsmen*, Emilia's love for her
childhood friend Flavina is rendered elegiacally, even as the love of Theseus
and Pirithous is allowed expression up to the eve of Theseus' marriage to
Hippolyta (1.3.55–92). Presented as always already in the past, and hence
irrecoverable, female homoerotic desire simultaneously was acknowledged
and mastered by male poets. Or, in my reworking of Holstun's terms,
symmetrical, 'feminine' homoerotic desire was granted signification only
after it was rendered insignificant.[13]

I am less interested in the male poets' containment of this desire, however,
than in the implicit power asymmetry that seems to constitute the homoerotic pair: the relative power of each woman is aligned according to her
denial of homoerotic bonds. It is the female, rather than the male characters
of these plays, who, by their silent denial of the other woman's emotional
claims, position homoerotic desire in the past. Female homoeroticism is
thus figurable not only in terms of the always already lost, but the always
about to be *betrayed*. And the incipient heterosexuality of the woman who
is recipient rather than enunciator of homoerotic desire comes to stand as
the *telos* of the play.

This staging of the eradication of homoerotic desire is replicated in the
Titania-Oberon subplot of *A Midsummer Night's Dream*. Titania is psychologically threatening precisely to the degree she upsets the homosocial
'traffic in women' formally negotiated by Egeus and Theseus in the opening
scene, and implicitly played out by Demetrius and Lysander in the forest.[14]

The changeling boy, child of Titania's votress and representative not only of her female order, but of female-oriented erotic bonds, is an object of maternal exchange between women. In inverting the gendered relations of the homosocial triangle, Titania not only 'effeminizes' the boy, but usurps patriarchal power. The child is the manifest link of a prior, homoerotic affection between women that doesn't so much exclude Oberon as render him temporarily superfluous. This affront motivates Oberon's attempt to humiliate Titania *erotically*, capture the boy, and secure him for martial, exclusively masculine, purposes.

The gendered and erotic scenarios enacted in these plays do not exemplify psychosexual *necessity* – that is, a developmental movement through progressive erotic stages – but an economic, political imperative: as each woman is resecured in the patriarchal, reproductive order, her desires are made to conform to her 'place'. Significantly, the homoerotic desires of these female characters existed comfortably within the patriarchal order until the onset of marriage; it is only with the cementing of male bonds through the exchange of women, or, in Titania's case, the usurpation of the right to formalize bonds through the bodies of others, that the independent desires of female bodies become a focus of male anxiety and heterosexual retribution.

In Shakespeare's plays, an originary, prior homoerotic desire is crossed, abandoned, betrayed; correlatively, a heterosexual desire is produced and inserted into the narrative in order to create a formal, 'natural' mechanism of closure. The elegiac mode of Shakespearean drama, however, which renders 'feminine' homoeroticism insignificant by situating it safely in the past, is supplanted in the history of the drama by a more immediate mode that not only locates such desire in the present tense, but depicts it as explicitly erotic. Thomas Heywood's *The Golden Age* and James Shirley's *The Bird in a Cage* both momentarily stage the temptations of a female-oriented eroticism; but they achieve temporal and psychological distance, not by the use of elegy, rather by employing mythological conceits and self-referential theatricality. Exuding homoerotic content within separatist female realms, the 'Ladies Interlude' (Act 4, scene 2) of Shirley's play, and Diana's virgin circle in Heywood's, repeat and extend the homoerotic pastoralism of *As You Like It* and *A Midsummer Night's Dream*.

The Golden Age is an episodic dramatization of the lives of Jupiter and Saturn, focusing, as does so much Greek and Roman myth, on military and erotic conquest. Act 2 of the play concerns Jupiter's attempted seduction and eventual rape of Calisto, daughter of his vanquished enemy, King Lycaon. Upon Calisto's refusal of Jupiter's offer of marriage, she flees her father's kingdom, joining Diana's virgin circle in the forest. Hot in pursuit, Jupiter disguises himself as a 'virago', and successfully infiltrates Diana's pastoral cloister.

According to the rule of Diana's order, her 'princesses' are paired off in

a manner reminiscent of heterosexual, monogamous marriage. When Diana
welcomes and prepares to accommodate Calisto, she asks Atlanta:

DIANA: Is there no princess in our train,
           As yet unmatch'd, to be her cabin fellow,
           And sleep by her?
ATLANTA: Madam, we are all coupled
           And twinn'd in love, and hardly is there any
           That will be won to change her bedfellow.
DIANA [to Calisto]:   You must be single till the next arrive:
           She that is next admitted of our train,
           Must be her bed-companion; so 'tis 'lotted.

(Collier 1851: 2.1)

Jupiter, of course, is the 'next admitted', who quickly vows Diana's
oath of loyalty and chastity; the circle's definition of chastity, however, is
explicitly defined as protection of one's hymen from *phallic* penetration:

ATLANTA: You never shall with hated man atone,
           But lie with woman, or else lodge alone. . . .
           With ladies only you shall sport and play,
           And in their fellowship spend night and day. . . .
           Consort with them at board and bed,
           And swear no man shall have your maidenhead.

To which Jupiter eagerly responds: 'By all the powers, both early and
divine,/If e'er I lose't, a woman shall have mine!' Not only is the *double
entendre* spoken directly to Diana, and not as a secretive aside, but the
huntress applauds Jupiter's vow – 'You promise well; we like you, and will
grace you' – and thereby grants Calisto as 'her' bedmate.

The continual reiteration of the concept of women lying in bed, 'consort'-
ing together as 'bedfellows' and 'bedcompanions', explicitly and matter-of-
factly poses erotic 'sport and play' between women as a 'chaste' alternative
to penetrative sex with 'hated man'. With their emphasis on being 'match'd',
'coupled', 'twinn'd in love', Diana's 'nymphs' pose monogamous, erotic
'virginity' as the natural expression of love between women.

When Jupiter quickly attempts to capitalize sexually on his good fortune,
however, Calisto resists. The play, however, takes no stand on whether her
resistance is due to an aversion to passion between women, because of
Jupiter's haste and aggressiveness, or because of some inchoate suspicion
regarding Jupiter's coercive designs:

JUPITER: Oh, how I love thee: come, let's kiss and play.
CALISTO: How?

JUPITER: So a woman with a woman may.
CALISTO: I do not like this kissing.
JUPITER: Sweet, sit still.
   Lend me thy lips, that I may taste my fill.
CALISTO: You kiss too wantonly.
JUPITER: Thy bosom lend,
   And by thy soft paps let my hand descend.
CALISTO: Nay, fie what mean you?

To which Jupiter offers the ambiguous response: 'Prithee, let me toy./I would the Gods would shape thee to a boy,/Or me into a man.' That Calisto's transformation into a boy would help Jupiter's plight adds the further titillation of male homoeroticism to a plot already full of erotic possibilities. This enticing possibility, however, is foreclosed as Jupiter forcefully asserts his 'rights' as a man, and carries Calisto offstage to be raped. The contrast between Jupiter's sexual assault and the loving ministrations of Diana's circle could not be more clear. And the ramifications for Calisto are tragic: eight months later, her pregnant evidence of heterosexual intercourse leads to banishment from Diana's society.

This theme of rape is doubled and complicated in *The Bird in a Cage*, as the Princess Eugenia is 'threatened' not only by the sexual advances of her male beloved, but by those of one of her ladies. But, perhaps more importantly, the strategies that Heywood employs to distance his depiction of homoeroticism are in evidence in Shirley's play as well. Not only does *The Bird in a Cage* import into its subplot a mythological past, but that subplot also focuses on the exploits of Jupiter. In addition, Shirley's dramatic device of a play-within-a-play heightens the sense of theatricality to which Jupiter's cross-dressing in *The Golden Age* merely alludes.

At the same time, however, the social context of *The Bird in a Cage* works to obviate the efficacy of these distancing mechanisms, with the play's role in a contemporary controversy pushing its meaning toward a material referent and verisimilitude. Satirically dedicated to the Puritan polemicist William Prynne, who attacked women actors as 'notorious whores' in *Histrio-mastix: The Players Scourge or Actors Tragedy* (1632–3), Shirley's play is implicitly a defence of Queen Henrietta, patroness of the Cockpit players for whom Shirley was principal dramatist. Just weeks before Prynne's publication, the Queen and her ladies had performed speaking parts at court in Walter Montague's *The Shepherd's Paradise*. Prynne's alleged libel against the Queen gave the authorities the chance they had been looking for to imprison him, inflict corporal punishment, and suppress his book. The gender and erotic consciousness expressed in *The Bird in a Cage* thus implicitly refers to the material reality of female royalty displaying and speaking her body not only in courtly but theatrical spectacle. A liminal moment in the history of the relation between theatricality and sexuality, Shirley's play thus renders problematic the use of those conventions that previously had governed depictions of female desire: the necessity of boy actors and the cross-dressing of homoerotically desiring female characters.

The 'bird in a cage' refers extra-theatrically to Prynne languishing in prison, and within the play to both the Princess Eugenia, confined with her ladies to a tower by her over-zealous father, and to her beloved Philenzo, who secretly enters her chamber disguised as a bird in an enormous cage. During their confinement, the ladies decide to pass the time by staging an 'interlude', the story of Jupiter's 'seduction' of Danaë, which replicates in miniature the themes of the main plot, with Eugenia acting the part of Danaë, and her lady, Donella, playing Jupiter. Significantly, Donella's impersonation of the lustful god is not burdened with cross-dressing, which makes even more remarkable the extent to which she discovers and articulates her own desire through the course of play-acting. As 'Jupiter', her twenty-eight-line amorous speech to the sleeping 'Danaë' ends with a self-admonition to forgo poeticizing and begin *acting*: 'But I rob my selfe of Treasure,/This is but the Gate of Pleasure./To dwell here, it were a sin,/ When *Elizium* is within./Leave off then this flattering Kisses,/To rifle other greater Blisses' (Shirley 1633:4.2. Sig H2v, 24–9). The threatened rape is interrupted by a bell announcing the surprise arrival of the bird cage, and, by means of this device, Philenzo's 'rescue' of Eugenia. Donella's response to this interruption is explicit and confused disappointment: 'Beshrew the Belman, and you had not wak'd as you did Madam, I should ha' forgot my selfe and play'd *Jupiter* indeed with you, my imaginations were strong upon me; and you lay so sweetly – how now?' (Sig H2v, 32–5).

In the context of Prynne's condemnation of the theatrical imagination and Shirley's implicit counter-argument in favour of it, Donella's erotic 'imaginations' are positively rendered. This affirmation of desire is voiced as well by the character Cassiana, who earlier remarked upon Jupiter's entrance: 'now comes *Jupiter* to take my Lady napping, we'l sleep too, let the wanton have her swinge, would she were a man for her sake' (Sig H2r, 36-Sig H2v, 1). That the 'wanton' *is* simultaneously Donella and 'Jupiter' is suggested by Cassiana's retention of female pronouns, which helps to materialize the pun embedded in Donella's wish: to play Jupiter in *deed*. In light of this, it might not be stretching erotic allusion too far to see in Donella's earlier response to Cassiana's impromptu poeticizing a bawdy joke about female arousal. Cassiana begins: 'Thinke Madame all is but a dreame,/That we are in – Now I am out – beame, creame./Helpe me *Katerina*, I can make no sence rime to't.' To which Donella puns: 'Creame is as good a Rime as your mouth can wish,/Ha, ha, ha' (Sig. H1r, 34–8).

The two rapes with which Eugenia is threatened invert conventional expectations: whereas Donella's erotic approach first seems to exist only in the realm of her imagination, and conversely, the disguised Philenzo's erotic demands appear as a real threat to the princess's safety, it soon becomes clear that it is Donella who is actually so transported with desire as to force herself upon her mistress, and that Philenzo only adopted the guise of rapist as a manipulative ploy.[15] And whereas the stage directions tell us that Philenzo 'discovers himselfe' to the princess (Sig. I1r, 12–13), Donella seems to have 'forgot [her] selfe' (Sig. H2v, 33) in precisely the way Prynne and other anti-theatricalists feared.

Despite the strength of Donella's 'imaginations', the dramatic process of Heywood and Shirley is, like Shakespeare, to pose eroticism between women as an option, only to displace it through the force of a seemingly 'natural', ultimately more powerful heterosexual impulse. The final closure of these erotic incidents, and the dominant economy of desire that these plays endorse, however, does not cancel out the erotic attraction between some female characters which is represented as a legitimate, if ultimately futile, endeavour.

In all of these plays, the displacement of the homoerotic by the heterosexual happens so 'naturally' that the *tension* between the two modes of desire is erased. But are these in fact *two separate* modes of desire? It would seem that for certain types of women, such a contiguity existed between female homoeroticism and heterosexuality that the direction of object choice hardly figured at all. At least, for female characters who did not challenge conventional gender roles – who did *not* cross-dress, who did *not* wear swords, who were not anatomically 'excessive' and who did not use 'illicit devices', whose gendered 'femininity' belied the possibility of 'unnatural' behaviours – desire may have been allowed to flow rather more freely if less sensationally between homoerotic and heterosexual modes. That in these plays such desire is ultimately reduced and fixed within the institutional prerogatives of heterosexual marriage – that the eradication of the 'feminine' homoerotic position to desire is precisely what must be *staged* – points to the political and economic use of women's erotic bodies within a patriarchal economy.

At issue here, it seems to me, is less sexuality or gender *per se*, than reproduction. These women's desires are untenable not, as is the case with transvestism, tribadism, or sodomy, because they are viewed as implicitly imitative and hence monstrous, but because they are essentially non-reproductive; such desire becomes an issue – becomes significant – only when the time comes for the patriarchal imperative of reproduction to be enforced. Woman's social role within a system of reproduction relies not only on her biological capacity to give birth, but on her willingness to perform that labour. It is only when women's erotic relations with one another threaten exclusivity, and thus endanger their reproductive 'performance', that cultural injunctions are levied against them. And it is precisely the cultural anxiety that women will fail to comply with this role, a role that is violently forced upon Calisto, that the drama obsessively articulates and assuages. It is hardly incidental that such theatrical liaisons are articulated only within the context of heterosexual courtship plots, where the expulsion of female relationships from the dramatic terrain resecures the promise of husbandly authority. The drama also suggests, however, that *if* same-gender erotic practices *could* exist coterminously with the marriage contract, there would be little cause for alarm. Heywood's Jupiter, for instance, shows no distress upon learning of Diana's separatist 'rule'; he merely tries to turn to his advantage the behavioural norms of a homoerotic environment. Although 'tribades' and 'sodomites' supplementing their bodies necessarily performed a certain amount of what Judith Butler terms 'gender trouble' (Butler 1991), the absence of outcry against 'feminine' homoeroticism suggests that it posed very little gender trouble at all. In the psychic landscape of the time, 'femmes' would be assumed available to give birth; tribades and sodomites would not.[16] The 'femme' involved with a tribade was seen as 'abused', the not altogether innocent victim of another woman's lust; her crime was correspondingly more minor, her punishment less severe.

Conceptual problems, of course, exist with my account. Perhaps most importantly, my analysis extrapolates a cultural *presence* from a discursive *silence*; it therefore could be accused not only of applying illegitimately twentieth-century categories to an earlier time, but of creating something quite literally out of nothing. To this charge, I can only answer that I find it inconceivable that within the vast array of erotic choices reported by early modern culture, 'feminine' bodies did not meet, touch, and pleasure one another.

Secondly, I presume that the erotic practices of 'tribades' and 'femmes' were radically discontinuous; that only 'tribades', for instance, used dildoes on their partners. But here we stumble across a certain circularity of definition: it is, after all, the penetrative use of a dildo or an enlarged clitoris that *defines* the 'sodomite' or 'tribade'. I confess ignorance as to the specific erotic acts in which early modern women may have engaged; but, in light of the fact that gynaecological texts encouraged men to arouse their wives by caressing their breasts and genitals, it seems implausible that women's pleasure was exclusively centred on penetration (Laqueur 1990; Johnson 1634; Pare 1573).

To what extent, then, can women's relationships with one another be perceived as 'resistant', 'oppositional', or 'transgressive'? To the extent that they existed coterminously with patriarchal prerogatives, not at all. They only *became* oppositional when perceived as a threat to the reproductive designs of heterosexual marriage. Whereas the 'tribade' and 'sodomite' functioned as magnets for cultural fantasies and fears – about gender, reproduction, monstrosity, and the ultimate instability of all such cultural categories – the 'femme' woman, who challenged neither gender roles nor reproductive imperatives, seems to have been so unworthy of notice that little note was taken of her at all.

In conclusion, there seems to have existed a radical discontinuity between, on the one hand, sodomy and tribadism, and their theatrical correlative in cross-dressing plays, and, on the other hand, a theatricalized 'feminine' homoeroticism that has no discernible material equivalent in the fantasized typologies in which early modern women were represented. Whereas the tribade and sodomite haunt essays, travel accounts, and gynaecological texts, femme–femme love seems to exist discursively solely as a theatrical invention. However, perhaps we can extrapolate from the drama itself the reasons for this disjuncture, for the absence of animus against 'femme-femme' love. For, if we have not interpreted the language of Helena, Hermia, Titania, Celia, Diana and Donella as homoerotic, it is not only because of our internalized homophobia, or because of our formalistic inclinations to privilege the final heterosexual teleology of these comedies, but because the palpable 'femininity' of these characters blinds us – and, I suspect, may have blinded many of their contemporaries as well – to the eroticism evident in their language of desire. Existing independently of the representational nexus of sodomy and tribadism, bodily supplementation and gender appropriation, these theatrical representations suggest that 'feminine' homoerotic desires were dramatized precisely because they did not signify.[17]

Notes

1 The quotation in full is:

> These lewdnesses are so detestable, that nothing needs to be said to increase their Horror: for Nature suffers almost as great a violence in *hearing* of them, as in the perpetration. It is wonderful, indeed, how it ever came into the thoughts of *Men* to commit them: but, as the Apostle says, (Rom. I. 20–28) when they gave them-selves up to Idolatry, God gave them up to vile affections; and the Devil put them upon going as much out of the way for wickedness, as he had brought them to do for their Religious Worship. They had changed the glory of the incorruptible God into Images of corruptible Men and Beasts, for Adoration: and therefore He left them to debase *themselves*; and turn the Channel of their Lusts, as well as their Devotions, from what was natural, to what was abhorrent from Nature; to their own Sex, and to brute beasts.
>
> (Disney 1729: 180)

2 See, for instance, Thersites' labelling of Patroclus as 'Achilles' male varlet, his masculine whore' in Shakespeare's *Troilus and Cressida* (5.1.15–17) and Hamlet's self-representation as a 'drab, a stallion' in *Hamlet* (2.2.588).

3 With the exception of recent work by Katharine Park and Lorraine Daston, little historical, theoretical, or literary investigation has been attempted on early modern female same-gender pleasure. Lillian Faderman's encyclopaedic historical overview of love between women devotes only two short chapters to the period prior to the eighteenth century, focusing mainly on Brantôme's *Lives of Fair and Gallant Ladies*. Judith Brown's archival work on the life of Benedetta Carlini is helpful, but in many ways is more revealing of religious than erotic

practices. The important work of James Holstun, Harriette Andreadis, and Elizabeth Harvey picks up the representation of Englishwomen's desires in the mid-seventeenth century, focusing primarily on the poetry of John Donne and Katherine Philips. And an important recent anthology, *Lesbian Texts and Contexts* (Kay and Glasgow 1990) discusses only nineteenth- and twentieth-century texts.

4 By means of this anecdote, Greenblatt positions his analysis of Shakespeare's *Twelfth Night*, which he views as a partial retelling of Montaigne's story, in relation to non-theatrical discourses; correlatively, he employs the play to support his claim that within the Renaissance imagination, transformations of identity occurred unidirectionally: from imperfect to perfect, from female to male.

5 Greenblatt retells another anecdote (originally recorded by the French physician Jacques Duval in *On Hermaphrodites, Childbirth, and the Medical Treatment of Mothers and Children* [Rouen, 1603]) of gender ambiguity, in this case occasioned not primarily by the adoption of clothes but by the confusions of the body. A female servant, Marie, revealed to the woman she loves, Jeane, that she was really a man. After consummating the vows they had made, to the apparently mutual enjoyment of each, the couple sought public approval of their love. Marie changed her name to Marin, and began wearing masculine clothing. The two were subsequently arrested, tried, and condemned. The crime for which both were convicted was sodomy; despite Marin's claim that the terror of the trial had caused his penis to retract, the court maintained that Marie was a tribade who had used her unnaturally large clitoris to abuse Jeane. It was only upon Marin's appeal to the Parlement of Rouen, which appointed a panel of doctors, surgeons, and midwives to repeat a medical examination, that Jacques Duval applied pressure to Marin's organs, and found there 'a male organ', which on second examination, 'ejaculated' in a manner consistent not with woman's expulsion of seed, but man's (Greenblatt 1988: 73–5). These French cases are also discussed by Daston and Park (1985) and Jones and Stallybrass (1991).

6 In France (but not in England) cross-dressing was a punishable offence. In England only class transvestism was a crime (Jones and Stallybrass, 1991).

7 For the distinction between desires and acts, see Smith (1991).

8 See, for instance, Nicholas Culpepper:

> Some are of opinion, and I could almost afford to side with them that such kind of Creatures they call Hermaphrodites, which they say bear the Genitals both of men and women, are nothing else but such women in whom the Clitoris hangs out externally, and so resembles the form of a Yard; leave the truth or falsehood of it to be judged by such who have seen them anatomized: however, this is agreeable both to reason and authority, that the bigger the Clitoris is in women, the more lustful they are.
>
> (Culpepper 1684)

The uniformity of French and English gynaecological texts is explained by their general dependence on previous authority, and especially their common inheritance of the Galenic model of heat.

9 According to Audrey Eccles, Bartholin referred to such women as 'Rubsters', and Dionis observed that 'there are some lascivious Women, who by *Friction* of this Part, receive so great Pleasure, that they care not for Men' (Eccles 1982: 34). Ambrose Pare included a section on such women in his original *Des Monstres et prodiges* (1573), but, according to Jean Ceard, he 'was forced to eliminate a section on lesbianism, with a graphic description of the female genitals, before

including *Des Monstres* in later editions of his collected works' (Pare 1573 [1971]: 26–7).
10 Sharp, however, takes care to minimize Englishwomen's culpability. In my edition she writes: 'In the Indies, and Egypt [tribades] are frequent', and another edition of her work adds these words – 'but I have never heard but of one in this Country' (Sharp 1671: 45). Sharp's displacement of the 'unnatural' on to other nations is totally conventional within the context of medical discourses that regularly employed nationalist paradigms of contamination and disease.
11 Despite my use of the term 'femme', I want to encourage the reader to resist viewing these women as prototypes of modern erotic identities, and to emphasize instead the risk of collapsing their difference into *our* desire for continuity and similitude.
12 See my *Desire and Anxiety* for an analysis of the connection between early modern homoeroticism and theatrical cross-dressing (Traub 1992).
13 In using the term 'feminine', I do not mean to reinscribe arbitrary binary gender designations. However, it seems fruitful to differentiate between those women who were charged with appropriating masculine prerogatives and those who were not.
14 The phrase 'traffic in women' was first coined by Emma Goldman in her critique of marriage as prostitution. It gained critical prominence through the work of Gayle Rubin. For the most powerful elucidation of homosocial triangles, see Sedgwick (1985).
15 By conflating rape with seduction, I self-consciously reproduce the ideology of the play, and in no way mean to endorse such a view.
16 In arguing that 'femme' women were not threatening because they did not disrupt the reproductive economy, I could be interpreted to mean that they were always sexually available to men. My point is merely that they were culturally *perceived* to be more available, more capable, more willing.
17 I would like to acknowledge Brenda Marshall, Susan Zimmerman, Margaret Hunt, Richard Burt, Linda Gregerson, and Will Fisher for giving me suggestions of where and how to look for female-centred desire. I would also like to thank the Gay and Lesbian Studies seminar participants at the Robert Penn Warren Center for the Humanities at Vanderbilt University for their insightful comments on an early draft. Finally, Misty Anderson provided timely research assistance and Kathy Cody gave invaluable help with the manuscript.

References

Andreadis, H. (1989) 'The Sapphic Platonics of Katherine Philips, 1632–1664', *Signs* 15: 34–60.
Anon (*c.* 1700) *Aristotles Complete Masterpiece*, London.
Bevington, D. (ed.) (1980) *The Complete Works of Shakespeare*, Glenview and London: Scott, Foresman & Company.
Bray, A. (1982) *Homosexuality in Renaissance England*, London: Gay Men's Press.
Brown, J. (1986) *Immodest Acts: The Life of a Lesbian Nun in Renaissance Italy*, New York and Oxford: Oxford University Press.
Butler, J. (1991) *Gender Trouble: Feminism and the Subversion of Identity*, New York and London: Routledge.
Collier, J. (1851) *The Golden and Silver Ages: Two Plays by Thomas Heywood*, London: Shakespeare Society.
Crooke, H. (1615, 1631) *A Description of the Body of Man*, London.
Culpepper, N. (1684) *A Directory for Midwives*, London.

Daston, L. and Park, K. (1985) 'Hermaphrodites in Renaissance France', *Critical Matrix* 1: 1–19.

Derrida, J. (1974) *Of Grammatology*, trans. Gayatri Chakravorty Spivak, Baltimore and London: Johns Hopkins University Press.

Disney, J. (1729) *A View of Ancient Laws Against Immorality and Profaneness*, Nottingham: Vicar of St Mary's.

Dollimore, J. (1991) *Sexual Dissidence: Augustine to Wilde, Freud to Foucault*, Oxford: Clarendon Press.

Eccles, A. (1982) *Obstetrics and Gynecology in Tudor and Stuart England*, Kent, Ohio: Kent State University Press.

Faderman, L. (1981) *Surpassing the Love of Men: Romantic Friendship and Love Between Women from the Renaissance to the Present*, New York: William Morrow.

Foucault, M. (1978) *The History of Sexuality*, vol 1, trans. Robert Hurley, New York: Random House.

Greenblatt, S. (1988) 'Fiction and friction', *Shakespearean Negotiations: The Circulation of Social Energy in Renaissance England*, Oxford: Clarendon Press, 66–93.

Halperin, D. (1990) *One Hundred Years of Homosexuality, and Other Essays on Greek Love*, New York: Routledge.

Harvey, E. (1989) 'Ventriloquizing Sappho: Ovid, Donne, and the erotics of the feminine voice', *Criticism* 31: 115–38.

Heywood, T. (1611) *The Golden Age*, London.

Holstun, J. (1987) ' "Will you rent our ancient love asunder?": Lesbian elegy in Donne, Marvell, and Milton', *ELH* 54: 835–67.

Jay, K. and Glasgow, J. (eds) (1990) *Lesbian Texts and Contexts: Radical Revisions*, New York and London: New York University Press.

Johnson, T. (1634) *The Works of that famous Chirurgion: Ambrose Parey, translated out of Latine and compared with the French*, London.

Jones, A. and Stallybrass, P. (1991) 'Fetishizing gender: Constructing the hermaphrodite in Renaissance Europe', in Julia Epstein and Kristena Straub (eds) *Body Guards: The Cultural Politics of Gender Ambiguity*, New York and London: Routledge, 80–111.

Kinney, A. (ed.) (1974) *Markets of Bawdrie: The Dramatic Criticism of Stephen Gossen*, Salzburg: Institut für Englische Sprache und Literatur.

Laqueur, T. (1990) *Making Sex: Body and Gender from the Greeks to Freud*, Cambridge, Mass., and London: Harvard University Press.

Pare, A. (1573) *Des Monstres et prodiges*, trans. J. Ceard, Geneva: Droz (1971).

Prynne, W. (1632–3) *Histrio-mastix: The Player's Scourge or Actor's Tragedy*, New York: Garland (1974).

Rubin, G. (1975) 'The traffic in women: Notes on the "political economy" of sex', in Rayna Reiter (ed.) *Toward an Anthropology of Women*, New York: Monthly Review, 157–210.

Sedgwick, E. (1985) *Between Men: English Literature and Male Homosocial Desire*, New York: Columbia University Press.

——(1990) *The Epistemology of the Closet*, Berkeley: University of California Press.

Senescu, F. (ed.) (1980) *James Shirley's The Bird in a Cage: A Critical Edition*, New York and London: Garland.

Sharp, J. (1671) *The Midwives Book*, London and New York: Garland (1985).

Shirley, J. (1633) *The Bird in a Cage*, London: Quarto.

Smith, B. (1991) *Homosexual Desire in Shakespeare's England: A Cultural Poetics*, Chicago: University of Chicago Press.

Stubbes. P. (1583) *The Anatomie of Abuses*, London.
Traub, V. (1992) *Desire and Anxiety: Circulations of Sexuality in Shakespearean Drama*, London and New York: Routledge.

Chapter 10

Sex and social conflict
The erotics of *The Roaring Girl*

Jean E. Howard

In the printed preface to *The Roaring Girl*, entitled 'To the Comic Play-Readers, Venery and Laughter', the play advertises an intention to address erotic matter in a comic fashion.[1] Venery, in its double meanings of (a) the practice or sport of hunting beasts of game, and (b) the practice or pursuit of sexual pleasure, dominates this text. Most of the venery is overtly sexual. Young men hunt maids, and gallants pursue city wives for sexual satisfaction inside or outside marriage. Yet not all of the venery of this text is so relentlessly heterosexual as this summary suggests, and the sexual hunt provokes other types of venery as well, as angry fathers hound, harass, and entrap their wayward sons, and angry husbands stalk cuckolding gallants. At the centre of this complex world stands Moll Cutpurse, Venus 'in doublet and breeches' (Gomme 1976: Preface, 1.14), a figure who not only provokes erotic desire and sexualized aggression in others, but who also remains an erotic subject in her own right. As such, she threatens her culture's conventions for managing female desire. By examining various aspects of 'venery' in this drama I hope to show several things: first, that this site of licensed 'play' affords glimpses of a landscape of erotic desire and practice whose contours cannot quite be mapped in twentieth-century terms; second, that the manifest contradictions surrounding the play's representations of sexuality, marriage, and gender roles suggest that these were contested cultural phenomena – the source of anxiety and conflict as much as of laughter; third, that homoerotic bonds between men subtend this textual world and are not always easily reconciled with cultural imperatives to marry and reproduce; and, finally, that female sexual desire remains the most intractable aspect of the play's sexual economy.

Recently, feminist, gay, lesbian, and queer critics (the four categories are not necessarily discrete) have emphasized the political necessity and the analytic utility of investigating sexuality as a relatively autonomous system of cultural meaning and site of social struggle, one that cannot simply be subsumed under an analysis of gender difference and hierarchy (Sedgwick 1990: 27–35; Traub, forthcoming 1992).[2] As Gayle Rubin has written, in revision of her own earlier conflation of sex and gender into one system,

'Gender affects the operation of the sexual system, and the sexual system has had gender-specific manifestations. But although sex and gender are related, they are not the same thing, and they form the basis of two distinct arenas of social practice' (Rubin 1984: 308). In this essay I will attend to the specificity of sexuality by looking at how sexual practices and desires are represented in this text and points of conflict within the sexual economy rendered visible. But at the same time I will try to show *interconnections* between sexuality and other systems through which social conflict was regulated and registered in early modern England, especially the effect on sexual practice of class antagonisms and of a gender ideology that sexualized the desiring, speaking, publicly visible woman and simultaneously made her a threat to man's gender dominance and to patriarchal constructions of 'the good wife'.

Like gender, sexuality has increasingly been revealed as less an essential biological given than a socially constructed, historically variable set of practices and ideologies.[3] As gay and lesbian scholars have made clear, homosexuality, for example, does not have one set of meanings through time. In discussing same-sex relationships in early modern England, Alan Bray argues that while there were certainly sodomitical acts committed in the Renaissance, they were not undertaken by 'homosexuals', that is, by people for whom same-sex sexual orientation constituted a primary category of identity or subjectivity.[4] Rather than a distinct identity, homosexuality constituted a potential within everyone, a point on a continuum of possible sexual practices (Bray 1988: 25). Consequently, there may have been more fluidity in the matter of object choice, especially for men, than is 'normal' today when homosexual and heterosexual are typically taken to signal unitary and fixed sexual identities. In addition, Galenic biological models depicting both boys and women as unfinished men may have enabled adult males – to some as yet undefined extent – to treat boys and women as interchangeable sexual objects (Laqueur 1990: 63–148). As I hope to show, however, a greater fluidity for men, at least, in the matter of sexual object choice did not mean that early modern England was a polymorphous paradise in which conflicts never arose between different modalities of erotic desire and sexual practice. Boys and women were 'the same' in their hierarchical relationship to adult males, but they were also 'different', if only in the crucial matter of their respective roles in reproduction. In addition, sexuality was certainly not 'free' in some absolute sense, but was regulated by the state, by village custom, by changing ideological imperatives.

Sodomy, for example, was a crime for which a man could die. Of course, for a long while sodomy was a comprehensive term for many 'devilish' or stigmatized practices including witchcraft, atheism, etc. Only gradually in the course of the sixteenth and seventeenth centuries did the term come to stress, in legal and popular discourse, anal penetration of one man by another, an act that to be prosecuted usually had to involve force and be perpetuated on a young child.[5] However, even though the definition of sodomy became more particularized as a specific sexual crime during this period, few were prosecuted for it. Despite a handful of notorious sodomy cases involving children or enemies of the state, there seems to have been wide cultural acceptance of what we would now call homosexual practices among Renaissance men, especially but not exclusively between men of unequal status or in clear positions of dependency and control such as servants and masters, students and schoolmen.[6] None the less, this form of sexual practice – as opposed to heterosexuality undertaken within marriage – was always potentially susceptible to severe punishment.

In texts that have survived, early modern English writers say less about sexual encounters between women than between men, though there *are* passages such as the report in Jane Sharp's *The Midwives Book* of women whose clitorises were so enlarged they could be used as penis-substitutes in sexual relations with other women. Writing of the clitoris, Sharp says:

> commonly it is but a small sprout, lying close hid under the wings, and not easily felt, yet sometimes it grows so long that it hangs forth at the slit like a Yard, and it will swell and stand stiff if it be provoked, and some lewd women have endeavoured to use it as men do theirs. In the Indies and Egypt they are frequent, but I never heard but of one in this Country, if there be any they will do what they can for shame to keep it close.

> (1671: 32)

Interestingly, the fear of what we would now call lesbian eroticism is projected on to the dark women of India and Egypt, though as Harriette Andreadis has pointed out in regard to Katherine Philips, some women were quite open about having intimate same-sex friendships with other women. What we don't know is whether such intimate relationships involved genital sexuality or if the erotic components of such friendships found other avenues of expression.[7]

If same-sex erotic relations were understood *differently* in the early modern period than they are today, the same is true for what we now call 'heterosexuality'. While marriage, and hence some degree of heterosexual activity, was the norm in Protestant England, sexual relations with women were often constructed as dangerous to men and compared, unfavourably, to the 'safer' and more ennobling realm of male friendship (Orgel 1989: 26; Rackin, forthcoming 1992). Men who displayed excessive passion for women were termed effeminate because they became like women in allowing passion to override their reason and self-control. Moreover, women themselves were often viewed as creatures with such strong sexual appetites that it was only with difficulty that men could retain proper control over these libidinous creatures. It is hardly surprising, therefore, to find misogyny and fear of women's sexual appetites informing a number of cultural productions from the period. On the other hand, while heterosexuality was often stigmatized as dangerous and demeaning to men, the late sixteenth and early seventeenth centuries also saw increased cultural emphasis upon marriage, especially among the middling sort, as the affective focus of their lives and not simply as an economic necessity (Belsey 1985: 192–221). Many texts from the period celebrate marriage and present women as the proper and 'natural' objects of masculine erotic desire.

This being the case, it is not surprising to find what Bruce Smith has termed a 'contest' in some literary works of the period between homoerotic male friendship and the claims of heterosexual marriage (Smith 1991: 64–7). Genre, of course, mattered a great deal in representing this contest. Read enough Renaissance romantic comedies and one might think the theatre was part of a vast bourgeois apparatus to make heterosexuality compulsory, though not necessarily in ways equally advantageous to both sexes. When a woman like Hermia in *Midsummer Night's Dream* gets to wed the man of her desires, this achievement is often coupled with the loss of the woman's voice, mobility, and independence. On the other hand, read enough Renaissance tragedy and one might think the Renaissance theatre was a vast aristocratic apparatus for weaning men away from heterosexuality since so many of these texts offer only representations of devouring, cuckolding, sexualized women and highlight the intense bonds and aggressions between men.

Yet to speak monolithically of the connection between sexuality and dramatic genre is of limited usefulness because it misses much of what was uniquely volatile and contradictory about the production of erotic desire at the site of the stage where, for example, even a heterosexual marriage plot was acted out, literally, by a man and a boy actor.[8] Moreover, not only did the stage mime the desire of fictitious persons, but commentators of the period remark upon it as a space where erotic desire flowed between spectators, as well. Some of that desire was provoked by happenings on the stage, but some by the conditions under which spectatorship occurred. Amphitheatre playing made spectators as visible to one another as were the players; and since those spectators were both men and women, anti-theatricalists worried aloud about the sexual outrages that might be perpetuated by same-sex or by opposite-sex partners either at the theatre or in the taverns and inns to which theatre-goers and actors would subsequently repair (Howard 1989: 31–49). I suggest that this particular theatre – with its all-male acting troupes, its mixed audiences (mixed by both gender and class), its penchant for plots of transvestite disguise, and its daylight conditions of playing such that stage and audience were equally spectacles – created conditions of erotic volatility in which desire could flow in many and often contradictory directions and where sexuality could become a staging ground for many forms of social struggle.

The conflicted terrain of erotic possibility

As a city comedy, *The Roaring Girl* stages erotic desire in a complex and often highly contradictory fashion that bears little resemblance to the treatment of 'venery' in the often timeless, relatively unlocalized world of Shakespearean romantic comedy. Urban and suburban spaces are particularized in this play, as are the social groups – young gallants, petty merchants, cutpurses and canters – who struggle for pre-eminence, and sometimes just for survival, in a cityscape that seems to fuel the fires of desire and to invite the intermingling of venereal and economic pursuits. In this setting sexuality repeatedly comes under scrutiny, and under contest, revealing an erotic terrain fraught with conflict and contradiction.

Consider, for example, a provocative and – to modern readers – puzzling moment in Act 4 when the hero, Sebastian, secretly brings his beloved, Mary Fitz-Allard, to his father's chamber. In typical comedy fashion, these two lovers have been scheming from the first scene of the play to outwit the covetous father, Sir Alexander Wengrave, who is blocking their marriage because he is worried about 'what gold/This marriage would draw from him' (1.1.79–80) and scorns Mary's dowry of five thousand marks (1.1.84). In Act 4, Sebastian meets Mary in his father's chamber. Moll Cutpurse, dressed 'in man's clothes' (4.1.39), accompanies the two lovers and, somewhat surprisingly, Mary *also* wears men's clothing. She is suited 'like a page' (4.1.39) in apparel rigged up by Moll's tailor. It is not altogether clear why this disguise is necessary. Mary is not like the plucky heroines of Shakespeare's plays who use their male disguises to protect themselves from sexual aggression during long pursuits of the men they love and whose disguises often are accompanied by a temporary assumption of masculine prerogatives of freedom of speech and action. Mary is a tamer version of these women, probably donning male disguise to enter Sir Wengrave's chamber unnoted, but hardly, like Portia, to argue in a courtroom or, like Rosalind, to educate her beloved as to the proper way to love a woman. The disguise, far from giving Mary the upper hand by concealing her identity from the world in general and her lover in particular, instead makes her more fully the object of Sebastian's erotic fancies. For example, when Moll, watching the two of them kiss, comments: 'How strange this shows, one man to kiss another' (4.1.46), Sebastian replies: 'I'd kiss such men to choose, Moll,/Methinks a woman's lip tastes well in a doublet' (4.1.47–8), and further, 'As some have a conceit their drink tastes better/In an outlandish cup than in our own,/So methinks every kiss she gives me now/In this strange form, is worth a pair of two' (4.1.54–7). The exchange simultaneously calls attention to the 'strangeness' of a seemingly same-sex erotic embrace, and also to its desirability.

Why is kissing a mannishly-clad woman so thrilling? Several answers are possible. One would stress the general transgressiveness of the scene and the setting. Sebastian is rebelling against his father by pursuing Mary, and at this moment he is doing so in his father's very chamber and in the company of a notorious roaring girl, Moll Cutpurse, who is *also* dressed as a man. In such a context, kissing the bride-to-be while she is dressed as a boy, 'outlandishly' transformed, could simply offer an added dimension of transgression to this highly transgressive moment. But another possibility is that it is not the context that makes the kiss 'worth a pair of two', but the very fact that Sebastian is kissing what looks, on the outside, like a boy; in sum, that his most intense erotic pleasure is what we would now call homoerotic in nature or, framed in accordance with Galenic notions of biology, it is the potential man within the young woman that constitutes the true object of Sebastian's desire.[9] Indeed, the name Sebastian itself in some quarters carried homoerotic connotations in the Renaissance, largely because of the long iconographic tradition of representing the arrow-pierced saint and his intimate relationship with Christ as 'an indirect ideal of homoerotic love' (Saslow 1977: 63).[10] Moreover, dressed as a page, Mary enacts the role of a gentleman's servant, one of the social positions most often marked out as constituting a culturally sanctioned object for a master's erotic investments.

The multiple sexual valences of this scene are further complicated, of course, by the fact that on the Renaissance stage Mary and Moll were played by male actors, not by women. While in performance the fact of the boy beneath the woman's clothes could usually have been ignored by playgoers, it could *also* at any time have been brought to consciousness by a self-reflexive gesture or comment. At those instances when audience attention is directed to the boy actor *as* boy, or when within the terms of a fiction such as *The Roaring Girl* a male stage character expresses delight at kissing a masculinely clad boy – at such moments a multiplicity of sexual possibilities open before the male spectator, in particular, a multiplicity fostered by the gap between the heterosexual imperatives of the marriage plot and the homoerotic reality of the material conditions of stage production and/or the expressed desires of particular male characters such as Sebastian.

Such moments seem to me productively multiple and contradictory in their erotic valences, making it impossible, for example, simply to characterize Renaissance stage comedy as an apparatus for producing bourgeois heterosexuality and channelling erotic energy into the emerging cultural form of companionate marriage. The stage drew upon, produced, and reproduced more than a single sexual discourse. At the level of the plot, plays ending in multiple marriages often contain a submerged, and sometimes an overt, resistance to heterosexual coupling. In *The Roaring Girl* that resistance is complexly staged. In the main plot, while Sebastian overtly pursues a heterosexual marriage, I have already commented on the fact that in doing so he finds particular piquancy in kissing his beloved when he/she is dressed as a man. Moreover, the aristocratic world in which he moves is largely a homosocial world devoid of women. Sir Alexander's house in the play's second scene is peopled entirely by men – Sir Adam Appleton, Sir Davy Dapper, Goshawk, Laxton, Greenwit, and other 'gentlemen'. Sebastian seems to have no mother. Among the gentlemen who at the play's end gather at Sir Alexander's are Sir Thomas Long and Sir Beauteous Ganymede, a pair whose names suggest, respectively, phallic endowment, and homo-erotic beauty.[11] In Act 5 Sir Thomas asks Jack Dapper about his 'sweet-faced boy' (5.1.23), and earlier Jack's father accuses him of wasting his money on worthless companions, including 'ningles/(Beasts Adam ne'er gave name to)' (3.3.62–3). Despite the fact the plot focuses on getting Sebastian married, the 'gentleman' class as a whole seems less interested in marriage than in various modalities of same-sex bonding.

Where marriage *does* get emphasized is in the middle-class subplot. Here issues of sexuality have their own complexity. Shakespearean comedy, of course, rarely moved beyond the portrayal of courtship to engage the actuality of marriage. City comedy frequently does, and in *The Roaring Girl* we have not only an aristocratic courtship plot involving Sebastian and Mary, but also the depiction of three actually existing marriages involving the Openworks, the Tiltyards, and the Gallipots. Women, in the form of wives, are very visible in this plot in contrast to their near absence in the aristocratic plot. However, even in this merchant world, homoerotic bonds cut across heterosexual ties between men and their wives; and, just as importantly, class antagonisms and gender conflicts affect erotic desire and performance in complicated ways. 'Venery' becomes a site of profound contradiction, and in attempting to resolve these contradictions, the play often shunts aside or silences the women, leaving their sexual desires per-petually deferred or unfulfilled.

Class antagonisms play a large role in structuring sexual relations in this plot. Ted Leinwand has argued that many of the stereotypes of city comedy embody class ideologies. For example, 'the merchant is revealed as the personification of the gentry's fears, and the clever gallant represents the gentry's will to sexual mastery at a time when its social and financial potency was uncertain' (Leinwand 1986, 123). In *The Roaring Girl* Laxton's and Goshawk's attempts to seduce Mistress Gallipot and Mistress Open-work in part validate Leinwand's thesis. These gallants are poor, especially Laxton, and what he most seeks through a liaison with Gallipot's wife is access to her husband's money.

But while these merchants *have* money, there are strong suggestions they are not satisfying sexual partners for their wives. Gallipot embodies one type of Renaissance effeminacy in that he dotes on his wife to excess, excusing every fault, making no demands, but, it is implied, leaving her sexually unsatisfied. As she rails at her 'apron husband' (3.2.30–1), 'your love is all words; give me deeds, I cannot abide a man that's too fond over

me, so cookish; thou dost not know how to handle a woman in her kind'
(3.2.23–5). By contrast, Mistress Openwork complains that her husband
spends himself sexually with other women, leaving her no source of
pleasure. This seems to be the basis for her anger in Act 2 at Moll who has
come to her shop to buy the shag ruff. When Master Openwork greets
Moll cordially, Mistress Openwork cries, 'How now, greetings, love-terms
with a pox between you, have I found out one of your haunts? I send you
for hollands, and you're i' th' low countries with a mischief. I'm served
with good ware by th' shift, that makes it lie dead so long upon my hands,
I were as good shut up shop, for when I open it I take nothing' (2.1.204–9).
These marriages of sexual lack seem to indict the merchant-class man for
impotency and the merchant-class woman for insatiability. Neither heterosexuality nor marriage seems very attractive in this depiction.

On the other hand, the gallants who hang about these merchant wives
are represented through yet another class-based stereotype, that of the
profligate aristocrat who has sold his family lands and whose degeneracy
can be sexually symbolized. None of these gallants actually sleeps with the
merchant wives, and the pun in Laxton's name suggests one reason. At least
symbolically, he lacks a testicle; he is, in Mistress Gallipot's disillusioned
words, 'a lame gelding' (4.2.38). The decaying branches of the aristocracy
are in no position to challenge or reform the merchant class. In the end the
wives are driven back to their husbands, not because these husbands become
more sexually satisfying, but simply because they at least have money: 'we
shopkeepers, when all's done, are sure to have 'em [the gallants] in our
purse-nets at length, and when they are in, Lord, what simple animals they
are' (4.2.45–7). She goes on to say, further, that when the gallants then
importune with the merchant wives for favour, these wives then must 'ingle
with our husbands abed, and we must swear they [the gallants] are our
cousins, and able to do us a pleasure at court' (4.2.53–5).

It is worth pausing at the verb. Exactly what is it to ingle with one's
husband? The *OED* glosses this very passage as 'to fondle with' one's
husband. But to me the verb also suggests to play the ingle, that is, the boy
catamite, with one's husband, possibly meaning to engage in anal sex with
him. While anal sex can certainly be part of eroticism between men and
women, it seems important that the wives, as they describe giving special
sexual pleasure to their husbands in order to wheedle something from them,
use a word bringing to mind the specific sexual act connected with the boy
partner, the ingle or Ganymede. In 1598 in his *A Worlde of Wordes*, John
Florio translated the Italian word *zanzerare* as 'to ingle boies, to wantonly
play with boyes against nature' (Florio 1598: 459), suggesting that the verb
'to ingle' *could* mean something more provocative and 'against nature' than
mere fondling.

While the homoerotic implications of Mistress Gallipot's speech are
indirect, they resonate in my mind with the stage moment in which

Sebastian takes double delight in kissing Mary dressed as a page. Such moments raise the possibility that for some men in this text erotic desire and pleasure are most intense when directed at and satisfied by other men or by women who assume the clothes or the 'positions' associated with the Ganymede.[12] In this play the cultural imperatives to marry seem strong, but it is not clear that erotic desire lines up neatly with cultural imperatives. Among the aristocracy the imperative to marry remains connected in this play to the consolidation and passage of land and property, but the Wengrave milieu contains no actual women except the women who will or might marry Sebastian and produce heirs and fortune for the Wengrave line.

For urban merchants the imperative to marry seems linked to economic realities of another sort. The merchant couples work together, keep economically afloat by dividing between them the labour of making their businesses profitable. The scenes involving these couples are studded with details reflecting the realities of a shopkeeper's life: getting cloth from Holland, preparing orders in a rush for valued customers, keeping abreast of the finery most sought after by the court gallants, as when Mistress Tiltyard tells Jack Dapper which feathers are most in fashion among 'the beaver gallants, the stone riders,/The private stage's audience, the twelvepenny-stool gentlemen' (2.1.133–4). But these unions are not depicted as erotically fulfilling. There is the unmistakable implication that, like female play-goers, the publicly visible, economically useful urban wives were experienced by men as threatening figures: sexually demanding, potentially unchaste, and probably more interested, as a daily matter, in riding the stone horse from on top than in submissively 'ingling' with their husbands. These women are sexually attractive only to such spouses as the effeminate 'apron husband', Gallipot, whose vapid doting only proves the point that such wives, if uncontrolled, emasculate men and cause them to lose their proper masculine dominance.

I will return to the issue of the relationship between female subordination and female sexual attractiveness to men when I discuss Moll, but the resolution of the citizen plot reveals the deep strand of misogyny running through the merchant plot. These clever, economically useful women who demand more sex, or different sex, than their husbands afford them, are shunted aside at the end of Act 4 so that an orgy of bonding can occur between the merchant husbands and the aristocratic gallants. Goshawk's machinations to achieve Mistress Openwork having been revealed, Master Openwork says: 'Come, come, a trick of youth, and 'tis forgiven./This rub put by, our love shall run more even' (4.2.215–16). In short, no contest involving a woman can disrupt male friendship. Class aggression pales before gender solidarity. Similarly, after Laxton has been exposed, Master Gallipot proclaims himself 'beholden – not to you, wife -/But Master Laxton, to your want of doing ill,/Which it seems you have not' (4.2.320–2). And as Master Openwork and Gallipot lead the way offstage to a feast of reconciliation, Gallipot's final words are: 'wife, brag no more/Of holding out: who most brags is most whore' (4.2.325–6). In other words, a woman who opens her mouth is a prostitute, a commonplace of the period (Stallybrass 1986: 126), but one suggesting why these talkative women frighten their husbands with the spectre of a female sexual demand they cannot answer, an independent subjectivity they cannot master. As this plot suggests, satisfactory sex for adult men seems to involve more than the sex, male or female, of the desired partner. Equally important is that that person be properly subordinate, whether he/she is an ingle, a wife, or a whore.

The Roaring Girl and her viol

Moll's presence in the play both complicates and clarifies these issues. She is made up, textually, of competing ideological strands. The contradictions prevent her from being read as an entirely unified subjectivity, but they also function to show what is at stake in her representation, what nexus of gender, class, and sexual contests her textual presence mediates. Some parts of her representation answer to a patriarchal anxiety about how modernity – here represented by the market place, urbanization, the whirl of fashion – have turned gender and sexual relations on their head. Seen from this perspective, Moll's cross-dressing objectifies disorder in order to put it to rights. We therefore find her intervening in the Wengrave plot on the side of the young lovers, since the father's attempts to block that marriage are unnatural and unjust. But we also find her attacking unmanly men and braggarts: men who lack the 'stones' appropriate to their sex. Watching Jack Dapper buy a feather, she is moved to remark that 'the gallants of these times are shallow lechers, they put not their courtship home enough to a wench, 'tis impossible to know what woman is thoroughly honest, because she's ne'er thoroughly tried' (2.1.290–3). She ends by saying 'Women are courted but ne'er soundly tried,/As many walk in spurs that never ride' (2.1.298–9). The emphasis is on men's failure to be sexual 'riders'. And the failings of braggart men are what she seems to reprove both when she trips up Trapdoor (2.1.334) and when she bests Laxton at sword play in Lincoln's Inn Fields (3.1.115–29). It is also important that when she is written in the ideology of 'correction', there is animosity between her and the merchant wives. At one point Moll wishes Mistress Openwork were a man so Moll could give her a beating, presumably to silence her tongue and chasten her independence (2.1.215–21). If Moll's 'corrections' worked, women would again be docile and men manly, and happy marriages would thrive.

Fortunately – and I use the adverb from my contemporary position as a modern feminist – there is much more to Moll's representation. First, the *fact* of her cross-dressing destabilizes the very essentialist binarisms that the 'corrective' cross-dresser overtly wishes to uphold. Moll not only dresses like a man, she behaves with all the ferocity and strength she seems eager to instil in men. She can fight and cant and smoke and support herself. The very fact she can do these things suggests that women are not inherently weak, silent, and dependent, nor men the only ones gifted with the sword. Moreover, Moll's connections with the shops of London and the commodities available from them further underscores how malleable are identities in a market place in which a commercial transaction can alter the self, right down, as Marjorie Garber has suggested, to the hint that Moll has acquired an artificial penis (Garber 1991: 223–4). One way to appropriate Moll as a radical figure is to stress those aspects of her representation that deconstruct the gender binarisms that underwrite patriarchal domination and to stress the way the expanding market economy, while increasing alienation and class exploitation, can also lead to results subversive of some forms of oppression, here the tyranny of an ideology of fixed gender characteristics. One's ability to transform one's appearance by the sartorial possibilities afforded by the market place thus becomes a potentially liberating phenomenon.[13]

Another way to appropriate Moll for radical purposes, and the one I will pursue, is to show how she lodges a critique of the specific material institutions and circumstances which oppressed women in early modern England. While many of Moll's actions point to a utopian future where oppressive hierarchies and binarisms have been undone, she also functions in the here-and-now of the play's world as an opponent of actually existing conditions that exploit women and other disadvantaged figures. To understand this aspect of Moll's representation and how she appears when read in a Marxist-feminist rather than a deconstructive-psychoanalytic problematic, it is necessary to examine how she functions in this text as erotic object *and* subject.

Interestingly, Moll *does* seem to function as erotic object in this text. Laxton, seeing Moll buying goods in the shops, dressed at that point as a woman, exclaims that he would 'give but too much money to be nibbling with that wench: life, sh'as the spirit of four great parishes, and a voice that will drown all the city: methinks a brave captain might get all his soldiers upon her' (2.1.169–72). This outspoken woman who often openly dresses as a man, doesn't marry, and roves about London buying things and consorting with canting underworld figures, is the most highly eroticized figure in the play. While Laxton actually tries to get her in a coach to speed off to a rendezvous in the suburbs, other men constantly speculate about Moll's genitalia, her erotic performance, and the possibility of engaging in sex with her. Trapdoor brags that when Moll's 'breeches are off, she shall follow me' (1.2.223), implying that in sexual intercourse he will take the lead which she typically takes in their daily relations of mistress and servant; later he tells her he has an immovable part 'to stand when you have occasion to use me' (2.1.327–8), again eroticizing their relationship. Alexander Wengrave, terrified Moll will enthral his son, and eager to cast her as a monster, says she casts 'two shadows' (1.2.132) and later alleges she has 'two trinkets' (2.2.74–5) in her breeches. The fact that the female Moll is personated by a male actor of course gives this accusation a particular piquancy in performance. Laxton, commenting on the sexual confusion engendered by Moll's cross-dressing, says that she 'might first cuckold the husband' (by sleeping with his wife) and then 'make him do as much for the wife' (by sleeping with the husband) (2.1.192–3). The point is that however odd and hermaphroditical Moll appears to some, she is constantly being discussed in erotic terms: as a potential bedmate, as one whose unfathomable 'double-ness' provokes speculation about her genital organs and her potential for a variety of sexual performances.

I would argue, moreover, that despite the fact Moll occasionally dresses as a man, in the first instance – though probably not exclusively – it is the *woman* in Moll that men seek, rather than the man. After all, from Moll's self-description, she hardly seems to embody the androgynous allure of the compliant young page, the part Mary assumes and the part usually seen as sexually attractive to adult men. Moll, however, is a loud, roving pipe-smoker: a roarer. This text, in fact, makes one long to know more about Elizabethan casting practices than we presently do. Was Moll played by the same type and age of actor as played Mary? Or was a slightly older, more full-bodied performer required, so that the contrast between the charming androgynous boy/woman and the more frightening, but alluring, hermaphroditical adult female could be registered? Whatever the casting choices made, what Laxton explicitly stresses when he fantasizes 'nibbling' with Moll is her prodigious female reproductive capacity (able to provide a captain with a whole regiment of soldiers), her enormous spirit (capturing the energies of four parishes), and her enormous voice (able to drown out all the city). He may in part wish to mate with her to produce a homosocial world of soldiers, but to achieve that end he has to acknowledge Moll's special reproductive capacities. Moreover, he has this fantasy of 'nibbling' with her while Moll is dressed in female clothing. At this moment she figures in his imagination as female excess, words spewing from an upper orifice, babies from a lower. In fact, the openness of her body is prefigured in the play's very title. A roaring girl, a version of the more common stage type, the roaring boy, is a woman given to copious, quarrelsome speech. To *be* a roaring girl is to have one's mouth open. Moll does, for a great deal of the play; and sometimes when it is open she is quarrelling and sometimes canting and sometimes just talking. And, of course, any woman whose mouth is opened in public spaces, in particular, is read as whorish, as incontinent with other bodily orifices as much as with the mouth.

What makes Moll erotically alluring, I think, is exactly what keeps her from being an example of the construction of femininity suitable for wives. Rather than sewn up, locked up, and quiet (remember that Mary first came to Sebastian's house dressed as a seamstress), Moll is open, excessive, mobile. Wives who exhibit the same characteristics are terrifically threatening because their openness seems to challenge husbands' proprietary rights in wives' bodies. But Moll is not a wife. She is, in fact, unmarried, notorious, and also lower class – hardly wife material for a Laxton or, as old Wengrave's horrified response attests, for a Sebastian. By contrast, Mary first comes to Sebastian in Act 1 as the docile seamstress, later as the androgynous servant, the page. While she is insistent in her pursuit of Sebastian, she always presents herself in properly subservient guises. Crucially, both Laxton and old Wengrave try to control the subversiveness of Moll, to subordinate her to them, by economic means. Assuming that money can buy her, Old Wengrave tries to get her to steal precious objects from his chamber so he can subordinate her to the power of the law (4.1.1–39). Laxton gives her money as he arranges their rendezvous in the coach. In fact, he gives her the ten angels (2.1.262) he received earlier in the same scene from Mistress Gallipot (2.1.93). The woman *from* whom he takes the money he does his best to avoid sexually (2.1.116–28); the woman *to* whom he gives it he does pursue sexually. The difference, obviously, has to do with Laxton's relative power in the two circumstances. In the first, he 'lacks stones' in relation to the economically prosperous middle-class merchants. Mistress Gallipot, while seen by him as sexually available, is not erotically stimulating, perhaps because she is powerful, if only economically, in ways he cannot control. But Moll lacks the cultural and economic status of the married merchant wife, and Laxton seems to feel that if he can further subordinate her by getting her to accept money for sexual favours, then he can enjoy the physical pleasures her openness seems to invite. Consequently, he tries to subordinate her with angels, a word whose punning associations with ingles (Rubenstein 1989: 12) raises the possibility, at least, that in turning Moll into his paid paramour, Laxton may want from her a variety of sexual pleasures, those associated with the ingle as well as with the woman as vessel of reproduction. What is clear, however, is that to act on his desires Laxton must symbolically subordinate Moll by making her his paid bedmate.

Moll, however, does not comply. While she initially accepts the ten angels from Laxton, when she meets him at Lincoln's Inn Fields she throws down his money, to which she adds ten angels of her own, and demands he fight her with swords for the lot. She then launches into a withering critique of his behaviour, a critique that reveals that in constructing the character of Moll, Middleton and Dekker tapped into discourses of radical protest (Shepherd 1981: 67–92) that provide the basis for a critique of the sex and gender systems that far exceeds the tamer demands for more manly men and womanly women voiced by Moll when she is represented as corrective 'reformer'. Moll is both a reformer and a radical. The voice of the latter is on display when she castigates Laxton for thinking 'each woman thy fond flexible whore' (3.1.71), a critique which ends

> In thee I defy all men, their worst hates,
> And their best flatteries, all their golden witchcrafts,
> With which they entangle the poor spirits of fools.
> Distressed needlewomen and trade-fallen wives,
> Fish that must needs bite or themselves be bitten,
> Such hungry things as these may soon be took
> With a worm fastened on a golden hook:
> Those are the lecher's food, his prey, he watches
> For quarrelling wedlocks, and poor shifting sisters,
> 'Tis the best fish he takes: but why, good fisherman,
> Am I thought meat for you, that never yet
> Had angling rod cast towards me? 'cause, you'll say,
> I'm given to sport, I'm often merry, jest:
> Had mirth no kindred in the world but lust?
> Oh shame take all her friends then: but howe'er
> Thou and the baser world censure my life,
> I'll send 'em word by thee, and write so much
> Upon thy breast, 'cause thou shalt bear't in mind:
> Tell them 'twere base to yield, where I have conquered.
> I scorn to prostitute myself to a man
> I that can prostitute a man to me,
> And so I greet thee.

>   (3.1.90–111)

This is a refreshingly economic explanation for prostitution and a stunning declaration of Moll's own freedom from the economic necessity that drives some poor women into the flesh trade, i.e., that makes them prey to man's ingling/angling rod. In doing so, she reverses the power relations that have made Laxton assume he can safely use her as an erotic object, a fond flexible whore. Elsewhere, in explaining why she won't marry, Moll offers a critique of the whole institution for being premised on female subordination. For a woman, marriage means loss of control and freedom: 'marriage is but a chopping and changing, where a maiden loses one head and has a worse i'th'place' (2.2.43–4). At such moments, Moll embodies a position much more radical than that she adopts when trying to 'adjust' men and women to the hierarchical positions society marks out for them. Rather than specifying the 'real' Moll (a task that assumes she is a self-consistent representation of a unified psyche), I wish to stress how thoroughly her representation is enmeshed in contradictions, a sure sign it is doing the work of mediating complex social tensions.

One thing Moll's representation foregrounds is the tension that exists in this text between the pressure of urgent female sexual desire and a patriarchal culture in which women's sexuality is in theory subject to masculine control and regulation. Consider, for a moment, a striking feature of this play: its insistent linkage of Moll with the playing of a particular musical instrument, the viol. The original Moll Frith gained some of her considerable notoriety from playing a lute on the stage of the Fortune Theatre. As Linda Austern has shown, women playing musical instruments – usually the small stringed instruments or the virginals – were considered to be erotically stimulating to men, the combination of feminine beauty and the beauty of harmonious sound acting together to arouse uncontrollable passion (Austern 1989: 427). Consequently, if women played, they were to do so in private, for their own recreation or the delight of family and husband, and never in public. Moll Frith was thus transgressive in playing her lute on the public stage.

Moll Cutpurse is even more transgressive in that her instrument is not the lute, able to be tucked decorously beneath the breast, but the viol, played with legs akimbo. Moreover, she seems to appropriate this instrument not so much to make herself an erotic object, as to express her own erotic subjectivity. In 2.2.18 she enters with a porter bearing a viol on his back, taking it to her chamber. In Act 4, when Mary and she, both dressed as men, go to old Wengrave's chamber to meet Sebastian, Moll actually plays upon a viol that is hanging on the wall. Her taking up of this instrument is the occasion for a great deal of bawdy banter concerning Moll's skills as a musician, whether or not she initiates the taking up of a gentleman's instrument, and whether or not, as some 'close' women say, it is unmannerly to play on such an instrument. At the climax of this jesting, Moll says she does not care what other women say. When they accuse her of lewdness she falls asleep and dreams. Then, in two songs, she recounts her dreams, which turn out to be about two 'loose' women, one of whom gads about London and 'lays out the money' (4.1.104) and comes home 'with never a penny' (4.1.109), the other of whom sleeps with a man from the navy while her husband is in prison. These 'dreams' seem to function, doubly, as angry indictments of the hypocritical 'dames' who would call Moll whore and yet seize sexual pleasure for themselves, and as wishful projections of a longed-for freedom for herself. Moll seems to acknowledge the latter reading when, the songs over, she says 'Hang up the viol now, sir; all this while I was in a dream, one shall lie rudely then; but being awake, I keep my legs together' (4.1.127–9).

This encounter is absolutely riveting in the way it acknowledges, insists upon, female erotic desire, while making clear the cultural imperatives that operate to shape, channel, and control that eroticism. Except in dreams, Moll cannot be an autonomous sexual subject and escape being called a whore. The men who obsessively comment on her sexuality speculate about her 'doubleness', her ability to play either the man or the woman's part in sexual encounters. Moll herself, when refusing Sebastian's marriage proposal, says: 'I love to lie o' both sides o'th' bed myself' (2.2.36–7) meaning, clearly, that she likes her independence, but perhaps also indicating she likes a certain unspecified variety in sexual partners and practices. My point, however, is not to define Moll's 'real' sexual orientation, since to do so is impossible. Instead, I want to emphasize that heterosexual marriage is the only 'legitimate' avenue open to Moll for acting on any of her sexual desires, whatever they might be. And marriage she rejects on political grounds as entailing an insupportable subordination and loss of independence. She is equally firm in refusing extramarital encounters with the braggarts Laxton and Trapdoor who would make her a bought woman or a sexual prize.

Yet Moll never denies her sexuality. She has and acknowledges her sexual dreams; she has and acknowledges her 'instrument', that viol with which she is so insistently linked, the fingering of which seems to symbolize her skill at clitoral masturbation, as well as her potential skill at manual stimulation of the male penis. When Sebastian describes Moll's skill as a musician to his father, he calls her a musician 'of excellent fingering' (4.1.168) with 'the most delicate stroke' (4.1.170). Sir Alexander immediately sees these as the skills of a whore servicing, and undoing, men (4.1.173). But on the stage when Moll actually plays her instrument what the spectator sees is a woman whose strokes and clever fingering occur in the space between her own legs.[14] Her viol suggests her own sexual instrument and her masturbatory playing of it a final defiance of patriarchal, phallus-oriented, sexuality. At the play's end, joking with Sir Alexander Wengrave, now her friend, Moll says: 'and you can cuck me, spare not:/Hang up my viol by me, and I care not' (5.2.253–4). She can imagine enduring public humiliation for female transgression as long as she can defiantly exhibit her viol, sign of the sexual being she is. Through her one realizes that the culturally sanctioned ways for women to express erotic desire may exact too high a price to be employed. For Moll there seems to be no way, outside of dream and solitary pricksong, to gratify eros without enduring an unendurable subordination and exploitation. Yet in her jaunty defiance she makes us feel she is no victim, that keeping her legs together, outside of dreams, and retaining her mighty voice, her outlandish dress and her mobility are preferable to any other bargain she might have struck with her culture.

The ending of the play, which leaves Moll defiantly outside the marriage fold and Mary submissively within, is a fine example of the significant contradictions of this text's handling of the 'comic' matter of venery. This drama doesn't tell a single or simple story about sexuality and its relationship to institutions such as marriage. In its inability to do so it reveals the pressure points in the culture's ways of making sense of its multivalent and changing practices. For example, while this text privileges marriage as the central fact of middle-class life and the necessary means for the aristocracy to reproduce itself and pass on its money, marriage *per se* is not depicted as an untroubled or attractive institution, and sexual desire does not lodge inside it easily. The play suggests that for some men this is because they find more compelling the erotic allure of the boy page, for whom the cross-dressed virgin stands as simulacrum, than the erotic allure of the woman in and of herself. While, at least for men, there seems to be more fluidity in object choice than our current ideology of fixed sexual identities allows, none the less there is an implicit contest between the pull of the homosocial world embodied in the Wengrave milieu and the male-female bond of marriage, a bond given actual depiction only in the offputting antagonisms visible in the citizens' marital alliances.

There is much evidence in the play, moreover, for the complex way in which erotic desire is intimately entwined with power relations. For adult males the subordination of the sexual partner seems necessary. In Mary's case, she assumes the clothes and the acquiescent manner of the young male servant, the page. In Moll's case, Laxton *tries* to subordinate her with the angels that turn a free woman into a whore. The most sexually shunned woman is, predictably, the outspoken, publicly visible, economically productive wife. She is legitimate, but not entirely subordinate, caught as she is in the nowhere land between the actualities of marriage as a functioning economic institution that demands her visibility and independence and the ideologies of acquiescent femininity associated with the concept of wife.

The play, moreover, while raising quite explicitly the problem of female sexual desire, provides schizophrenic solutions to its satisfaction. While Mary supposedly gets her desire satisfied by marriage, the absence of actual wives in the Wengrave milieu, coupled with Sebastian's pleasure in her page's disguise, makes one wonder whether Mary-as-woman will continue to exist in any real form after marriage, and whether *her* sexual desires will be fulfilled. Certainly the experience of the citizens' wives is not encouraging. Moll, by contrast, resists marriage, knowing that whatever pleasures the institution affords to women are fundamentally premised on her subordination. What remains, for Moll, are the eroticisms of solitary fantasy and self-pleasure. Importantly, no sustaining community of women, parallel to the male homosocial and homosexual networks visible behind the foregrounded heterosexual couplings of the text, exists to absorb Moll. The citizen wives gossip with one another, but are jealous of Moll, and while Moll is kind to Mary, their female friendship does not seem to embrace the degrees of intimacy implied by the presence of a Sir Beauteous Ganymede among the men.

In short, *The Roaring Girl*'s representations of venery are fraught with frustrations and antagonisms. Much more starkly than in Shakespeare's comedies, for example, the idealizations of the heterosexual romance plot clash with the competing investments of male homoeroticism and the negative, satirical conventions by which middle-class marriage was frequently represented in misogynist literature and city comedy. The result is no green world of laughter and fulfilled desire, but the rough inequalities of an urban landscape of friction and of difference, in which desire, especially woman's desire, finds no easy fulfilment.

Notes

1 All citations from *The Roaring Girl* refer to the New Mermaids edition edited by Andor Gomme (1976). For rigorous and generous readings of this essay I am especially grateful to Mario DiGangi, Phyllis Rackin, and Susan Zimmerman.

2 The word *queer* is a hotly contested one in gay and lesbian scholarship. For discussion of the term and for examples of 'queer critical practice', see *Social Text* 29 and *Differences* 3, 2, especially the lead essays by Warner (1991) and de Lauretis (1991) respectively. I use the term *queer* to indicate alternatives to normative heterosexuality. The value of the word for me lies in its ability to draw attention to sexuality as a primary site of oppression, but also of collective possibility and resistance, in a way that sidesteps the usual gendering and division of marginalized sexualities into gay, lesbian, and bisexual categories.

3 In the last decade there has been an enormous amount of work done on historicizing sexuality. Michel Foucault's *The History of Sexuality: An Introduction* (1980) remains a key text for literary and historical scholars.

4 Since Bray's book, debate has continued on the question of whether, for men, non-heterosexual emotional investments and practices constituted the basis for identity formation or a lifestyle in early modern England. While both Smith (1991) and Bredbeck (1991) accept the view that only the nineteenth century saw the emergence of 'the homosexual' as a medical/legal category, both also seem to entertain the idea that in some writing of the period there was 'the possibility of a homosexual subjectivity' (Smith 1991: 223). For Bredbeck's (1991) argument that such a subjectivity arises only 'subjunctively', in the imagined difference from the sodomitical monster of legal discourse, see especially Chapter IV, 'Tradition and the individual sodomite', pp. 143–85.

5 For a careful account of the legal discourses concerning sodomy in sixteenth- and seventeenth-century England see Smith (1991: esp. 42–55).

6 Alan Bray (1988: esp. 48–56) has called attention to the ways early modern hierarchies of status, age, and economic power underwrote homosexual practices in schools, universities, households, the theatre and other social sites. For discussions of forms of homoerotic bonding between men of the same age and status in early modern literature see Smith (1991: 31–77).

7 For a good discussion of the difficulties of finding an appropriate language to talk about same-sex female intimacy in the early modern period, see Andreadis (1989).

8 There is now a considerable literature talking about the gender and sexual implications of cross-dressing on the Renaissance stage. I summarize much of that literature in my essay 'Crossdressing, the theatre, and gender struggle in early modern England' (1988). See also Orgel (1989).

9 Thomas Laqueur (1990: esp. 63–148) provides a stunning analysis of the one-sex Galenic model of human anatomy widely held in the early modern period. Literary scholars such as Stephen Greenblatt (1988: 66–93, especially 92) have referred to Laqueur's work in suggesting 'an apparent homoeroticism in all sexuality' in the early modern period. I would argue that there *are* many representations of homoeroticism in early modern texts, representations which a heterosexist criticism has often been unable to acknowledge. On the other hand, there are many cultural reasons for this besides the existence of Galenic biological

models, including the relatively late age of most marriages and the existence of many exclusively male institutions such as universities, Inns of Court, etc. In addition, as Greenblatt also acknowledges, much effort was expended in early modern England to secure gender difference and to promote heterosexual passion and its institutionalization in marriage. I therefore find it more useful, rather than stressing that at some level all sexuality was homoerotic, to emphasize the mixture of erotic interpellations operating on individual subjects, especially male subjects. The drama at times represents the negotiation of these competing interpellations as untroubled and at times as vexed and contestatory.

10 I am indebted to Mario DiGangi for pointing out to me the homoerotic signifi- cance of Sebastian's name and for pointing me toward both the Saslow article (1977) and one by Cynthia Lewis (1989) in which she explores the late mediaeval and early Renaissance associations of St Anthony with St Sebastian as embodi- ments, among other things, of homoerotic attraction. Obviously, the existence of these visual traditions gives further weight to a homoerotic reading of the Antonio-Sebastian friendship in *Twelfth Night* and the relationship between Antonio and Bassanio in *The Merchant of Venice*, Bastiano being the Italian diminutive for the name Sebastian (Lewis 1989: 205).

11 For excellent work on the significance of the names in this play see Garber (1991).

12 What I find impossible to resolve is the degree to which, when a woman 'ingles', her partner's pleasure depends on her being 'like a boy' at that moment or on her being 'like a *submissive* woman'. I think we are dealing here with two complexly related variables: sex (male/female) of object choice and status (subor- dinate/superior) of object choice. Though Galenic biology, at least, did not provide a basis for establishing sexual difference in modern terms, the culture generated many other ways of thinking about male and female as different 'kinds'. I cannot accept, therefore, the absolute interchangeability of woman and boy as social and sexual categories, though there was obviously more slippage between them than we can easily imagine today. *Both* the sex and the relative power and status of the sexual object seem factors in the erotic economy of this text.

13 The numerous sartorial transformations of various characters in this play give strong support to the position that the market destabilizes various traditional means of marking identity, since appearance can be altered at will. Moll, of course, takes the lead in sartorial alterations of self. In her first stage appearance she attempts to purchase a shag ruff; later she discusses with a tailor's messenger the measurements for a new pair of Dutch slops. It is probably the same tailor she later employs to make up a suit of men's clothes for Mary Fitz-Allard to wear when going to the chamber of Sebastian's father. Moll, of course, sometimes appears in women's clothes – a frieze jerkin, safeguard and short dagger, and sometimes in men's – breeches, doublet and sword. Hers are the most startling transformations of self, but other characters also remake themselves: Trapdoor appears in Act 5 as a wounded soldier; Mary Fitz-Allard comes on stage dressed at various times as a seamstress, a lady, and a male page; Greenwit tries to use a wig to pass as a summoner; the citizens' wives don masks as they are contem- plating setting off for Brainford; and foolish Jack Dapper tries to make himself a proper gallant by buying a feather at Tiltyard's shop.

14 I call attention to Moll's autoeroticism to in part affirm the possibility of female sexual pleasure in a textual world thoroughly dominated by concerns with men's erotic desires and fulfilments, and also to call in question the contemporary

presumption that sexualities, whether heterosexual or homoerotic, involve primarily alloerotic relations. In this regard see Sedgwick (1991).

When I had finished this essay Bruce Smith found and gave to me the following poem which he had discovered in a mid-seventeenth century (1655) miscellany entitled *Wits Interpreter, The English Parnassus* compiled by one J. C. (John Cotgrave?). Many of the poems in the volume date from the early seventeenth century. The poem in question, 'The Violin', quite explicitly eroticizes the virgin's playing of the viol in ways suggesting autoeroticism.

The Violin

To play upon a Viol, if
A Virgin will begin,
She first of all must know her cliff,
And all the stops therein.

Her prick she must hold long enough,
Her backfals gently take;
Her touch must gentle be, not rough,
She at each stroak must shake.

Her body must by no means bend,
    But stick close to her fiddle:
Her feet must hold the lower end,
    Her knees must hold the middle.

She boldly to the bowe must flie,
    As if she'd make it crack;
Two fingers on the hair must lie,
    And two upon the back.

And when she hath as she would have,
    She must it gently thrust,
Up, down, swift, slow, at any rate
    As she herself doth list.

And when she once begins to find
    That she growes something cunning,
She'll nere be quiet in her mind,
    Untill she find it running.

(123–4)

References

Andreadis, Harriette (1989) 'The Sapphic Platonics of Katherine Philips, 1632–1664', *Signs* 15, 1: 34–60.

Austern, Linda (1989) ' "Sing Againe Syren": Female Musicians and Sexual Enchantment in Elizabethan Life and Literature', *Renaissance Quarterly* 42: 420–48.

Belsey, Catherine (1985) *The Subject of Tragedy: Identity and Difference in Renaissance Drama*, London and New York: Methuen.

Bray, Alan (1988) *Homosexuality in Renaissance England*, 2nd edn, London: Gay Men's Press.

Bredbeck, Gregory W. (1991) *Sodomy and Interpretation: Marlowe to Milton*, Ithaca: Cornell University Press.

de Lauretis, Teresa (1991) 'Queer Theory: Lesbian and Gay Sexualities, An Introduction', *Differences* 3, 2: iii–xviii.

Florio, John (1598) *A Worlde of Wordes or A Most copious and exact Dictionairie in Italian and English*, London.

Foucault, Michel (1978) *The History of Sexuality: An Introduction*, vol. I, trans. Robert Hurley, New York: Random House.

Garber, Marjorie (1991) 'The logic of the transvestite: *The Roaring Girl*', in David Scott Kastan and Peter Stallybrass (eds), *Staging the Renaissance: Reinterpretations of Elizabethan and Jacobean Drama*, New York and London: Routledge.

Gomme, Andor (ed.) (1976) *The Roaring Girl* by Thomas Middleton and Thomas Dekker, New York: W. W. Norton.

Greenblatt, Stephen (1988) *Shakespearean Negotiations*, Berkeley: University of California Press.

Howard, Jean E. (1988) 'Crossdressing, the theatre, and gender struggle in early modern England', *Shakespeare Quarterly* 39, 4: 418–40.

—— (1989) 'Scripts and/versus Playhouses: Ideological Production and the Renaissance Public Stage', *Renaissance Drama* 20: 31–49.

Laqueur, Thomas (1990) *Making Sex: Body and Gender from the Greeks to Freud*, Cambridge, Mass.: Harvard University Press.

Leinwand, Theodore B. (1986) *The City Staged: Jacobean Comedy, 1603–13*, Madison: University of Wisconsin Press.

Lewis, Cynthia (1989) ' "Wise Men, Folly'Fall'n' ": Characters Named Antonio in English Renaissance Drama', *Renaissance Drama* 20: 197–236.

Orgel, Stephen (1989), 'Nobody's perfect', *South Atlantic Quarterly* 88, 1: 7–29.

Rackin, Phyllis (forthcoming 1992) 'Historical Difference/Sexual Difference', in Jean Brink (ed.), *Privileging Gender in Early Modern Britain*, Kirksville, Missouri: Sixteenth Century Journal Publishers.

Rubenstein, Frankie (1989) *A Dictionary of Shakespeare's Sexual Puns and Their Significance*, 2nd edn, London: Macmillan.

Rubin, Gayle (1984) 'Thinking sex: notes for a radical theory of the politics of sexuality', in Carole S. Vance (ed.) *Pleasure and Danger*, Boston: Routledge & Kegan Paul, 267–319.

Saslow, James M. (1977) 'The Tenderest Lover: Saint Sebastian in Renaissance Painting: A Proposed Homoerotic Iconology for North Italian Art 1450–1550', *Gai Saber* 1: 58–66.

Sedgwick, Eve (1990) *Epistemology of the Closet*, Berkeley: University of California Press.

—— (1991) 'Jane Austen and the Masturbating Girl', *Critical Inquiry* 17: 818–37.

Sharp, Jane (1671) *The Midwives Book*, London.

Shepherd, Simon (1981) *Amazons and Warrior Women: Varieties of Feminism in Seventeenth Century Drama*, New York: St Martin's.

Smith, Bruce R. (1991) *Homosexual Desire in Shakespeare's England: A Cultural Poetics*, Chicago: University of Chicago Press.

Stallybrass, Peter (1986) 'Patriarchal Territories: The Body Enclosed', in Margaret W. Ferguson, Maureen Quilligan and Nancy Vickers (eds), *Rewriting the Renaissance: The Discourses of Sexual Difference in Early Modern Europe*, Chicago: University of Chicago Press, 123–42.

Traub, Valerie (1992) *Desire and Anxiety: Circulations of Sexuality in Shakespearean Drama*, London and New York: Routledge.

Warner, Michael (1991) 'Introduction: Fear of a Queer Planet', *Social Text* 29: 3–17.

Index